Playing Before an Overflow Crowd

THE STORY OF INDIAN BASKETBALL IN
ROBESON, NORTH CAROLINA, AND ADJOINING COUNTIES

Tim Brayboy and Bruce Barton

CHAPEL HILL
PRESS, INC.®
Chapel Hill, North Carolina

Cover Image reprinted by permission from Henry T. Locklear
Cover and book design by Laura Weakland.
Typeset by Brenda Mangum.

Published by The Chapel Hill Press, Inc.
300-A Franklin Square
1829 East Franklin Street
Chapel Hill, NC 27514

ISBN Number 1-880849-52-6
Library of Congress Catalog 2002110606
Printed in the United States of America

Any additions or corrections to the book may be sent to either:

Tim Brayboy
916 Union Street
Cary, N.C. 27511-3756

Bruce Barton
P. O. Box 362
Pembroke, N.C. 28372-0362

TABLE OF CONTENTS

Acknowledgments

The authors give special thanks to the following people and institutions:

To school superintendents, principals, teachers, and staff of Cumberland County Schools, Hoke County Schools, and the Public Schools of Robeson County for their invaluable help in providing information important to this publication.

To the Public Schools of Robeson County, Indian Education Resource Center for the use of its archival records.

To the University of North Carolina at Pembroke for its support, and to university photographer, Bobby Ayers, for his magnificent photograph search abilities.

To the Louis Round Wilson Library staff in the North Carolina Collection at the University of North Carolina at Chapel Hill for their assistance with reference materials, particularly microfilm that contained important basketball news reports published in *The Robesonian*.

To *The Robesonian* (Lumberton, NC) for reprint permission.

To *The News-Journal* (Raeford, NC) for reprint permission.

To *The Fayetteville-Observer* (Fayetteville, NC) for reprint permission.

To *The Carolina Indian Voice*, (Pembroke, NC) for long and broad publicity of this project, and for reprint permission.

To the Division of Communication and Information, NC Department of Public Instruction for informational materials.

To Charlie Adams and the staff of the North Carolina High School Athletic Association, Chapel Hill, NC, who provided many kinds of support.

To all the former coaches and their families who contributed written and oral information, photographs and their time: Albert Hunt; Danford Dial, Sr.; Marvin Lowry; Ralph Hunt; "Ned" Sampson; Delton Ray Locklear; Wilton Cummings; James Howard Locklear, Sr.; James F. "Buddy" Bell; Bobby Dean Brayboy; Mary Sanderson; Lucy Oxendine Thomas; Pauline Bullard Locklear; Sara Bullard Locklear; Tommy D. Swett; and Hartman Brewington.

To the former high school basketball players, too numerous to list, for sharing newspaper clippings, photographs, and oral histories.

To Lumbee Indian historians: James Moore of the Prospect community; Ray Chavis of the Fairmont/Fairgrove community; and Welton Lowry of the Pembroke community.

To the many school patrons and parents of former athletes who shared photographs.

To Brenda Mangum, Shirley Banks and Laura Weakland for their competent and cheerful assistance that went beyond typesetting and graphic art. They were godsend angels.

To Barbara Braveboy-Locklear, who provided valuable editorial assistance.

Finally, we are grateful to our wives, Byrtis Dial Brayboy and Barbara Sampson Barton for their many acts of support, including turning on the porch lights time after time after time.

THIS BOOK IS DEDICATED IN MEMORY OF DANFORD DIAL, SR. AND RALPH HUNT

and all the former "Indian" basketball players, coaches and fans.

Danford Dial Remembered, by Bruce Barton

Danford Dial, Sr.

Danford Dial was a passionate man, no matter what the venue, no matter what the moment or the issue. He was passionate about life.

He was strongly identified with the Prospect community where he grew up as a boy and later became principal of Prospect High School. He always fought for the boys and girls and demanded more from them than they initially thought they had it in themselves to give. He set high standards for his students, first in the classroom, then as principal. It seemed that he always forced us to give our very best and then some.

I knew him as a junior at Pembroke High School in the school year 1957-58, when he taught there. What a year that was. "Mr. Dan" taught us Spanish that year because no one else was available to teach it. He taught it possibly with a Prospect accent and I still remember some of the language from the old Spanish book - *El Camino Real* ("*The Royal Road,*" as I recall). Did you know that "Mr. Dan" had a crooked finger that he often pointed at whoever he was most upset with at the moment? He cared and he could get provoked easily, especially in the classroom.

"Mr. Dan" also coached basketball for a few seasons, not many because he could hardly stand the youthful imperfections of his players. Pembroke native Paul Brooks told me a story recently of the time that "Mr. Dan" whipped him at half time for not following his X's and O's. The moral of the story is that Paul Brooks loved "Mr. Dan," and all of his players did, and I did too, from my vantage point in the classroom, reading aloud from the *El Camino Real* Spanish book.

And he gave Bibles away as a Gideon, and he fought furiously to save Old Main on the UNC-P campus. I always gave "Mr. Dan", my daddy, Lew Barton, Janie Maynor Locklear, along with Brantley Blue, the lion's share of credit for saving the historic building. I can see him now marching down 3rd Street in Pembroke with a stop sign in front of him, demonstrating and raising cain to Save Old Main, the historic building on the UNC-P campus that he cared so much about and where he got his start as a student and lifelong learner.

And he tried to stand up for Indian people at Prospect High School in the early 70s before integration confused us even more than we were confused at the time. The Civil Rights movement overran his efforts, but he tried to be a warrior, a champion, for his people. He was way ahead of his time.

I remember him in the last few years of his life at many gospel music concerts. Both "Mr. Dan" and I love(d) gospel music, songs from the heart. We often waved across the auditorium between gospel music acts when we found ourselves in the same place at the same time. It was always good to see "Mr. Dan."

We miss you "Mr. Dan", for your life and your passion.

Mr. Danford Dial, 80, died Friday (Nov. 10, 2000) in Southeastern Regional Medical Center in Lumberton. We extend sincere condolences to his family and wide circle of friends.

Ralph Hunt Remembered, by Bruce Barton

Ralph Hunt

I'll miss "Mister Ralph." Even though we were close in age (I am 59, "Mister Ralph" 66), I always referred to Ralph Hunt as "Mister Ralph." I suppose it was the respect I felt for him shining through.

I went to his funeral Monday, Nov. 20, 2000 at New Bethel Methodist Holiness Church near Rowland and listened intently as he was eulogized by Rev. James Harold Woods and Rev. Crafton Chavis. And Sheriff Glenn Maynor gave a few remarks about his mentor, and mine, "Mister Ralph." I agree with every remark, and every song and prayer. Many dignitaries turned out, but most of us there were ordinary working folk who get up every morning and work for a living. "Mister Ralph" WAS OUR HERO, OUR FRIEND, OUR MENTOR. His silence spoke volumes to us because he never said anything until it was time. His words were pregnant with meaning when he did deign to speak after thoughtful deliberation. And he was usually on the mark, including calling elections complete with estimated figures. He was uncanny about prognosticating elections, and reading the minds and intents of his many friends, and his few enemies.

Ralph Hunt and I, along with Tim Brayboy and many former players, coaches and fans, are involved in remembering Indian basketball as we practiced it between 1939-1967 when the schools were foolishly segregated. In spite of that, many of us remember those days with fondness, and we have already organized, had our first annual banquet, and are now writing a book about that great sports and social phenomenon in our camp – Indian basketball. "Mister Ralph" was the first chairman of our board of directors. I suspect he would be pleased if, in lieu of flowers, you decided to make a contribution to the Indian Basketball Alumni Association, P.O. Box 362, Pembroke, North Carolina 28372. Plans will be announced soon for our second annual banquet, and plans for the future... including the anticipated publication of the "about 80%" complete book.

Note: Danford Dial's eulogy appeared in Bruce Barton's "As I See It" column November 16, 2000 in The Carolina Indian Voice *Newspaper. Ralph Hunt's eulogy appeared in the "As I See It" column November 23, 2000.*

"My father was a self-made man. He believed in what was right for students. If you did not know him when he was alive...you never will."

Danford Dial, Jr., Prospect High School

FORWARD

The stories related in "Playing Before an Overflow Crowd" will certainly bring back many memories for coaches, athletes and the communities that so avidly supported their athletic teams. And that is good, because one of the slogans we use at the North Carolina High School Athletic Association is that high school sports can provide "a memory forever," and this book helps to chronicle many of those memories.

For some, however, this will be all new ground. The idea that there was a state association, a western association, an association for predominantly black high schools and then a conference for predominantly native American schools is a shock and surprise for many. That would be particularly true for today's student-athletes who have only known integrated schools, all of which are members of the same statewide athletic organization.

But that's another reason why this book is important. We cannot really know where we're going unless we know where we've been, and this book makes sure that this part of history is not overlooked or forgotten.

Tim Brayboy, one of the co-authors, has made a great suggestion. He believes strongly that students who have never been in a segregated school system ought to read "Playing Before an Overflow Crowd." For the native American youngster, it may bring up questions that you may want to have explained by an older adult, a grandfather or grandmother who actually experienced high school athletics under these circumstances. I'm sure they'll have some very interesting stories to relate. Certainly some great names in our state's athletic history got their start at one of these schools and played on some of these teams.

The amazing thing, though, is despite lack of facilities or some of the other trappings of an athletic program – much basketball was played outdoors, for instance – these teams still competed hard, took pride in what they did, were cheered by their supporters and received good coaching from dedicated, conscientious individuals. In that sense, today's coaches and athletes have just built upon the long-standing traditions established in so many communities across our state, regardless of the economic setting, racial composition or location.

The North Carolina High School Athletic Association is proud that these schools and their communities are part of the NCHSAA today, but we also can't forget what has gotten us to this point. Tim and Bruce have done an excellent job of researching this great journey, and we think you'll enjoy the ride as you learn about another interesting aspect of our great state.

Charlie Adams, Executive Director
North Carolina High School Athletic Association

A relatively quiet rite of passage occurred in 1968, when Indian high schools in Robeson and adjoining counties disbanded their athletic conference and joined the North Carolina High School Athletic Association. Since the 1920s, the Indian athletic conference had competed in inter-school athletics. The conference offered baseball, basketball, and football as competitive sports for male students and basketball for high school female students. Though all three sports were offered, time after time, it was basketball that received the widest support from the Indian community.

The Lumbee Indian community in Robeson County, where much of the athletic competition took place, consists of four sub-communities. Tribal members commonly identify their place of residence by one of three ways. The first is the sub-community of which there are four: Prospect, Pembroke, Fairgrove, and Saddletree. Some of these communities date back as far as the mid-1700s. All are distinctively Indian. There are many different settlement areas within these sub-communities. For example, Saddletree includes the Indian settlements of Magnolia, Mt. Olive, and Antioch. The settlements of Reedy Branch, Green Grove, Fairgrove, and Ashpole are generally grouped under the name of Fairgrove. The church is the second identifier. When Indians refer to Sandy Plains, Harper's Ferry, Burnt Swamp, New Hope, and a host of others, they are referring to a specific "Indian" church. The third Indian identifier applied is a school: for example, Union Elementary, Union Chapel, and Piney Grove. Lumbees seldom refer to townships in the context of residency. They reserve that designation for political expression. Individual Lumbees maintain that they can tell the place of residence of an individual by his or her accent; that people from Saddletree, Pembroke, Prospect, and other settlements have distinctive speech patterns.

The speech patterns among the Indians may vary, but one constant remains: the memories of the way Indian high school basketball was played in Robeson and adjoining counties during the years from 1939 until 1967, when the county Indian high schools disbanded their athletic conference. Though the Indian athletic conference was formed in the 1920s, our search for printed news materials covering respective schools' athletic activities during the decades of 1920 and 1930 was largely unsuccessful. Unfortunately, there is little printed information about Indian high schools' basketball reign in Robeson County, North Carolina, during the 1940s, 50s, and 60s. We felt these facts alone were enough reason to write the story about basketball's dominance as an Indian high school sport during that era. Perhaps the most compelling reason the story must be told now is that time is running out on gathering information from coaches and athletes who actually participated in competitive high school basketball during the 1940s and 1950s and early 1960s. For instance, Indian basketball stalwarts Ralph Hunt and Danford Dial died within days of each other in November, 2000.

In our goal to gather data for this book, we utilized the willingness of various news media to inform the general public regarding the project. Additionally, we solicited the assistance of living coaches, athletes and patrons of the historically Indian high schools profiled throughout the book. Individuals representing the tribal community gathered and shared bits of information during several public meetings held in Robeson County. Soon thereafter, a group was organized and adopted the name of The Indian Basketball Alumni Association, Inc. Committees within the organization intensified efforts to collect materials that would move the project ahead. Research at the University of North Carolina at

Chapel Hill revealed microfilm showing a profound disparity in Robeson County's daily newspapers' coverage of the county's racially segregated high schools. *The Robesonian* newspaper did, however, print coverage of most of the Indian high school basketball tournaments. A wealth of information about the Indian athletic conference was given us by retired basketball coaches and players now living in Robeson County.

Formed in the 1920s, member schools of the Robeson County Indian High School Athletic Conference were governed by the rules and regulations of the Robeson County Board of Education. Championships were organized, supervised and administered by the school principals. Original school membership included Fairmont, Green Grove, Magnolia, Pembroke, Piney Grove, Prospect, and Union Chapel. After the 1942 school year, high school students from Piney Grove were assigned to Magnolia, reducing the Conference to six schools. In 1951, high school students from Union Chapel were assigned to Pembroke. By 1952, a new school opened near Fairmont. High school students from Fairmont and Green Grove were assigned to the new Fairgrove High School, reducing the Athletic Conference to four schools. In 1966, Hawkeye High School, an Indian school in Hoke County, and Les Maxwell High School, located in Cumberland County, joined to form the Tri-County Indian High School Conference. That conference disbanded in 1968 when the member schools joined the North Carolina High School Athletic Association.

With grant monies from the Federal Administration, a gymnasium was constructed on the campus of Cherokee Indian Normal School, now UNC-Pembroke, in 1939 and 1940. Prior to the completion of the gymnasium in 1940, all Indian high school post-season basketball tournaments were played on outdoor courts. This modern facility had a regulation basketball court 94 feet in length and 50 feet in width. It had a seating capacity of over 1,000 and featured modern showers and dressing rooms for boys and girls. Additionally, the brick building contained coaches' offices, classrooms,

and storage areas. The school, whose name was changed to Pembroke State College for Indians in 1941, allowed Indian high schools to use the school gymnasium for some regular season games, in addition to posting season tournament play that took place on the campus throughout the 1940s and 1950s and into the early 1960s. Some early 1960s Indian high school post season tournament play took place in Lumberton's Recreation Center housed in the armory building (now the Bill Sapp Recreation Center). In 1952, Pembroke High School hosted its first post season ttournament play in its newly-constructed gymnasium located just yards away from the site of the Pembroke college. A year later, new gymnasiums opened on the campuses of Fairgrove and Prospect High Schools. The Magnolia High School gymnasium opened in 1954.

This book is merely a beginning and not an end unto itself. Every game has not been covered, nor has every player been mentioned. This is where we find ourselves at this juncture in time. We do not turn away from praise, however faint, but acknowledge fully that all errors fall back to our side of the ball.

It is our hope that these stories evoke fond memories of the Indian high school basketball games as they were played before an overflow crowd.

Tim Brayboy and Bruce Barton

INTRODUCTION
THE WAY THE GAME WAS PLAYED BACK THEN
AND
A HISTORY LESSON

It began with a March 31, 1998 news brief in the local newspapers
(*The Robesonian, The Fayetteville Observer, The Carolina Indian Voice*):

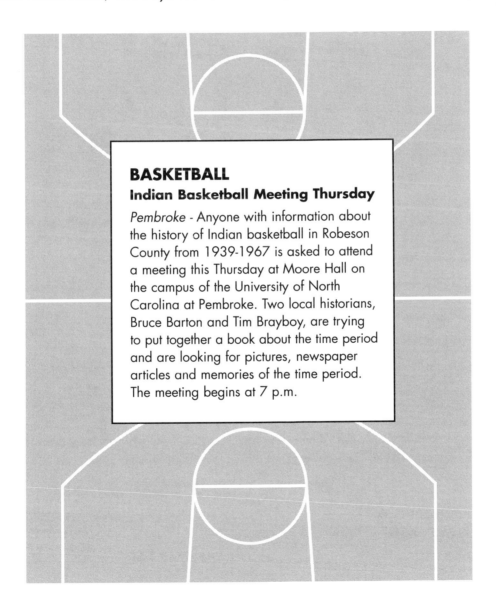

BASKETBALL
Indian Basketball Meeting Thursday

Pembroke - Anyone with information about
the history of Indian basketball in Robeson
County from 1939-1967 is asked to attend
a meeting this Thursday at Moore Hall on
the campus of the University of North
Carolina at Pembroke. Two local historians,
Bruce Barton and Tim Brayboy, are trying
to put together a book about the time period
and are looking for pictures, newspaper
articles and memories of the time period.
The meeting begins at 7 p.m.

Local basketball players were the first to respond to the public inquiry.

Photo by Gary Wayne Locklear

They are pictured (back row), left to right:

Gary Wayne Locklear (Pembroke High School, 1962-1966); Kenneth Ray Maynor (Pembroke High School, 1949-1953); Bobby Eugene Jacobs (Pembroke High School, 1957-1960); Hartman Brewington (Pembroke High School, 1956-1959); Danford Dial, Jr. (Prospect High School, 1962-1966); James F. "Buddy" Bell (Magnolia High School (1947-1954).

Front row, left to right:

John W. "Ned" Sampson (Pembroke High School, 1944-1947); Delton Ray Locklear (Pembroke High School, 1944-1947); Tim Brayboy (Pembroke High School, 1953-1957); Bundy Ross Locklear (Pembroke High School, 1950-1954); Oceanus Lowry (Pembroke High School, 1953-1957).

> "There were no age limits back then, teams had players playing high school sports who served in World War II. These veterans were over twenty one years old."
>
> **Delton Ray Locklear,** Pembroke High School, Class of 1947

> "The caliber of play was high quality. Given the opportunity many of the players could have played anywhere. They were just that good."
>
> **Les Locklear,** Magnolia High School

Indian History:
Men Seek to Keep Athletic Memories

This article by Earl Vaughan, Jr., appeared in *The Fayetteville Observer-Times* April 7, 1998

PEMBROKE – Bruce Barton stood in front of a blank easel, surrounded by memories living and written. The half dozen men with him in UNC-Pembroke's Moore Hall were athletes from another era. Thinning hair. More girth. Canes. Bifocals. But their memories of a time of segregation, a time when Indian high schools in Robeson County could only play against each other, were intact.

Barton fears those memories are dying. That is why he is working to produce a written history of the all-Indian high school basketball days from 1939-67. He's doing it one step at a time, by talking with the men still living who were part of the history.

Last week's meeting at UNC-Pembroke was the latest in a series designed to capture that history for the record. Barton and men like Ned Sampson and Danford Dial Jr. and Tim Brayboy came armed with annuals and scorebooks and their own recollections.

Barton, founder of the Carolina Indian Voice newspaper, had his easel to record as much of the history as he could. He was one of the few men in the room who didn't play high school basketball during the period of segregation. "In 1939, they stopped teaching high school courses at the university and built a high school with some of that New Deal money," Barton said.

Indian basketball was born when schools like Union Chapel, Pembroke, Prospect, Magnolia, Green Grove and Fairmont Indian School came along. The latter two eventually became Fairgrove. Les Maxwell High School from Cumberland County and Hawkeye High School from Hoke County joined.

Photo by Marcus Castro

Tim Brayboy, left, and Bruce Barton are gathering information for a book on Indian high schools.

All-Indian League

Together, they formed an all-Indian basketball league, since they were barred from competing with the white and black schools in Robeson County.

"It was board policy," said Tim Brayboy, a 1957 graduate of Pembroke High and long-time employee of the State Department of Public Instruction.

"There was no interaction within the races by rule of the Robeson County School Board," said Brayboy. "But we were able to schedule teams outside. We played Wadesboro, Rockingham, Hamlet, teams from Montgomery County."

And they played each other. From 1939 until 1967, the highlight of the basketball season, possibly the whole year, for the Indian schools, was the annual Indian tournament. It was held on the campus of then Pembroke College, in an old gym that seated about 1,000 fans.

"That was the big social event," said Ned Sampson, father of University of Oklahoma coach Kelvin Sampson. Ned Sampson played at Pembroke High from 1945-47, went on to Pembroke College and eventually coach in the Indian league.

"When you had the tournament, everybody would show up," Sampson said. "Prospect, Pembroke, Magnolia. Each community supported their school."

Unique Atmosphere

Photo by Marcus Castro

Ken Maynor, left, and Danford Dial, Jr. hold team photos of their Indian high school basketball team.

Ken Maynor played on two Indian tournament championship teams at Pembroke from 1950-53. He said there's nothing like the atmosphere of the old Indian tournament. "The highlight of the Indian schools was basketball," he said. "It was sort of the king of sports."

Instead of mourning at being limited to playing against only Indian schools, Maynor said the various communities reveled in the competition. "We would fill the gym to the rafters at the college," he said. "It was a big celebration playing our rivals, something to look forward to. I'd compare it to our Lumbee homecoming on the Fourth of July."

Danford Dial Jr. lived the thrill of the Indian tournament as both the son of a coach and a player. His father, Danford Dial, coached at Pembroke and Prospect

during the 1960s. The younger Dial played during the Indian leagues last days, from 1962-66, winning a championship with Prospect in 1965. Dial said the players of his day had no idea segregation was about to end.

"We were in our own little realm, in our own little area," he said. "To me, it made it more special.

Photo by Marcus Castro

Danford Dial Jr. points to his face in this photo of the 1964-65 Prospect High School Indian championship basketball team.

Bragging rights. It meant quite a bit. There was a rivalry between Pembroke and Prospect you could not believe."

Dial thinks basketball has changed a lot for the better today. Better coaching. Better athletes. A more complex game. But there are some things he misses about the days of the Indian league.

"Simplicity of life," he said. "You knew where you were going. You knew how you were going to get there. It was all laid out for you. At least it was for me."

Like Barton, Dial fears the history of the Indian league will soon be lost if it's not preserved now. He thinks it should be saved for a special reason. "There are many people who made a lot of sacrifices to get us where we are now," he said. "They all need to be remembered. If it hadn't been for those men in all those different communities and schools, I don't know how we would have all survived. It opens the door for somebody, somewhere. There would never have been a Kelvin Sampson."

That is what Barton wants to preserve as well.

"Basketball was a phenomenon of the times," Barton said. "The athletic competition was our outlet. There was more excitement back then. It reminds me of a Final Four."

Barton hopes to gather as much history as he can from the men who lived it, and get the book published by the end of the year. It can't happen too soon for Ken Maynor. "There is nothing on record," Maynor said. "It's a civilization gone with the wind."

THE WAY THE GAME WAS PLAYED BACK THEN...

In a look back on those glorious "Indian" high school days between 1939 and 1967 one can see clearly now that those were hard times, and that players sacrificed to play basketball. The games were played many times after farm crops were gathered or in between the gathering of the life-giving crops of tobacco and cotton and corn or whatever else could be grown in Robeson and adjoining counties to help put food on the table and a little bit of money in parents' pockets.

In retrospect, those were good days, too, in part, because of the spiritual nature of the game of basketball; the symbolic measurement of life itself where decisions were made and carried out to either victory or defeat. Indian people learned to never give up, and to work as hard as they humanly could, and then to dig a little deeper to find the essence of what they were about as a person and as a group – the segregated Indians of Robeson, Hoke and Cumberland counties.

Little was known about welfare back then, and most people worked diligently to get whatever it was that they got. They worked for what they had and were reminded often of the biblical admonition to "work by the sweat of the brow." And also that if one did not work then, of course, the ultimate penalty was not to eat. And people helped each other, sharing common travails and joys. Family members helped pick the cotton, crop the tobacco, raise the barns and just be good neighbors.

There were not many discussions about who they were. They knew who they were back then. They were Indians by birthright, by community, by choice, by segregation, by where they lived and with whom they played. They went to church every Sunday to worship with their own and to be preached to, mostly, by their own Indian preachers.

They went to school by themselves. Schools were strictly segregated; the Indians, blacks and whites each had their own schools and their own athletic programs; never playing each other. And musings were heard from time to time in sweaty and inadequate gymnasiums on Indian school campuses. "How would we do if we played Lumberton or Red Springs?" And secretly, in the deep recesses of their collective hearts, they thought that they would probably have won the game, or at least held their own, but it was not to be. Indians could only play Indians back then when the game was sacred and important to them as a life builder, as a way to explore the reality of their inner selves. They learned a lot about themselves when they played "Indian" basketball. They learned that basketball is a microcosm of life itself, and how they play the game is an indicator of what kind of person they are and will become.

Back then, in 1939, the Indians of Robeson and adjoining counties were officially named Cherokee Indians of Robeson County, and that would remain the name until 1953 when Rev. D.F. Lowry led a movement to change their name to Lumbee, in geographic honor of the ever-flowing Lumbee River nearby.

"Because of segregation during this time, there was no interscholastic athletic competition among the white, Indian, and black schools in Robeson County. The Indian high schools were able to schedule basketball games with white schools from Scotland, Richmond, Anson, and Montgomery counties in North Carolina and McColl High School in South Carolina."

Tim Brayboy, Pembroke High School
Class of 1957

When the English ships landed on the North American shores at Roanoke Island on the North Carolina coast, in the late 1500s, the Englishmen found Indians already there. The Englishmen were surprised to find that Indians were an amalgamation too, alike but different at the same time. The on-rushing Englishmen found Algonquians, Iroquoians, and Siouan Indian people. Within these linguistic stocks were the Tuscarora, Cheraw, Catawba, Cherokee, and sundry other tribes. The Indians were living in relative peace with one another. Six tribes were historically significant. These were:

- Hatteras, with whom the whites first came in contact on the shores of what is now North Carolina;

- Saponi, who were helpful in developing trading alliances between white traders and the sundry Indian groups;

- Tuscarora, the largest and most important and most warlike tribe of eastern North Carolina, with whom the whites had the most deadly Indian war in North Carolina's history;

- and the Cheraw and Pee Dee, both encountered in the Pee Dee Drainage Basin at the time of white contact in 1735; and the Waccamaw who were located on Drowning Creek as early as 1725.

Since records were not kept that long ago, it is not known how many Indians lived in North Carolina when the first white man came.

And in the throes of segregation of those days, many Indians turned to Christianity as their balm in Gilead. Lumbee historian Adolph Dial, who co-authored a history

> **"The idea of trusting your fellowman and the belief in a heaven beyond served to comfort, yet, in a ruthless world, also to impoverish many Indians."**
> **–Adolph L. Dial**

of the Lumbee, wrote, "The effects of Christianity were morally rewarding but sometimes socially debilitating. The idea of trusting your fellowman and the belief in a heaven beyond served to comfort, yet, in a ruthless world, also to impoverish many Indians." Dial also astutely noted that "The Lumbees' religious adherence caused them to accept their lot in life passively, thus slowing their progress politically and economically. It has only been since World War II that the Lumbee community emerged into the outside world in a measurable way." The churches seem to have changed too.

Until 1835, the Indians of Robeson and adjoining counties enjoyed the same rights and privileges as their white neighbors. It was a busy time, a time of raising families, putting down roots along the Lumbee River. The land seemed big enough for all people, no matter what their shade or hue of skin color. It seemed almost idyllic here along the dark stream.

But 1835 brought an ill wind, and the winds blew until it erupted into the Civil War where every institution, ideal and even different life-styles were brought into question. The South seemed called upon to answer questions about slavery and its way of doing business and how it treated its people. Politicians took refuge in laws and in 1835 the State of North Carolina amended the state constitution to deny people of color, including the Indians, THE RIGHT TO VOTE, BEAR ARMS, ATTEND SCHOOLS AND OWN PROPERTY. In 1854, the General Assembly even made it a criminal offense to marry outside one's race.

And this was the law of the land until 1868 when the Reconstruction Act restored the rights of citizenship to the Lumbee, but not the right to attend white schools. There were no Indian schools, and the Indians refused to attend the woefully inadequate black schools.

They were legislatively kept in ignorance for 50 years until 1885, a landmark year in the history of the Indians of Robeson and adjoining counties, when they were named Croatan Indians by the State of North Carolina. This period of 50 years is referred to by the Indians as the darkest period in their history. The lack of education for the Indians resulted, ironically, in an enmity between the Indians, blacks and whites that still exists today.

A North Carolina legislator, Hamilton McMillan, a Red Springs native, somehow worked and began to champion the cause of the Indian, resulting in a law (as noted earlier) being passed in 1885 that named the Indians of Robeson and adjoining counties, "Croatan Indians." The act authorized separate schools for the Indians. The fruit of this legislative vine will become Croatan Normal School in 1887, now the University of North Carolina at Pembroke. Thus, after 50 years of neglect, the Indians had their own school system. It was separate, unequal and inadequate, but it was theirs! And they rejoiced and worked hard to build schools for their children. This act that ratified the people as an Indian tribe by the State of North Carolina might be considered the historical highwater mark for the Indians of Robeson and adjoining counties.

In 1911, the state again renamed the Indians. They became simply, "Indians of Robeson County" because the name "Croatan" had become a mark of derision by the local white and black and, even some elements of the Indian communities. The legislators two years later renamed the Indians, "Cherokee Indians of Robeson County." They remained Cherokees until 1953 when they received the name that they are mostly known by today – Lumbee!

Inside this social incubator, the Indians flourished in spite of the legislative restraints. The game of basketball became a symbolic metaphor that helped to define them as a people. They love basketball because it tests their athletic and spiritual prowess better than any other game. They were tested and could not take refuge elsewhere. They had to learn to play the game honestly, by the rules. And the best team usually won. A basketball court seems, in a symbolic way, to represent life itself. It has boundaries and rules, and a goal – to win by hard work and perseverance. Basketball, more than any other game, seems to reward the one who works the hardest. Basketball players most times cannot finesse their way to victory or play outside the lines.

And the camaraderie might have been the greatest reward for playing the game. The sense of belonging, of loving your teammates, although the rough-hewn Indian youngsters probably would never have said it out loud. But, within the confines of the heart, the player truly loved his/her school, coach, and teammates and wanted to win because of the glory associated with the victory. Basketball comforted them, allowed them to become better people than they were. Basketball, the great equalizer, taught Indian youth, both boys and girls, important life lessons. And all of them, the fans, the administrators, the coaches and the players, are better for the experience of Indian basketball in Robeson and adjoining counties, especially during that interesting time between 1939-1967 until integration broke their ranks and thrust them into a frightening world unknown to many of them.

According to the 2000 census, there were 99,551 American Indians living in North Carolina. Information received from the N.C. Commission of Indian Affairs shows there were 46,896 American Indians in Robeson County, 4,691 in Cumberland County; and 3,852 in Hoke County.

Rev. D.F. Lowry led the movement to name the Indians of Robeson and adjoining counties LUMBEE. In 1905, Rev. Doctor Fuller Lowry received the first diploma issued by the Croatan Normal School for completing its "Scientific Course." This photograph of Lowry (right), shown with Bruce Barton, then editor of The Carolina Indian Voice newspaper, and his daughter, Brandi, was taken in 1975. Rev. Lowry died in 1977 at age 96.

A HISTORY OF EDUCATION

AND

THE COLLEGE GYMNASIUM

A History of Education:

From Croatan Normal School to University of North Carolina at Pembroke

Evolution of Names: 1887 — 1996

1887	Croatan Normal School
1911	Indian Normal School of Robeson County
1913	Cherokee Indian Normal School of Robeson County
1941	Pembroke State College for Indians
1949	Pembroke State College
1969	Pembroke State University
1996	The University of North Carolina at Pembroke

The First Building — 1887

Photo courtesy of UNC-Pembroke Archives

In 1887, under the influence of Honorable Hamilton McMillan, a N.C. Legislator from Robeson County, a law passed providing for the establishment of a normal school for the Indians of Robeson County. "For the payment of teachers' salaries and for no other purpose,"

$500 dollars were appropriated. The Indian citizens of the county contributed funds and labor and thereby secured a building to conduct a school. It was located about one and one-half miles northwest of Pates, on an acre of land bought from Rev. William Jacobs for $8. Rev. W. L. Moore was the first principal. The enrollment was 15. The Legislature appointed Rev. W. L. Moore, James Oxendine, James Dial, and Preston Locklear as members of the board of trustees. These men were given authority to associate with themselves three other Indian citizens of the county, and they selected Malachi Locklear, Benjamin Chavis, and Isaac Brayboy. In 1889, the appropriation was raised to $1,000 and remained the same for many years. In 1903, the Legislature made an appropriation of $100 for ceiling and seating in the first building. Rev. D. F. Lowry received the first diploma issued by the school in 1905, having completed a scientific course.

The Second Building — 1909

Photos courtesy of UNC-Pembroke Archives

In 1909, the normal school was moved to the present site near Pembroke. The Indians purchased a ten-acre tract at $50 an acre and had it deeded to the State Board of Education, and also contributed $600 toward the building of this house, the General Assembly having appropriated $2,000 toward the cost of the building.

Prof. H. L. Edens moved the school to Pembroke with little interruption and graduated the second student in the history of the school, John A. B. Lowry, in 1912.

The "college" was named INDIAN STATE NORMAL COLLEGE from 1911-1913.

The University of North Carolina at Pembroke
One University Drive
P. O. Box 1510
Pembroke, North Carolina 28372-1510

NEW WALLS RISE ON PEMBROKE GYM AFTER ORIGINAL WALLS DESTROYED
Officials Silent As to Reason For Replacement Of Brick

Articles appeared in *The Robesonian*, Friday, January 27, 1939, pages 1 & 8

REQUIREMENTS OF WORK QUESTIONED

Construction work on a gymnasium for Cherokee Indian Normal School at Pembroke has been resumed amid piles of brick and crumbled mortar from previously raised walls of the building, torn down after an inspection revealed structural weakness.

Officials' silence cloaked the condemnation proceedings, but left unrefuted the statement by a local bricklayer that he had been instructed, while at work on the project, to flush the walls with mortar only when an inspector was on the job, and that he quit work because he could not meet a requirement to lay from 2,000 to 2,500 brick in an 8-hour day.

Brick masons now are building new walls under the surveillance of an inspector unofficially reported to be devoting his entire time to the project. He succeeds a part-time inspector who had been employed jointly by two architects to inspect the gymnasium and two other projects, at Pembroke and Fairmont.

Ross Shumaker of Raleigh, architect for the gymnasium, said he had been asked to withhold all information for publication about the project, and declined to state whether a full-time inspector had been employed, but admitted: "That it seemed advisable to have additional supervision."

WALLS OPENED

Representatives of the state which is sponsor for the gymnasium building, and the PWA (Public Work Administration), which is aiding in its construction with a grant of federal funds, broke open and inspected sections of the walls last Saturday. An informed source stated one section of the waist-high wall, about 16 feet in length, was found to be considerably weaker than usual for a wall of that type, while another section opened for inspection showed some weakness, though not enough to affect the building. A third section opened it was reported, showed sound workmanship.

Work was stopped on the day of this inspection, and Mr. Shumaker visited the gym Monday. Part of the walls subsequently were torn down, and new courses of brick across, were started. The architect stated, however, that the weak section of the wall would not actually have made the building dangerous to occupy if it had gone unnoticed. Satisfactory arrangements for further construction have been made, he said.

Failure to flush a wall of this type would leave three courses of brick standing independently without joining mortar in between. From either side of the wall, the omission in the center ordinarily would not be detected.

DEFECTS REPORTED

Refusal of officials to give any explanation for the destruction of the original walls and raising of new ones also lent plausibility to unofficial reports that the construction defects were not found by inspectors in the course of regular inspection of the building, but by workmen who had either been discharged or had quit work because of greater demand for a greater quantity of production than they were able to meet.

Importance of that aspect of the matter, was emphasized by W.S. Griffith, contractor and construction supervisor for the Griffith Construction Co. of Rockingham, N.C. who became infuriated and told a *Robesonian* reporter to get off the building location when the reporter asked him about his requirements for bricklayers.

Previously, Mr. Griffith had denied making a requirement that bricklayers employed on the project should lay 2,500 brick a day, and declared he had "not signed anything" specifying that as a necessary qualification for applicants for work.

HIS OWN BUSINESS

When asked what requirements he did make, he replied that was "his own business," and pointed out the nearest way off the lot.

Fifteen hundred brick a day is regarded by local masons as a "good" average for one man to lay in an 8-hour day on an outside 12 1/2 inch wall such as the Pembroke gym project calls for. No one questioned on this point said he knew of any brickmason who could do a satisfactory job on such a wall at a speed as high as 2,500 brick a day.

BALKS AT INSTRUCTIONS

However, C.D. Falls of Lumberton, R. 4, one of several brickmasons who quit work on the project, said he did so after being advised by the foreman that Mr. Griffith had issued orders for the masons to lay between 2,000 and 2,5000 brick a day. Mr. Falls said he and several others declined to go to work under those terms, and that he came to Lumberton, reporting the incident to Walter R. Smith, PWA resident engineer.

Mr. Falls said he also had been ordered to stop flushing the brick with mortar on the sides of the inside course, though in some 20 years of bricklaying he had never known of the outside walls of a public building being constructed without flushing of the brick. When he was stopped, he said he was told not to flush unless an inspector was on the job. He also said he called to the attention of Byron Burney of Lumberton, part-time inspector on the project, that the construction was not being done correctly.

Now employed on a Laurinburg PWA project, Mr. Falls said he had heard no complaints there about his work or speed.

Contractor Griffith volunteered the statement that he had not fired anyone because of failure to lay a minimum number of brick in a day, but because of incompetence and "sloppy" work.

When questioned about the replacement work going on around him, Mr. Griffith's first reply was that he had admitted making a mistake, but that practically everyone connected with the project had made mistakes and that the others would admit theirs.

The Griffith Construction Co. was low bidder on the gymnasium project, and also has the contract for construction of a high school building near the Normal campus. The high school building was reported unofficially to have been inspected and found satisfactory.

Complicating the situation from the contractor's standpoint are requirements of the PWA that in so far as possible, local labor shall be used on the project, preference to be given workmen listed with the State Employment service. The PWA also sets a minimum wage scale ranging from 35 cents an hour for laborers and $1.10 an hour for brick masons.

This photograph of the Pembroke State College for Indians gymnasium appeared in THE LUMBEE TATTLER in 1941. An interesting aside is the fact that the Indian people of Robeson County were not named Lumbee until 1953, some 12 years later. The modern and spacious building was a mere two years old when this photograph was taken.

All the brick masons supplied him by the Lumberton Employment office, Mr. Griffith said, have not been first-class workmen.

CHEROKEE INDIAN NORMAL COLLEGE GYMNASIUM

The College Gymnasium, a spacious building, modern in all details, was erected during the season of 1938-39 with a grant from the Public Works Administration. The facility has a regulation basketball court with a dimension of 94 feet in length and 50 feet in width. It has a seating capacity of one thousand, with fold-up bleachers on the main floor and permanent seats in the upstairs balcony. Featured are modern showers and dressing rooms for separate gender. Additionally, the brick building contains coaches' offices, classrooms on each end of the balcony, a downstairs recreation room and storage areas. Restrooms for the public are downstairs.

The school, whose name was changed to Pembroke State College for Indians in 1941, allowed Indian high schools to use the gymnasium for some regular season games in addition to post season tournament play that took place on the campus through the 1940s and 1950s and into the early 1960s. By the mid-1950s, all four Indian high schools had on campus gymnasiums.

When the English E. Jones Health and Physical Education building opened in 1972, the College Gymnasium was used by the college Media Department. The Media Department vacated the gymnasium in 1987, leaving the building vacant for two years. School officials seeing no more use for the "Old Gymnasium" made the decision to raze the building. The historic building was demolished in 1989.

The building contained dressing rooms, showers and lockers for men and women athletes. All of the Indian high schools in Robeson County held a basketball tournament in the gymnasium each year in March. The "college", now the modern University of North Carolina at Pembroke, also provided many of the amenities needed to put on a basketball tournament, including referees and security. Sell-out crowds were the order of the day, and Indian basketball players, fans and coaches looked forward each year to "tournament time" when excitement filled the air. Looking back, maybe the community should have politicked to save the building as a testament to a time when Indians learned the real lessons of life on the hard wood floor of the "gym" at "the college."

CHEROKEES MEET WINGATE DECEMBER 12

Pembroke, December 8, 1940 - The Cherokee Indian Normal College five will open its basketball season in the new gymnasium here next Tuesday night, meeting the strong Wingate Junior College team at 7:30.

The contest will be part of a program dedicating the new gymnasium on the Indian College campus. The College band will furnish the music.

Coached by Foy Martin, Wingate presents one of the strongest cage outfits in North Carolina Junior College circles. Coach J.P. Sampson's Cherokees have the prospects this season and the contest is expected to be hard fought.

Photo courtesy of UNC-Pembroke Archives
Pembroke State College Gymnasium, 1946.

The historic "Old Gymnasium" demolition, 1989.

"Robeson County Indian High School Basketball 1939-67...This was an era so important in our lives. High school basketball was important to the players and coaches. However, it was very important to the patrons of the community, too. It provided the people a social outlet. In the 1940's and 50's there was not much for a person to do except work on the farm or around the home. There was no television, few people had electricity, maybe a battery radio, had no money to go to a movie. High school sports were about the only thing for entertainment. The basketball tournament at the college was the social highlight for the year for most people."

Ray Chavis, historian, Fairmont Indian High School

English E. Jones Health and Physical Education Center

The Center is named for English E. Jones who was President (1962-1972), Chancellor (1972-1979) of Pembroke State University. The Center was designed by the architectural firm of Jordan, Snowdon and McVicker Inc., of Laurinburg, NC. Speros Construction Company of Maxton, North Carolina was the general contractor.

The Center opened in the fall of 1972 and is located in the western part of the campus. The building covers 96,000 square feet. It has five classrooms, an administrative suite that includes the intercollegiate athletic offices, a conference library, area for seminars and an audio-visual lecture, and a classroom seating 150. Faculty and coaches' offices are located along the front halls of the building. The building is completely air-conditioned.

The varsity gym has a maple floor, and a seating capacity of 3,000 for basketball. The auxiliary gym has a rubberized floor. The main gym includes an area for three basketball courts, eight badminton courts, and four volleyball courts. Gymnastics and other sports can take place in the auxiliary gym. The locker room area accommodates 2,100 people.

Other facilities include an indoor swimming pool with six lanes and a separate diving tank. The area around the pool is equipped with permanent bleachers, seating 275. A laboratory is used in teaching courses in the physiology of exercise. An athletic training room is used for treating athletic injuries. Areas are also provided for weight training plus steam or sauna baths, and a large room to store physical education equipment, supplies, uniforms, and towels.

The exterior of the building consists of face brick and exterior masonry wall. The pool area is built of concrete with the remainder of the building constructed from steel frame.

The architects say five miles of wood pilings were used in the building, 800 tons of steel, 100,000 concrete blocks and 400,000 face brick.

By Gene Warren

Photo courtesy of UNC-Pembroke

THE SCHOOLS

ROBESON COUNTY INDIAN HIGH SCHOOL ATHLETIC CONFERENCE AND TRI-COUNTY INDIAN HIGH SCHOOL ATHLETIC CONFERENCE

The Robeson County Indian High School Athletic Conference began interscholastic athletic play in the 1920's. Original members of the conference were: Fairmont "Indian", Green Grove, Magnolia, Pembroke, Piney Grove, Prospect, and Union Chapel. In 1951 because of school consolidation the member schools were reduced to: Fairgrove, Magnolia, Pembroke and Prospect. Before consolidation, championships were conducted in football, basketball, and baseball for boys; basketball and softball for girls. After the schools consolidated, football was dropped from athletic programs, which left basketball and baseball for boys. Basketball remained the same for girls. Athletics were governed by the Rules and Regulations of the Robeson County School Board of Education. Championships were organized, supervised and administered by the school principals. The post-season basketball tournament was held most times in the Pembroke State College gymnasium before overflow crowds.

In 1966, Hawkeye (Hoke County) and Les Maxwell (Cumberland County) joined the Robeson County schools to form the Tri-County Indian High School Athletic Conference. The schools joined the North Carolina High School Athletic Association in 1968, ending a period of segregation with grateful hearts to the recalled deeds of those ordinary citizens. We honor their achievements as a very precious legacy.

October 12, 1999, the North Carolina High School Athletic Association recognized the accomplishments of these schools with a plaque put on permanent display in the Simon F. Terrell Building, North Carolina High School Athletic Association, Chapel Hill, N.C.

Photo by Glenn Swain, *The Robesonian*

Charles Adams, executive director, North Carolina High School Athletic Association and Tim Brayboy share a moment before the unveiling of the plaque recognizing the accomplishments of the Indian high schools in Robeson and adjoining counties.

Robeson County Indian High School Athletic Conference

Photo by John Bell, *Touch of Life*

Dedicated October 12, 1999 at the North Carolina High School Athletic Association Headquarters in Chapel Hill, North Carolina.

"This organization began interscholastic competition in the 1920's, under the auspices of the Robeson County Board of Education. Original members were Fairmont, Green Grove, Magnolia, Pembroke, Piney Grove, Prospect and Union Chapel.

Championships were held in several sports, organized and administered by the school principals. The popular post-season basketball tournament was held at Pembroke State College. Consolidation reduced the membership to four, and then in 1966 Hawkeye (Hoke County) and Les Maxwell (Cumberland) joined the Robeson County Schools to form the Tri-County Indian High School Athletic Conference.

In 1968, The schools joined the North Carolina High School Athletic Association. But many athletes and coaches first got the opportunity to participate in this conference, another important part of the tradition that is now the NCHSAA."

- *Text by Rick Strunk*

Taking part in the official unveiling of the plaque noting the history of the "Robeson County Indian High School Athletic Conference" at the headquarters of the North Carolina High School Athletic Association in Chapel Hill on October 12, 1999 were, left to right, Charles Adams, NCHSAA executive director; Tim Brayboy, former basketball player; Ronnie Chavis, former player and now Athletic Director of the Public Schools of Robeson County; and Barry Harding, who also played basketball.

Photo by Glenn Swain, *The Robesonian*

Photos by Glenn Swain, *The Robesonian*

LEFT TO RIGHT: James Frank Scott (Pembroke), Oscar Oxendine (Green Grove) and Cecil Hammonds (Green Grove) were three of the former basketball "old timers" who attended the unveiling of the plaque at the North Carolina High School Athletic Association headquarters in Chapel Hill, NC, on October 12, 1999.

Arriving for the ceremony at the NCHSAA headquarters in Chapel Hill were former foes, Kermit Chavis (Magnolia) and Tim Brayboy (Pembroke). Now longtime friends, Chavis and Brayboy, both point guards for their respective teams, had some celebrated battles on the hardwood when basketball was the game of choice for most Indian communities. Chavis and Brayboy played basketball in the late 1950s.

Also present for the unveiling of the plaque recognizing accomplishments of Indian high schools were (left to right) Margaret H. Chavis, Director of Indian Education for the Public Schools of Robeson County; Bruce Barton, an employee of Indian Education; Purnell Swett, former Superintendent of the Public Schools of Robeson County;

Barry Harding, Superintendent, Public Schools of Robeson County; and Robert Deese, member, Board of Education, Public Schools of Robeson County. Swett (Pembroke) Harding (Magnolia) and Deese (Pembroke) all played basketball with varying degrees of success.

FAIRGROVE HIGH SCHOOL

Photo courtesy of Fairgrove High School

Alfred Hunt, Johnny Hunt, right
Fairgrove High School 1966

"Every game we played hard, this was the only way we were coached. We owed it to the fans who came to see us play."

Horace Hunt, Fairgrove High School
Class of 1957

Fairgrove High School opened in the 1952-53 school year. The consolidated school was built to accommodate the high school students from Fairmont Indian High School and Green Grove High School. Fairgrove gets its name from the two schools.

Fairgrove was built on land purchased from Julie Mitchell. The school is located approximately two miles southwest of town limits of Fairmont, North Carolina. Albert Hunt, who was principal at Fairmont Indian School, was the first principal at Fairgrove School.

The advisory committee to Fairgrove School when the school opened were: John Will Hunt, Ollen Brooks, Willie Oscar Strickland, Fred Hunt, Sam Sanderson, and James Rogers.

The Fairgrove attendance district in 1952 was from Lumberton's 5th Street East and from Long Branch along the Lumber River to the South Carolina line.

The school year 1981-82, high school students from Fairgrove and Rowland were assigned to the new South Robeson High School. Subsequently, Fairgrove became a middle school with grades four through eight.

Although total racial integration was completed in the early 1970's the ethnic composition of the school continues to be predominantly American Indian. Fairgrove Middle School serves the following groups: American Indian, African American, Hispanic, Caucasian, and multicultural.

Today, Fairgrove Middle School is part of a rural farming community and is located in southeastern Robeson County. The school is approximately two miles west of the Fairmont town limits on Fairgrove Road. Craig Lowry is the school principal, the son of Adna Lowry who was principal when the facility was a Union School, K-12.

Fairgrove Interscholastic Athletic Program

Bringing together the students from Fairmont Indian and Green Grove High Schools paid immediate dividend to the Fairgrove High School athletic program. The boys basketball team won the conference post season basketball tournament in 1955, 57, 58, 59, 62, 63, and 64. The boys teams were blessed with outstanding student athletes and coaches. Coaching the teams were: Albert Hunt, Adna Lowry, Sr., Leon Hunt, Ralph Hunt, Sanford Hunt and James F. "Buddy" Bell. Albert Hunt, Adna Lowry, Sr. and Ralph Hunt served the school as principals.

The girls team won the conference post season basketball tournament in 1960 and 61. They played in the tournament championship in 1954, 56, 58, and 59. Coaching the teams were: Albert Hunt, Adna Lowry, Sr., Reese Locklear, and Ralph Hunt.

Photo: 1967 Fairgrove High School Yearbook, *Fairgrovian*

1967 FAIRGROVE HIGH SCHOOL CHEERLEADERS

FRONT ROW: Brenda L. Oxendine, Nora D. Rogers, captain; Becky Hunt, Shirlean Carter.

BACK ROW: Myrtis Eddings, Angelita Oxendine, Peggy Hammonds, Co-captain; Elizabeth A. Mitchell, Brenda K. Mitchell.

1956-1957 FAIRGROVE GIRLS BASKETBALL TEAM

Photo: 1957 Fairgrove High School Yearbook, *The Fairgrove*

STANDING LEFT TO RIGHT: Coach Reese Locklear, Virginia Oxendine, Vashtie Jacobs, Lee Hunt, Treva Hunt, Dorothy Hunt, Martha Hunt, Linda Hunt, Assistant Coach Mary Myrtle Hunt.
KNEELING, LEFT TO RIGHT: Janice Sealey, Clara Locklear, Lillian Hunt, Annie Ruth Oxendine, Doris Locklear and Lena Gray Hunt.

MAIN ENTRANCE

FORWARD

The pages of history tell an impressive story of the rapid progress our country has made. The pages of this annual tell an impressive story of the progress and accomplishment of our annual staff.

We commend the staff for a job well done.

PRINCIPAL

Sponsored By   ROWLAND IMPLEMENT CO.   Rowland

Copy from the 1953 *Fairgrove Annual*, the yearbook of the new school. Fairgrove School's first year in operation was the 1952-53 school year. First year Principal Albert C. Hunt is also shown.

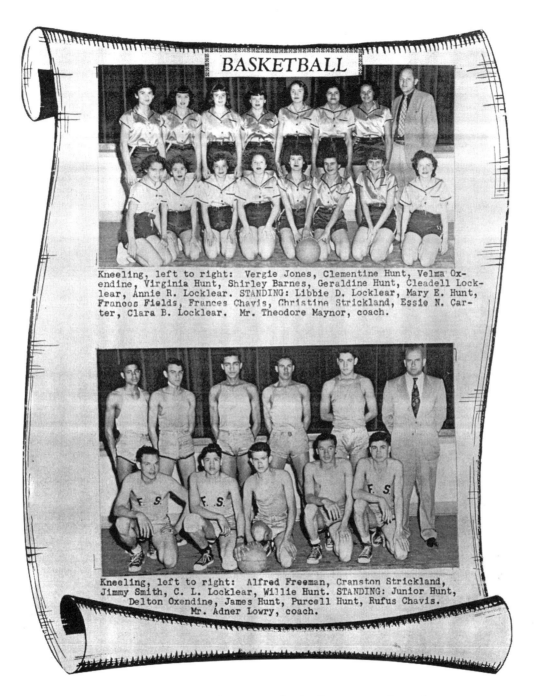

BASKETBALL

Kneeling, left to right: Vergie Jones, Clementine Hunt, Velma Oxendine, Virginia Hunt, Shirley Barnes, Geraldine Hunt, Cleadell Locklear, Annie R. Locklear. STANDING: Libbie D. Locklear, Mary E. Hunt, Frances Fields, Frances Chavis, Christine Strickland, Essie N. Carter, Clara B. Locklear. Mr. Theodore Maynor, coach.

Kneeling, left to right: Alfred Freeman, Cranston Strickland, Jimmy Smith, C. L. Locklear, Willie Hunt. STANDING: Junior Hunt, Delton Oxendine, James Hunt, Purcell Hunt, Rufus Chavis. Mr. Adner Lowry, coach.

1953 Fairgrove girls and boys basketball teams and coaches. Copy from the *Annual*, the year book of Fairgrove High School

Fairgrove School 1965, Most Athletic
Timmy Hunt — Betty Fay Locklear

Photo courtesy of Betty Fay Locklear Brewington

BETTY FAY LOCKLEAR BREWINGTON, started playing basketball at a very young age on the family farm with her nine brothers and sisters. She played a total of seven years at Green Grove and Fairgrove High School. She was voted most athletic in her 1965 graduating class. Residing in Southgate, Michigan 33 years, Betty graduated from Chrysler Institute of Engineering and Central Michigan University. She is a 24-year employee of Daimler-Chrysler Corporations' Glass division. The daughter of the late Horace Locklear and Savannah Locklear of Saddletree, Betty was married to the late Willie Brewington. She has one son, Shane, and one grandson, Tyler.

Photo courtesy of Public Schools of Robeson County

Fairmont Indian High School merged with Green Grove and re-opened as Fairgrove High School in 1952-53 school year.

The site of the former Fairmont Indian School was located in the Northeast section in the town of Fairmont, North Carolina, at the corner of Morro/Marvin, and Stafford Streets. An open canal serves as a boundary to the property. The canal serves to drain water from the low lying insulated site. Today, the site where the school buildings stood has public housing that is administered by the Town of Fairmont Housing Authority and a recreation park administered by the Robeson County Parks and Recreation Department. During the history of the Fairmont Indian School three different buildings were constructed on the site. The first building was constructed in 1900. The wood building was used for several years. A second wood building was constructed to accommodate increased student enrollment.

The school building was used by the American Indian people several years for church services until they were able to construct their own building, which they did in the late 1920s. In 1928 the second building was destroyed by fire. Church officials of the recently constructed Cedar Grove Baptist Church located in front of the site of the school, opened its doors and allowed the church building to be used until a new school could be constructed. The third school building was constructed on the site where the other school burned. The four-room wood building was a union school, serving students in grades 1-11. (Note: North Carolina State Board of Education requirements for high school graduation at this time were the completion of eleven years.) A cafeteria was attached, thought to be the only one at this time among the American Indian schools in Robeson County.

In the late 1930s, Fairmont Indian School administration and staff began preparations to become an accredited school. The Robeson County Board of Education employed A.B. Riley as principal of Fairmont Indian School. Riley, certified as a principal, had served as principal at Pembroke Normal School. Through Riley's help Fairmont Indian School was accredited in 1938.

Several people served as principals of the school: A.B. Riley, Kermit Lowry, Delton Lowry, Jenny Smith, and Albert Hunt.

Fairmont Indian School closed at the end of the 1951-52 school year. All students, grades 1-12 were assigned to the new Fairgrove School. Fairgrove School opened the 1952-53 school year. The consolidated school was built to accommodate the student body from Fairmont Indian School and the students in grades 7-12 from Green Grove School. Fairgrove gets its name from the two schools. Albert Hunt was assigned to be the first principal of Fairgrove School.

Fairmont "Indian" High School Shows Remarkable Progress

This article appeared in the *Odago*, a literary publication at the Cherokee Indian Normal School (December 14, 1937).

The history of the school at Fairmont shows the remarkable progress in education in this part of the country.

In 1927 the schoolhouse was a two-room building. This house was burned, and the session was completed at Pleasant View Church. In spite of this disaster, the school was re-organized the same year with the appointment of G.E. Spaulding as chairman of the board. The other members were Oscar Hunt and James Hunt, the latter being a member of the previous board.

In response to a request made by this committee, the county board of education made an appropriation of $3,000 to erect and equip a four-room building. School work began in this building in the session of 1928-29.

But elementary schooling did not meet all the educational needs and demands of this section. It was realized that here was the logical place for the location of a high school. Aroused by the desire for higher education, the trustees of Fairmont, Piney Grove, Ashpole Center, New Bethel and Henderson schools held a meeting which resulted in the creation of a high school plan, with Fairmont as its center. The action taken at this meeting was approved by the county authorities and a Fairmont high school was started on its way.

Beginning with students contributed from the seventh grades of these supporting schools, the Fairmont High School has grown from an institution having only one high school teacher to a State accredited school with four instructors in high school and six in the elementary grades.

The latest step in this story of progress was the completion during the current year, of a splendid new high school building, erected on an appropriation of $11,000. This building has seven rooms and a spacious auditorium. One of the seven rooms is occupied by a well-equipped home economics department.

There are approximately 440 students in school, of whom about 75 are in the high school department.

Present Committee – G.E. Spaulding, J.W. Sampson, George Ransome.

Present Faculty, High School – Bradford Lowry, Principal, A.B. Riley, Mildred Lassiter, Frances Shaffner.

Elementary – Mary Warriax, Pearl Hammonds, Ludahlia Wilkins, Carl Maynor, A.G. Dial.

Photo courtesy of Public Schools of Robeson County

1950 FAIRMONT INDIAN HIGH SCHOOL GIRLS BASKETBALL TEAM

FIRST ROW: Sadie Oxendine, Frances Chavis, Delois Chavis, Margie Oxendine, Sue Sanderson.

BACK ROW: Clara Locklear, Lucille Locklear, Christine Strickland, Margaret Hunt, Clois Chavis, Velmer Smith, Anna Sanders, Coach Albert Hunt.

Interscholastic Athletics at Fairmont Indian School

Although small in enrollment, the athletic teams measured up well against other teams in the Robeson County Indian High School Athletic Conference. In 1945, the boys basketball team, coached by Carlie Oxendine, won the post season basketball tournament after a close contest with Green Grove by the score of 22-16. Captain Clifford Oxendine, playing at forward for Fairmont, was high scorer with nine points. Written records are not available to support the results of the 1947 boys post season tournament, but information received from an eye witness has Fairmont High School winning the tournament. Others coaching the Fairmont boys team were Herbert Oxendine and Adna Lowry.

Photo courtesy of Public Schools of Robeson County

1951-1952 CHAMPIONS

FRONT ROW, LEFT TO RIGHT: James B. Oxendine, James S. Hunt, James A. Hunt, Holland Clark, Zeb Oxendine.
BACK ROW: Delton Oxendine, Lankford Sanderson, Purcell Hunt, Earl Hammonds, Len Hunt and Coach Adna V. Lowry.

GREEN GROVE SCHOOL

Green Grove School originated in 1887 as a result of the 1885 North Carolina General Assembly mandate to establish separate schools for American Indians residing in Robeson County. School was first held in Reedy Branch Baptist Church. The church was located on a rural dirt road (now State Road 2422) approximately two miles east of McDonald, North Carolina. The school site was later moved and a one room wooden building was erected on what is now State Road 1003. This school was named Joe Branch School. As student enrollment increased, another room was added to the building.

Joe Branch School existed until the early 1920's. In August of 1921, the Robeson County Board of Education purchased two acres of land from Elizabeth Townsend by guardian Mary G. Bain for the construction of a new school. These two acres are a part of the present day site, located on rural State Road 2422, near Reedy Branch Baptist Church. A four room building was constructed on this site and given the name Green Grove School, from the beautiful grove of oak trees surrounding the area. The original building was destroyed by fire in 1929. Immediately, plans were made to rebuild another school at the Green Grove site. This phase of construction included two separate buildings: One five classroom school building and a house for teachers. The five classrooms were eventually sub-divided to provide accommodations for high school students.

In 1940, a four room brick structure was constructed adjacent to the main building. This building now is used for second and third grade classrooms. As student enrollment increased additional classrooms were needed. In December 1943, three and four tenths acres of land were purchased by the Robeson County Board of Education from Sam C. Floyd to be used for school construction.

Main High school building on Green Grove Campus.

Photos courtesy of Public Schools of Robeson County
Home Economics Building on Green Grove campus in 1940's.

During the 1943-44 school term, the main building was once again destroyed by fire. Reedy Creek Baptist Church provided their church for Green Grove Elementary school students and faculty, grades one through six. During the 1944 fall school term, these students and faculty used a school in the McDonald community. This school had become available when the McDonald School students were assigned to a school in Rowland, North Carolina.

In 1952, a new school was constructed at the Green Grove site. This modern brick building was designed and constructed as an elementary school.

The year before, the Robeson County Board of Education had approved the consolidation of Fairmont Indian and Green Grove High Schools. By the high school students leaving, this allowed the elementary students from the McDonald School to return to Green Grove School.

Today, Green Grove School consists of a four-room brick structure built in 1940 located adjacent to the main building. This building is currently being used for second and third grade classrooms. The main building has ten classrooms (Pre-Kindergarten through second grade), administrative offices, a cafeteria, a teacher's lounge, a gymnasium/auditorium, rest room facilities, and a storage room. A media center is located on the northeast side of the main building. Green Grove serves six ethnic groups: American Indian, African American, Hispanic, Caucasian, Asian, and Multicultural. Presently there are 350 students. Green Grove School is part of a rural farming community located in southeastern Robeson County, approximately six miles northeast of the city limits of Fairmont, North Carolina on State Road 2422. The campus contains 9.24 acres of land.

There are several economic structures that govern the general aspects of the community. A low percentage of the families rely upon agriculture for their livelihood. However, a few families use farming to supplement their income from other occupations. Most families in the community are employed by manufacturing located in Robeson County.

Many changes have occurred since its inception. Green Grove School stands as a symbol of pride to the community, and to the many former students, teachers, administrators, and patrons who were part of the school's valued history. These citizens can look back in time to memories of events that transpired, some without any consequence even at the time they were a reality; some with a poignancy that is indescribable; some comical, some tribal, some tragic but all part of their human existence. Those in charge of the school today continue to provide a quality education for all the students.

Interscholastic Athletics at Green Grove High School

The foundation and development of the interscholastic athletic program at Green Grove School in the 1940's was under the leadership of coaches Herbert G. Oxendine and Joe Sampson. These two men, through hard work and willingness of the student athletes, developed basketball teams that were a force for other conference teams.

The boys team won the conference post season basketball tournament in 1946. They played in the championship game in 1942, 1945, and 1947. The girls team never advanced to a championship game.

Photo courtesy of Public Schools of Robeson County

1948-49 GREEN GROVE BOYS BASKETBALL TEAM

FRONT ROW: Rucious Hunt, Oscar Oxendine, William Hammonds, Earl C. Scott, Weldon Hunt.

BACK ROW: Coach Herbert G. Oxendine, James F. Hunt, H.B. Chavis, Buddy Swett, Willie Swett, Carlie Hunt.

Herbert Grantham Oxendine (1913-66)

Photo courtesy of Linda Ellen Oxendine

Herbert G. Oxendine was born November 7, 1913, to William Arthur and Maude Woodell Oxendine. He died suddenly on December 14, 1966. He was married to the former Deborah Dial.

Oxendine was the father of four children: Linda Ellen, Richard Arthur, Miriam Denise, and Herbert Grantham, Jr.

He attended the Robeson County School System and was graduated salutatorian of his class at Pembroke High School in 1934. Not only was he a dedicated student but was also endowed with a very good athletic ability. Oxendine attended McKendree College in McKendree, Illinois during his freshman year, then returned to his hometown to attend Pembroke State College for his sophomore and junior years. He later received his Bachelor's degree from Western Carolina University. In 1953, Oxendine received an Ed.D. in Education from Boston University.

During his life, he achieved many goals which were beyond recognition in the tribal community for his time. He was among the first of the Lumbees to receive his Ed.D. His master thesis was entitled "A Survey of Outdoor Science Interest at the Fifth and Sixth Grade Levels."

His employment was as diverse as his interests. He received an Honorable Discharge as a Major in the U.S. Air Force after serving in World War II. At Green Grove High School, he served as coach and teacher for three years, teaching science and mathematics. He was also employed at Fairmont High School, Fairmont, NC. His last terms of employment were at Pembroke State College for 12 years before his death. While there, he served as director of Student Teaching, director of Summer School, freshmen class advisor, Dean, manager of Bookstore, and coach of girls basketball.

Other significant achievements of Oxendine include a board director of Tri-County Community Action, Inc.; secretary of Pembroke Kiwanis Club and "Kiwanian of the Year" (1966: director of Odom Children's Home; deacon, Sunday School Superintendent and director of training at First Baptist Church in Pembroke, NC.

In recognition of his diligent and outstanding work, the Science Building at Pembroke State University and the Pembroke Senior High Football Field were named in his honor.

Oxendine was a mentor to many Indian students and was also a volunteer who added his talents and energies to Indian basketball.

- Lumbee Regional Development Association Archives

Photo courtesy of Public Schools of Robeson County

1948-49 GREEN GROVE GIRLS BASKETBALL TEAM

FRONT & CENTER: Coach Herbert G. Oxendine.

FRONT ROW, LEFT TO RIGHT: Helen Hunt, Mazie Jacobs, unidentified, Margaret Hunt, Elaine Hunt, Thedis Ray Hunt, Louise Chavis, Margaret Strickland, unidentified, unidentified.

BACK ROW, LEFT TO RIGHT: includes members of boys team) William Hammonds, Oscar Oxendine, Rucious Hunt, Weldon Hunt, H. B. Chavis, Carlie Hunt, Earl C. Scott, James F. Hunt, Willie Swett, Buddy Swett.

The History of Hoke County Education

One of the tenets of mankind is that, "Nothing is simple." This holds true as one attempts to put together a logical sequence of events that leads to the Hoke County High School of today. Compounding the complexity of the situation is the fact that until 1969, Hoke County was one of the few counties in North Carolina that had three separate school systems – Indian, black, and white. Each of the three suffered in the early days the same problems that plagued other small, rural communities. The population was scattered across the county in isolated microcosms that suffered from similar problems, a lack of resources. Gradually, as the population increased and the need for better and better education became evident, leaders of all three races began to see the wisdom of consolidation. The 1940's was a decade of new, small buildings that soon became obsolete, with consolidation the end result.

This treatise of Hoke County High School attempts to deal briefly with the three separate systems as separate entities that merged in September, 1969 into one strong institution that has made the entire community proud.

The history of American Indian Education in Hoke County, North Carolina is clouded by a lack of records. However, some facts are available and certain assumptions can be made with a reasonable degree of certainty.

As was the case with most small schools of all races in rural North Carolina, it was a story of several small schools that eventually closed and or were consolidated. Such was the case with Jacob's Point, Macedonia, and Antioch Indian.

Jacob's Point is first mentioned in the Hoke County Board of Education minutes of April 6, 1914: "Several Croatans from Antioch Township came before the Board to petition for a school. Their petition was considered favorably though no definite action was taken..." Dan Newton and James Locklear were appointed to raise funds for the purchase of the Jacob's Point school house, the County was to pay one half the cost of the same.

On August 19, 1914, the Hoke County Board of Education passed, "that we sell Jacob's Point School House and site to the Indians for $150.00, and that a committee of the Jacob's Point school be instructed to confer with authorities of St. John's Church to see the chance for conducting school in the church this year..."

Further reading of the minutes of the Hoke County Board of Education, and the early mention of Jacob's Point, it might be inferred that this school came into being while Antioch Township was still a part of Robeson County, North Carolina. This school was in operation as late as 1933-34.

Though Jacob's Point is first mentioned in the Hoke County Board of Education minutes, in 1914, it is referred to at least by in reference in a deed dated February 27, 1894 as part of Public School district #20. Reference is Robeson County Book RRR-741. This deed is held by Elizabeth Matthis Brown. The site of the old school is on the south side or SR 1130, .2 miles east of X of SR 1128. This was a one room building and stands as of this time, though in a dilapidated condition. When Jacob's Point closed, the students then went to Antioch Indian School, which was located just in front of Mt. Elim Baptist Church.

The Antioch Indian School opened the school year of 1935-36, the school was a two-room building for grades one through eight. School administrators and teachers that served Antioch School were; Kinlaw Jacobs, Mary Lee Goins, James E. Dial, Mary Liza Locklear, Eleanor Dial, Wilson Chavis, and Georgeanna Dial.

Macedonia was a one room school whose beginning is unclear. The site was between the cemetery of present day Macedonia Methodist Church and the church itself, right at the intersection of SR1113 and SR1118. Administrators and teachers that served Macedonia School were: Carrie Moore Dial, Libby Bryant, Johnny Bullard, Jessie Bell Chavis, Libby Hunt, and Cattie Bell Bullard.

According to an article in *The News Journal,* Raeford, North Carolina, dated September 3, 1953, Macedonia School antedated another school that burned about 1933. The students that had attended this school were then transported to Robeson County. After transporting the students to Robeson County for several years, the Hoke County Board of Education passed to build a school at a different site. The new one room school served students in grades one through eight. One teacher was employed to teach all grades. The school building was used by the community as a church.

During these racially segregated times, American Indian children in Hoke County who wanted to further their education beyond the eight grade, attended high schools in neighboring Robeson County.

During all these years the main leadership in the fight made by the American Indians of Hoke County for better schools was furnished largely by Elisha Dial, Sr. (August 15, 1890 – August 31, 1980) and Rodney Locklear, Sr. (December 8, 1889 – February 6, 1973). In 1916, Elisha Dial came to Hoke County from Robeson County, as did many other American Indian families. When Dial arrived there were no schools for American Indian children. Realizing the need for his children and other American Indian children to have their own schools. He and Rodney Locklear, with community support, petitioned the Hoke County Board of Education to provide a school for American Indian children. The Board of Education with the support of School Superintendent W. P. Hawfield, schools were built.

Consolidated Indian School

In its inception in 1952, the new school built for the American Indian citizens was more than a consolidated school to the community. It was a source of great pride. It was the first modern educational facility with adequate space, a lunchroom, indoor rest rooms, and later to be added gymnasium. Of most importance, the school offered a high school curriculum leading to a diploma. The school was the result of a long struggle by the American Indian people to acquire quality education in Hoke County. The new school was a symbol of growth and respect that the people had attained.

The new school was named "Consolidated Indian School." Students from Antioch Indian and Macedonia Indian schools made up the student body. According to Winford Rogers, grandson of Elisha Dial, Sr. "I was one of the first dozen Hoke County Indian ninth graders." He and two others, James Anderson Maynor and Johnny Branch, made up the first high school graduating class.

Rogers would go on to college, get a degree and teach at the high school.

James H. Dial, who was principal at Antioch Indian School, was the first principal at the Consolidated Indian School. All the teachers who were teaching at Antioch and Macedonia, were assigned to the new school.

The school year 1954-55 Spurgeon M. Bullard succeeded James H. Dial as principal. During Bullard's term as principal, the school underwent two name changes. In 1954-55 school year the name was changed to Hoke County Indian School. In the 1958-59 school year, Bullard's last year as principal of the school, Lew Barton, a teacher at the school, came up with the name "Hawkeye." The name was sanctioned by Bullard and the school committee, including the chairman, Elisha Dial. Newman Oxendine succeeded Bullard as principal, he was succeeded by Earl Hughes Oxendine, who was principal when consolidation of the high schools was transmitted by the Board of Education. At its April 1, 1968 meeting, the Hoke County Board of Education changed the name of Hawkeye school to South Hoke Elementary School to be effective with the 1968-69 school year. At the same meeting, the Hoke County Board of Education passed a resolution calling for the consolidation of Upchurch High School, Hawkeye, and Hoke High School.

Laughlin MacDonald contributed to this history

Photo by Tim Brayboy

South Hoke School, once known as Hawkeye School.

Interscholastic Athletic Program at Hawkeye High School

In 1959, Bobby Dean Brayboy was employed as the first Physical Education teacher and full time athletic coach at Hawkeye. The same year a gymnasium was constructed at the school. Brayboy with assistance from school custodian staff, painted lines for the basketball court on the bare cement floor in the gymnasium. Brayboy organized boys and girls basketball teams. It was through his efforts that school officials from Hawkeye, Les Maxwell School, and Eastern Carolina School organized the Tri-County Indian High School Athletic Conference.

During Brayboy's tenure the faculty and students adopted the "Hawk" as the school's mascot. In 1961, Brayboy was drafted into the military service.

Forace Oxendine followed Brayboy as Physical Education teacher and Athletic coach. He expanded the athletic schedule to include baseball for boys. Oxendine was an outstanding athlete while attending Pembroke State College. He had played professional

Photo courtesy of Eva Brayboy

BOBBY DEAN BRAYBOY participated in athletics at Pembroke High School and Pembroke State College. In 1959, he became the first Physical Education teacher and athletic coach at Hawkeye School. Brayboy organized the school's boys and girls basketball teams for interscholastic competition. In 1961, the teacher and coach was drafted into military service. Captain Brayboy retired from the United States Navy after 20 years of service.

baseball, advancing to the triple-A level. He organized a strong baseball program at Hawkeye. One of his players, Durant Cooper, signed a professional contract with the Chicago White Sox, advancing to the triple-A level with the White Sox organization. Oxendine expanded the basketball and baseball schedule at Hawkeye to include the Indian high schools from neighboring Robeson County. Darkness fell on the school and community January 31, 1965 when the popular coach was killed. Oxendine's death occurred just days before the conference post season basketball tournament.

Hartman Brewington, who was assistant coach to Oxendine, succeeded him as the head coach. Brewington was coaching when Hawkeye and Les Maxwell High Schools joined the Robeson County High Schools to form a new Tri-County Indian High School Athletic Conference. The two schools were successful in the new conference. In 1966 Hawkeye played Pembroke High School for the tournament championship. Les Maxwell played Magnolia High School in the 1967 tournament championship game. Brewington left Hawkeye in 1967. Gerald Maynor coached the teams the 1967-68 school year. This was the last year for high school students at the school. On July 1, 1968 a resolution was passed

and ordered transmitted by the Hoke County Board of Education calling for the consolidation of Upchurch High School, Hawkeye High School and Hoke County High School.

A partial list of male players is: James Albert Hunt, Earl Lowry, David Earl Locklear, Leslie Locklear, Julian Pierce, Sheldon Pierce, Charles Barton, Elisha Dial, Jr., Harold Brewer, Carlton Locklear, Durant Cooper, Bobby Cooper, David Earl Bullard, Henry T. Locklear, Luther Locklear, Phil Pierce, Charlie K. Locklear, Jimmy McMillian, Willie Faye Jacobs, Donald Ray Oxendine, James Ed Locklear, Joel Dial, Jr., Ozell Jacobs, Muriel Jacobs, Don Woods, Charles Dial, Pete Oxendine, Jensen Locklear, Jimmy Ray Lowry, Ray Jones, Oscar Jacobs, Garfield Watkins, Henry Lloyd, Harvey Goins, Ray Carter, Larry Brewer, and Stoney Locklear.

A partial list of female players is: Glenda Sue Oxendine, Helen Locklear, Evelyn Carter, Everlina Carter, Brenda Oxendine, Joyce Locklear, Geannette Locklear, Carol Jane Locklear, Helen Locklear, Mary Catherine Locklear, Lella Faye Bullard, Ruth Dial, Glenna Oxendine, Anita Oxendine, and Gracey Lee Chavis. Cheerleaders: Betty Lou Bullard, Mary Lois Hunt and Peggy Revels.

Photos courtesy of Henry T. Locklear

1962 HAWKEYE BOYS AND GIRLS BASKETBALL TEAMS WITH COACH FORACE OXENDINE

Photos courtesy of Henry T. Locklear

Hawkeye High School Basketball Team with Coach Forace Oxendine left and Principal Earl Hughes Oxendine, standing far right

1966 Hawkeye High School Cheerleaders

1955-63 HAWKEYE ALUMNI

Hawkeye High School alumni with Wilson Chavis, far right, former basketball coach and assistant principal.

SCHOOL WILL DROP NAME OF CHIEF

by Lucy Gray Peebles
The News-Journal, Raeford, NC, April 11, 1968

Photo courtesy of Margaret Chavis

Elisha Dial, a leader in getting better schools for Indians in Hoke County.

"Hawkeye School" will soon be a name of the past.

A large number of school patrons who signed a petition to the effect wanted it that way, and the Hoke County Board of Education complied with their wishes and passed a motion to make it legal. It is the name that is to be abolished-not the school.

The institution will continue to exist and to grow but when the doors open next fall, it will be South Hoke School.

The name, "Hawkeye" is all right with some of the old timers regardless of this day and time of progress, consolidation and integration. They know that the school was named for an old realistic or legendary Indian Chief. Some other Hoke County Indians, however, want the name changed to something a little more sophisticated – a name that will benefit students of any race, and a name that school people nationwide will understand without explanation.

The board of education took the action at a recent meeting after a delegation with lengthy petition asked that the school be given a new name.

The school was dubbed "Hawkeye" back in 1952 when the new brick structure was built and two county elementary schools, Mt. Elim and Macedonia, were consolidated so Indian children in Hoke would have advantage of a high school education. Schools operating prior to that offered nothing higher for them than an eighth grade education.

A teacher, Lew Barton, came up with the "Hawkeye" suggestion. It was sanctioned by Principal S.M. Bullard and the school committee.

E.L. Dial, a committee man at the time, agreed, and he still doesn't see too much wrong with it, he says.

The 78-year-old man, known by many friends of all races as Elisha Dial, came to Hoke in 1916 and lived here four years before there was an Indian school. When his brood began to approach school age, he started to worry. he liked living in Hoke County, but if the children couldn't get schooling here, he would have to go back to Robeson County like other Indian families had done.

Dial made up his mind to go to the superintendent. He was a hard worker and an ambitious man who would go to bat for his family and for his fellowman, no matter what the race. He was respected by all. The superintendent, W. P. Hawfield, listened. He told Dial to find 20 pupils and he could have a school. Dial found 30 pupils and a teacher.

A vacant building at Jacob's Point near McCormick's Mill Pond was used for the one-room school. The enrollment grew year after year until the place was running over and the teacher had more than he could do. Many children walked three miles or more to classes, including all 10 of the Dial boys and girls.

By that time, K.A. MacDonald had become superintendent. Dial came to the office and asked for another teacher and more space. MacDonald agreed that the need was urgent and the larger building was erected at the other end of the pond. It was used for a school during the week and for church on Sunday. The religious name of Mt. Elim was adopted.

"We (the Indian patrons) were hard-working people and for recreation we would, on special occasions, have an all-day gathering at Mt. Elim. There would be chicken and fish and things that we rarely ever got at home." Dial often added to the festivities by buying everybody a set-up of ice cream.

Elisha Dial was raised with Old Prospect School right next door, but his father had bought a large piece of land, which was just about all water and woodland and the son stopped school at an early age and spent his days clearing land, while his father worked for someone else to bring in enough money to pay for the property and feed the family.

It taught him a lesson, he declared, a lesson that, "hard work and that only will get you the things you need and want." It was a lesson Dial relied upon throughout his life to feed his family of a dozen mouths and to eventually accumulate a 140-acre farm and a home.

He instilled in his children the same lesson, but was determined that they would have some book learning, too. Each of them went as far as the existing school would carry them. They, too, now have their own homes.

Winford Rogers, a grandson of Elisha Dial, was one of the first dozen Hoke County Indian ninth graders. He and two others, James Anderson Maynor and Johnnie Branch, made up the first high school graduating class at Hawkeye.

When Earl Oxendine, the present principal, came to follow Newman Oxendine as the new school was in its tenth year. There were 500 students. Now several building programs and six years later, there is a spreading plant and 740 students with an annual graduating class of about 20.

Early Indian Education in Cumberland County

The education process for American Indian students in the Cumberland County schools was an arduous development for their parents. Indian families were determined to get a school for their children, and their tenacity paid off when the Cumberland County Board of Education voted to build an elementary school in the community where the majority of the American Indians lived. In school year 1939-40, Cade Hill Elementary School opened. Built on a two acre site, the building was wood construction and consisted of two classrooms. Nevertheless, the school became the pride of the Indian community for whom it served.

The majority of administrators and faculty who served the school were Indian educators from adjoining Robeson County. Leona Lowry Woodell of Pembroke, North Carolina was the first principal of the school (1939-41). Others serving in that capacity were: Parree Janet Jacobs (1941-42); Maggie Lucas (1942-43); Carrie Lee Dial, who served two terms (1943-44) and (1946-47); Jessie Belle Hunt (1944-46); Purcell Locklear (1947-48); Marvin D. Spaulding (1948-49), and William Castor Locklear (1949-56). Besides being principal, these individuals taught a full class schedule. Because there were no high schools in Cumberland County for Indian students to attend during this time, students graduating from Cade Hill Elementary School attended Eastern Carolina High School, an all-Indian school in adjoining Sampson County. This circumstance proved to be a hardship on students who were forced to travel as many as 70 round-trip miles daily in order to get a high school education during these racially segregated years.

In order to accommodate the ever-growing American Indian population, and with the strong support of County School Superintendent, F. Douglas Byrd, Cumberland County appropriated funds for a new school that would be built in two phases on a site in east Fayetteville, North Carolina, three miles from downtown and less than one mile from the Cape Fear River at 102 Indian Drive. Les Maxwell Elementary School, named for school board member, E.L. "Les" Maxwell of Stedman, North Carolina, opened in school year 1956-57, albeit under the protest of local Indian parents and patrons who viewed the design and construction of the straight, single story wing with its hallway and classrooms on each side and flat roof line to be of poor quality.

With the opening of the new elementary school, Cade Hill Elementary School closed for students at the end of school year 1955-56. The second phase of construction on "Les" Maxwell School was completed in 1957. The design and construction matched the earlier phase and resulted in an L-shaped appearance. A library measuring approximately 10-feet by 10-feet was built within the wing to serve the 60-70 high school student enrollment. With the completion of this phase, Indian students in Cumberland County were afforded their first-ever opportunity to attend their own

Photo by Tim Brayboy

Les Maxwell School closed at the end of the 1968-69 school year.

high school. Two principals served Les Maxwell School during its brief history. Jesse Maynor of Robeson County was the first, serving from 1956-68. H. Dale Tompkins of Fayetteville served the 1968-69 school year. The majority of the school's teachers commuted from points in Robeson County each day. The first senior meeting requirement for graduation from Les Maxwell High School was Joyce Morrison. The candidate, wishing not to graduate alone, requested and was granted a graduation deferment from school officials. She was awarded her high school diploma in official ceremonies the following year. The annual number of high school graduates never exceeded ten in any given school year. The school closed to students at the end of the 1968-69 school year. American Indian students were reassigned to other schools in Cumberland County as school officials worked to complete a desegregation mandate.

Interscholastic athletics played an important part in the education of the students at Les Maxwell School. The scope of this program was small. There were basketball and baseball for boys, and basketball for girls. Athletic facilities were limited. The school did not have a gymnasium; basketball teams practiced and played on a clay court. Inclement weather hindered use of the outside court, for both play and practice. Constant use of the clay court by local citizens often resulted in severe indentations in areas beneath the baskets. Repairing and smoothing the site became a ritual for athletic coaches before each team practice. Some regulated games were played on the clay court. Lime was used in marking boundaries. On occasions when the supply of lime was depleted, actual earth drawings were made to show boundaries for play. Some gestures of support for the athletics program came from the local business community. For instance, the posts supporting wooden backboards were donated by electrical utilities companies. In 1963, Cumberland County Schools paved the clay basketball court with asphalt. Other outdoor athletic facilities included a combination baseball/softball field. There was adequate outdoor space for physical education activities.

Coaches in elementary grades at Les Maxwell School began a modified interscholastic athletic program before the high school was added. Curtis Moore and Wilton Cummings, both teachers at the school, were instrumental in starting a basketball program for students in grades seven and eight. A veteran coach, Moore's record dated back to the early 1940's when he coached championship teams at Prospect High School in Robeson County. Through their network with their coaching neighbors in Robeson County, these men were able to schedule games with Magnolia, Fairgrove, Prospect, and Pembroke Schools. They also scheduled games with Eastern Carolina School in Sampson County and Hoke County's Hawkeye School. When the high school opened at Les Maxwell School, Moore continued to coach seventh and eight grade teams while Cummings took reins as high school coach. Through the work of Cummings, Les Maxwell School joined with Eastern Carolina High School in rural Clinton, NC and Hawkeye High School in rural Raeford, NC to form the Tri-County Indian High School Athletic Conference. In addition to playing conference schools, Les Maxwell played Prospect, Magnolia, and Fairgrove High Schools as earlier noted. The conference scheduled each other four times during the season; then had a season ending tournament.

Finances for interscholastic athletics at the school were very minimum. The beginning of the program found the school without funds to buy uniforms for the players. The Les Maxwell School community was rural, and Indian parents identified with the employment and socio-economic conditions of the period. They had no money to buy uniforms for their children. In a display of unashamed determination, the boys wore blue jeans and tee shirts while the girls wore dress shorts and tee shirts during regulated play. The teams played several seasons in this type attire before uniforms were purchased. During this period of racially segregated school systems, athletic coaches became more than instructors. They were like good Samaritans, coming to the aid of their basketball teams. Their gestures of

Photo courtesy of Wilton Cummings

1961-62 LES MAXWELL GIRLS BASKETBALL

FRONT: Farella Locklear, Peggy Brewington, Mae Gibbs, Cerosha Brewington.

BACK: Anita Ammons, Linda Evans, Betty Brewington, Coach Wilton Cummings, Mary Goins, Evelyn Groves, Carolyn Maynor.

Photo courtesy of Carrie Moore Dial

1959 Les Maxwell Boys Junior Varsity Basketball Team, with Coach Curtis Moore.

kindness shined brightest on road trips to play other schools. On times when Les Maxwell School traveled to Robeson County to play Prospect or Pembroke High Schools, coaches would arrange for the teams to eat at Cozy Corner Restaurant, a local landmark located between the Prospect community and the town of Pembroke. The meals were a gift to the players from Coach Wilton Cummings, owner of the business situated in the corner of a busy crossroads in the heart of Indian country.

Joining the Les Maxwell School coaching staff at the beginning of the 1961 school year, Tommy Dorsey Swett became the coach of the high school boys team, lightening the coaching load of Cummings who had served as dual coach for boys and girls. Cummings continued as coach of the girls basketball team. Through efforts of the coaches more Indian students became involved in the basketball program. There

were many student participants on the Les Maxwell teams. Some boy participants over the years were: Morgan Gibbs, Jerry Grove, Jimmy Ray Jacobs, Clarence Goins, James Hardin, Charles Ray Goins, Stanly Goins, Delton Goins, Floyd Gibbs, Ellison Hunt, Glenn Bryant, Leonard Gibbs, Caldwell Hammonds, James Gibbs, Ted Jones, Granville Hammonds, Andy Evans, Bobby Locklear, Ronnie Melvin Locklear, Vernon Emanuel, Charles Hunt, Martin Locklear, Howard Maynor, J.L. Jacobs, Lester Chavis, Norman Locklear, William Dale Oxendine, Eddy Ammons, Earl Bledsoe, Alford Maynor, Earl Oxendine, E.J. Locklear, Lennis Watts, Phillips Watts, and team manager Cecil Goins.

Some girls who played on the Les Maxwell basketball teams over the years were: Mayanna Gibbs, Irene Gibbs, Maxine Bullard, Melrose Goins, Mary Etta Goins, Shirley Goins, Bessie Mae Goins, Betty Hunt,

Brenda Fay Hunt, Joyce Morrison, Betty Joyce Brewington, Anita Ammons, Linda Evans, Cherosia Brewington, and Gloria Goins.

All three Indian basketball coaches, Moore, Cummings, and Swett resided in Robeson County, a one-way commute of 40-45 miles. On road games, the coaches transported players back to the school campus. Those having no means of transportation home were given a free ride there by one or more of the coaches. After these "away" games, it was not uncommon for these coaches to arrive back to their respective Robeson County homes hours past midnight.

In 1965, Eastern Carolina High School in Sampson County closed, reducing membership of the Tri-County Indian High School Athletic Conference to two schools. In 1966, Les Maxwell and Hawkeye High Schools joined with Fairgrove, Magnolia, Pembroke, and Prospect High Schools in Robeson County to form as the Tri-County Indian High School Athletic Conference. Les Maxwell's boys' basketball team, coached by Swett, competed well in the conference. In 1967, playing Magnolia High School for the tournament championship, the team lost to the Magnolia team in overtime. This would be the last game Swett coached for the Les Maxwell team. He accepted a non-coaching position with the Robeson County Schools. His leaving meant changes in the Cumberland County Indian school. The coaching team had been together at the school since 1961, and had contributed immeasurably to the good of the east Fayetteville community. Their years of countless selfless acts were noticed by grateful Indian families in the rural community. The Les Maxwell boys' basketball team would play two more seasons under the leadership of a new coach before the end of the 1968-69 school year. Indian students were reassigned to school districts where their families lived. This major change in the social and academic fabric of the American Indian students and their parents created a lasting effect on their lives.

MAGNOLIA SCHOOL

In 1885, the first structure for Magnolia School was erected approximately one mile south of the present campus. It was a one-room log building, named after Magnolia Baptist Church. Later a new one room school was constructed across the road from the northwest corner of the present Magnolia School campus. In 1902, the school was moved to the present campus. A partition was added, dividing the building into two class rooms. In 1928, four more rooms were added to accommodate the increased student enrollment.

In 1931, B. G. School consolidated with Magnolia. In 1933, Frank Epps assumed dual roles as the first principal and teacher of the school. In 1935, additional land was purchased, including a four room house that was used for classrooms. In 1937, Blue School consolidated with Magnolia. Disaster struck in 1938 when the school was destroyed by fire. With funds from The Federal Emergency Administration of Public Works, a new six-room modern brick building, including an auditorium, was constructed. In 1940, the high school was accredited by the North Carolina Board of Education.

By 1950, the physical structure had grown from a one room building to the largest school in Robeson County. One building included 12 new classrooms, a two room agriculture department and another building with 15 classrooms and a cafeteria. It was during this time Smyrna and Barker Ten-Mile Schools consolidated with Magnolia. In 1955 a new gymtorium, an elementary building, and a library were added. By 1958, the enrollment had increased to 1,553. With the increased enrollment, new construction included classrooms and a science laboratory.

In 1988, a pre-kindergarten class was implemented. In 1989, because of more student enrollment, six new

Photo courtesy of Magnolia School
Magnolia School circa 1950

classrooms were added. In 1990, the Robeson County and City Boards of Education merged as The Public Schools of Robeson County. This merger brought consolidation. High school students from Magnolia were assigned to St. Pauls, Lumberton, Red Springs, and West Robeson High Schools. Thus ending an important era to the students, alumni, and patrons of Magnolia High School. Today, Magnolia School is open to students from pre-kindergarten through eight grades. The campus consists of seven buildings and a greenhouse.

Interscholastic Athletics

The informal, enthusiastic relationships that frequently characterize interscholastic athletic programs provide a natural background for effective group and individual guidance. The school administration and athletic coaches at Magnolia High School developed a cordial relationship with their student athletes. Frank Epps, a school principal and one of the administrators of the Robeson County Indian High School Athletic Conference, held a cordial relationship with his fellow school principals.

The school principals organized and administered the athletic conference and the post season tournaments.

Magnolia High School athletic teams were coached by outstanding people. Margolis Sanderson was the boys coach in the late 1930's and early 1940's.

Magnolia's basketball success occurred in the 1950's and 1960's under the leadership of coach Ned Sampson. Sampson, who had been a star athlete at Pembroke State College, brought to his high school team the same leadership qualities and teaching skills he had developed as a player. Under coach Sampson's leadership, Magnolia boys won many games on simple fundamentals. The team won the post season tournament in 1967, finishing second in 1954, 55, 60, and 61. When the Robeson County Indian High Schools joined the North Carolina High School Athletic Association in 1968, Magnolia High School boys team matched up well against schools in their assigned conference. Sampson would leave Magnolia High School for a teacher/coach position at Pembroke High School. Kermit Chavis, a former player of Coach Sampson would succeed him as coach.

The winning achievements of Magnolia High School girls teams were better than that of the boys. Under the coaching of Eugene Chavis in the late 1940's, the girls won the post season tournament in 1946 and was runner up in 1950 and 1951. Coach Chavis was a teacher of fundamentals and discipline. He developed a program for girls basketball that the other coaches in the conference patterned their programs by. After Chavis gave up his coaching duties, Ned Sampson took on the dual role of coaching the girls team. Under Coach Sampson's guidance the girls won the conference tournament in 1957. Narva Lowry Maynor also coached the girls team for several years.

1948 Magnolia High School

Photos courtesy of Magnolia School

GIRLS BASKETBALL

FRONT ROW: V. Emanuel, M. Bell, O. Locklear, A. R. Lowry, T. McGirt.

SECOND ROW: S. Locklear, G. Locklear, L. Maynor, A. Locklear, G. Godwin, R. M. Locklear, Coach Eugene Chavis.

BOYS BASKETBALL

FRONT ROW: J. Hammond, G. Oxendine, C. Locklear, B. F. Hammond, O. Cummings.

SECOND ROW: Coach Robert McGirt, M. Locklear, L. Locklear, T. Locklear, L. Blanks, L. E. Hammond.

Photo by Elmer W. Hunt, Sr.

MAGNOLIA HIGH SCHOOL
1957 – Girls Basketball Champions

PICTURED FROM LEFT TO RIGHT ARE:

KNEELING: Olivia Emanuel, Linda Revels, Alice Ree Locklear, Mattie Brewer, Louise Chavis, Lucy Locklear, Lestine Locklear.

STANDING: Ancie Dale Sampson, Mabel Blanks, Ruth McNeill, Patsy Ann Locklear, Geraldine Spaulding, Catherine McGirt, Lucy Jane Locklear, Mary Kate Jones.

Photo courtesy of Magnolia School

1942 MAGNOLIA HIGH SCHOOL
BOYS BASKETBALL TEAM
with Coach Joseph Sampson

MAGNOLIA VARSITY CHAMPS

Text and photo from *The Lumbee* newspaper published in Pembroke, NC, Thursday, March 2, 1967.

Magnolia's varsity team won the Tri-County Indian Conference tourney last Saturday night in Pembroke and are representing the conference in the district Class A tournament at Buies Creek. Players are, from left, front, Harry Canady, Harry Maynor, Samuel Oxendine, Jimmy Maynor and James S. Locklear. Back row, Billy Blanks, Tonto Locklear, Tony Hunt, Jimmy Hammonds, and Coach Ned Sampson. Canady and Oxendine were named to the all-conference team following the tournament.

Magnolia High School to Host Final Homecoming Feb. 8

From *The Robesonian*, Lumberton, NC, Sunday, February 3, 1991

Photo courtesy of Barbara Braveboy-Locklear

John Sampson

On February 8, 1991, Magnolia School will hold its final Homecoming activities starting at 11 a.m. with a reception in the Media Center for all Alumni. From 1 p.m. until 3 p.m. there will be an Alumni game.

At 8 p.m., Magnolia will be playing host to the Bulldogs of St. Pauls High School. These festivities will be the final farewell of an important era. To help make this a memorable occasion, Mr. John W. Sampson, a former Magnolia High School coach, and better known as "Mr. Ned" to his former athletes and friends will serve as the Grand Marshall for these events.

He grew up in Pembroke and graduated from Pembroke State College in 1953. While at Pembroke State "Mr. Ned" was well known for athletic skills, especially basketball."Having a chance to play against such professionals as Dick Groat will always be special," said Sampson.

After college, Sampson began his teaching and coaching career at Magnolia. He remained coach there for 15 years (1953-1968). During this time, a new Gymnasium was built (1956) and two of his teams won championships. The Varsity Girls in 1957 and the Varsity Boys in 1967. "Mr. Ned" served the community well and was an inspiration to many students, teachers, and friends.

Because of his intense involvement and commitment in sports he has been asked to return and serve as the Grand Marshall for these events. He is married to Eva Brewington Sampson, a nurse at Pembroke State University, and they have four children.

Ursula Kay Freeman, a teacher at Cary Elementary School, Karen Sampson, a pharmacist at Eckerds in Charlotte, Kelvin Sampson, head basketball coach at Washington State, and Suzanne Sampson, a physical therapist at the Good Samaritan Hospital in Phoenix, Arizona.

His parents are Ms. Bertha Sampson and the late Mr. Clifton Sampson, Sr. Mr. Sampson retired in 1983 and lives in Pembroke.

It has been said by a former basketball player, Mattie (Lucy) Brewer Bell, "There's no other person like our coach, "Mr. 'Ned'."

PEMBROKE HIGH SCHOOL

Photo courtesy of Pembroke High School
Pembroke High School circa 1950

1939 was a red-letter year in Pembroke because that was the year Pembroke High School came into existence. 1939 was the year "the college," now vibrant and alive as UNC-Pembroke, decided to concentrate on "normal" work and turn the high school out on its own. A brick building with ten modern classrooms and a large auditorium, was built on a site just west of the college campus. The building and the land were valued at $25,000, a mighty sum in 1939.

J.R. Lowry became the first principal. He also taught mathematics. The other teachers were: Ruby Bailey, French and English; H.H. Cummings, Agriculture; Mary Livermore, English; Willard Locklear, Mathematics and Civics; E.T. Lowry, Science; Rhoda Lowry, Home Economics; and Dorothy Oxendine, English and Civics.

Grades were 8th through 11, with 229 students enrolled the first year. The curriculum included ten courses, and the library boasted 480 books.

As with the early days of Indian education, records are scant and it was not until 1947 that Pembroke High School had its first four-year diploma. 1958-59 was the last year the eighth grade attended school in the high school; after that, the grades were 9th through 12th. Growth precipitated more buildings, including

another classroom, a music room and a gymnasium in 1952-53.

The educational shepherd through all of the steady growth was Elmer T. Lowry, who replaced J. R. Lowry as principal after the first year. Elmer T. Lowry stayed as principal until 1964 when Newman Oxendine replaced him at the helm.

Some tidbits show the growth at Pembroke High School: for instance, in 1963-64 there were 74 graduates, and graduates topped themselves in 1967-68 with 146. In its last year of existence, there were 11,017 books in the library and the course offerings had increased to 24. And there were 40 teachers for the 918 students enrolled. The buildings had increased in value to $1,393,000.

The buildings today are fully operational. Title IX (Indian Education) of the Public Schools of Robeson County utilizes the main building as its administrative offices, and includes a modern art gallery, museum, library and computer lab. The CIS Charter School uses one of the buildings, and the Shining Star Pre School uses the old music wing and some storage space in the gymnasium. The gymnasium, officially named "the Adrian B. McRae Gymnasium", is ticketed for restoration in the very near future, and the main building sports a new roof with new windows planned too.

As noted, the Pembroke High School was built in 1939 with PWA (Public Works Administration) funds, and served as the segregated Pembroke "Indian" High School from 1939 until the new high school opened on Deep Branch Road in 1968. The building was used as a junior high school before Indian Education moved into the historic building in 1992. The building was designated as a structure on the National Register of Historic Places in 1991.

The gymnasium, which opened the 1952-53 school year, was named for Adrian B. McRae, member, Robeson County Board of Education. The gymnasium still stands on the old campus site, though in a state of neglect.

Photo from Robeson County Indian Education Resource Center Archive Collection

At the main entrance of the historic school building is a bronze plaque that reads:

Federal Works Agency
Public Works Administration
John M. Carmody
Federal Works Administrator
Franklin D. Roosevelt
President of the United States
Pembroke High School 1939

Interscholastic Play

Pembroke High School won its share of championships, receiving credit for a championship in 1940 although the local newspapers do not list a score nor the other participants. Pembroke had many great players, including the storied "Ned" Sampson, and his brother, Kent Sampson, who scored a record 51 points as the Eagles defeated Fairgrove 93-58 in the Robeson County Indian Tournament semi-finals in 1966. Sampson set an all time scoring record in the tournament with 22 field goals and seven free throws. Sampson had scored a previous season high 46 before topping his own record.

Thomas Oxendine, Jr., is reported to have coached both the boys and girls basketball teams to the 1951 tournament championships. Other coaches at Pembroke High School were: Margolis Sanderson, Dorsey V. Lowry, Joseph Sampson, Wayne Maynor, Fred Lowry, Danford Dial Sr., Delton Ray Locklear, Jim Cook, Jydor Locklear and others.

The boys basketball teams at Pembroke won championships in 1942, 1944, 1947, 1951, 1953, 1954, 1956, 1960, 1961, and 1966. The girls won championships in 1951, 1953, 1954, 1955, 1956, 1958, and 1959.

Coach Joseph Sampson

Coach Joseph Sampson was a graduate of Pembroke State Teacher's College. For four years he was a member of the football, basketball, and baseball teams of that college.

After serving as coach for Magnolia and Green Grove for five years, Coach Sampson came to Pembroke High School in 1947. He established a record at the school superior to those in the past years. His record was as follows: Football – won 17 games, lost 11. Basketball – won 53 games, lost 15. Baseball – won 18, lost 9.

Coach Sampson was liked by all his students because he was cheerful and friendly at all times.

Boys Basketball

Pembroke High School acquired a record of 17 wins and 1 loss in an overtime period. Coach Joe Sampson's boys defeated some of the strongest semi-pro basketball teams of eastern North Carolina. The highlights of the season were the smashing triumph over Lilesville High School of Anson County, 26 to 13; and Pembroke High School's defeat of Lillington All Stars 46 to 28. Their only loss came in a game with Hamlet All Stars after Pembroke's players had received very little rest the previous night because of a long trip to another school. The season closed with Pembroke High School winning the trophy awarded to the victor of the Indian Basketball Tournament. Pembroke defeated Green Grove in the finals of the tournament 51 to 19.

1947 Basketball Season

Pembroke	30	Magnolia	12
Pembroke	36	Fairmont	14
Pembroke	30	P. State C	12
Pembroke	26	Lilesville	13
Pembroke	38	Magnolia	12
Pembroke	46	Lillington	18
Pembroke	35	Rockingham	10
Pembroke	26	Hamlet	29
Pembroke	13	Pembroke J.V.	12
Pembroke	30	Magnolia	12
Pembroke	40	Fairmont	16
Pembroke	21	Lillington	18
Pembroke	27	Green Grove	18
Pembroke	39	Magnolia	16

Tournament

Pembroke	23	Chapel	14
Pembroke	51	Green Grove	19

Photos courtesy of Pembroke High School

1947 PEMBROKE HIGH BOYS BASKETBALL TEAM

FIRST ROW: Delton Ray Locklear, Billy Lowry, Ned Sampson, Joseph Oxendine, Zeb Lowry, Jr.

SECOND ROW: Earl Locklear, Molon Strickland, Russell Oxendine, Jr., Jennings Jacobs, Kenneth Brooks, Hoover Lloyd.

THIRD ROW: Coach Joe Sampson.

1948 PEMBROKE HIGH BOYS BASKETBALL TEAM

FRONT ROW: John Archie Cummings, Tolbert Lowry, Luther Oxendine, James Dial, Lindbergh Martin.

BACK ROW: Eyrtle Ransom, Orville Lowry, Denver Oxendine, Cancel Chavis. Coach, Wayne Maynor.

Photo: 1951 Pembroke High School yearbook, *The Challenger*

Photo: 1951 Pembroke High School yearbook, *The Challenger*

PEMBROKE HIGH SCHOOL GIRLS
1958 ROBESON COUNTY INDIAN HIGH SCHOOL ATHLETIC CONFERENCE TOURNAMENT CHAMPIONS

FRONT: Barbara Ann Locklear, Vashti Chavis, Joan Lowry, Sylvia Lowry, Norma Jean Sampson, Betty Joyce Locklear.
BACK: Deola Oxendine, Henrietta Locklear, Edna Berry, Patsy Locklear, Jeanette Bell.

1958 PEMBROKE HIGH SCHOOL BOYS BASKETBALL TEAM

FRONT: Tecumseh Brayboy, James Harris, Noah Woods, Benford Lowry, Bobby Strickland, Holland Locklear, Billy Ray Locklear.
BACK: John L. Locklear, Jr., Leverne Oxendine, Howard Brooks, William Brant Lowry, Bobby Jacobs, Hartman Brewington, Jerry Revels, Lynwood Sampson, Walter Oxendine, Jr.

PEMBROKE HIGH SCHOOL BASKETBALL COACHES

Danford Dial, Sr.

Photo: 1946 Pembroke State College
yearbook, *The Indianhead*

Joseph Sampson

Photo: 1952 Pembroke High School yearbook,
The Challenger

Delton Ray Locklear

Photo: 1957 Pembroke High School yearbook,
The Challenger

Fred Lowry

Photo: 1957 Pembroke High School
yearbook, *The Challenger*

Tom Oxendine, Jr.

Photo: 1941 Pembroke State College
yearbook, the *Lumbee Tattler*

Jydor Locklear

Photo: Courtesy of Joy Brayboy Locklear

PHOTOS NOT AVAILABLE:
Margolis Sanderson, Dorsey V. Lowry, Wayne Maynor, Jim Cook.

Girls Basketball

Photo: Pembroke High School archives

Girls basketball had been in progress for only two years at Pembroke High School in 1947. Great improvement was made and more interest was shown from game to game. Coach Joe Sampson developed a fighting team. The only conference defeat was by Magnolia High School girls who defeated Pembroke High School in the finals of the tournament 19 to 21.

FIRST ROW: Audrey L. Jacobs, Madge Black, Frances D. Godwin, Frances D. Oxendine, Vanice Lowry, Kathryn Lowry.

SECOND ROW: Left - Joyce Jacobs, Manager; Right - Gladys Chavis, Asst. Manager.

THIRD ROW: Faye Maynor, Daphane Lowry, Doris Jones, Carolyn Sampson, Eva Mae Locklear, Helen Sampson.

Cheerleaders

The cheerleaders of Pembroke High School were Audrey Lee Jacobs, Joyce Locklear, and Madge Black. Elma Louise Ater and Ruby C. Dial were faculty instructors.

Photo: Pembroke High School archives

1947 CHEERLEADERS

Joyce Locklear, Audrey Jacobs, Madge Black.

Photo: 1957 Pembroke High School yearbook, *The Challenger*

1957 CHEERLEADERS

TOP: Mary Dicie Locklear, MIDDLE: Meskiel Wilkins, BOTTOM: Linda Ruth Lowry.

Photo: 1960 Pembroke High School yearbook, *The Challenger*

PEMBROKE HIGH SCHOOL
1960 ROBESON COUNTY INDIAN HIGH SCHOOL ATHLETIC CONFERENCE TOURNAMENT CHAMPIONS

FRONT ROW, LEFT TO RIGHT: Bobby Eugene Jacobs, Jimmy Ray Locklear, Walter Oxendine, Leverne Oxendine, William Brant Lowry, Steve Jones.

BACK ROW, LEFT TO RIGHT: Coach Jim Cook, Holland Locklear, Bemus Blue, Billy Ray Locklear, Benford Hardin, Gervais Oxendine, Tecumseh Brayboy, team manager.

PEMBROKE EAGLES WIN TOURNAMENT

Reprinted from *THE LUMBEE* newspaper, spring, 1966

Pembroke High's favored varsity and jayvee basketball teams romped all over their opponents Saturday night to win the championship of the Robeson County Indian Tournament.

Since the high school is not allowed to participate in further district playoffs, the Pembroke team offered to take on the tournament winners from the Robeson County league, the Littlefield Hornets and winner of the NC High School Athletic Conference, Maxton R.B. Dean.

In the Saturday finals, the PHS Eagles defeated the Hawkeye Hawks 52-23 and the Junior Varsity won by 44-37 over Fairgrove.

A capacity crowd watched as Pembroke was able to break the zone defense set up by Hawkeye in the first quarter, and post a 23-3 lead which was considered the determining factor in the game.

Gary W. Locklear led the way for Pembroke in the first quarter with his superior height by rolling away and shooting over his opponent's head. Locklear was also top scorer in the game with 22 points.

Pembroke used a 2-3 zone throughout the game which limited Hawkeye to mostly outside shots, and this enabled Pembroke to post a 35-13 lead at intermission.

During the first half, Hawkeye had their problems in making field goals, and as a result, they connected on only 3 goals and 7 free throws. Pembroke was more settled, and managed to follow up most of the shots from outside on tip-ins by Locklear, and follow-up shots by Kent Sampson.

Hawkeye had plenty of scrap and hustle throughout the game, especially in two brothers, Ozell Jacobs and Muriel Jacobs. The Jacobs brothers accounted for most of the Hawkeye rebounds, and Muriel accounted for most of their points with 8 with the rebounding ability

of Hawkeye Pembroke was still able to control both boards in most situations with 6'7" center Gary W. Locklear, 6'5" forward Kent Sampson and 6'1" forward Chester Chavis.

The second half began with Pembroke getting the tip-off, and Richard Oxendine lost the ball on a fast break. Hawkeye took possession and held it for 1 minute and 58 seconds before they attempted a shot which Ozell Jacobs made good.

During the remainder of the half, Hawkeye set up a man for man defense, and relied on ball control to hold Pembroke's scoring down, but they were unable to overcome the difference in scoring made by Pembroke in the first half.

Gary W. Locklear of Pembroke was followed in scoring by Kent Sampson with 18 points. Hawkeye did a good job in holding down Sampson's scoring, because in the semi-finals he netted 51 points, and finished with a tournament average of 34.5 points along with a season average of 32 points.

Muriel Jacobs of Hawkeye was followed in scoring by Ozell Jacobs and Joe Lowry with 4 points.

In the first game of the evening, Pembroke's junior varsity won the championship for the seventh time in as many starts in a thrill-packed game over Fairgrove.

Fairgrove stayed on the game all the way until the final seconds.

Charles Graham led the scoring for Pembroke with 13 points.

EAGLES CHALLENGE WINNERS

Reprinted from *THE LUMBEE*, newspaper

WINNING EAGLES, 1966 – Pembroke High School Eagles won the final round and championship of the County Indian Tournament last week with a 52-23 win over Hawkeye. The winning team above is (left to right)

FIRST ROW: Mike Clark, guard; David Hunt, guard; Jerry Chavis, guard; Richard Oxendine, guard; Coach Jydor Locklear.

SECOND ROW: Gary L. Locklear, guard; Chester Chavis, forward; Gary W. Locklear, center; Kent Sampson, forward; and Houston B. Locklear, forward.

Pembroke High School Principal Newman Oxendine and basketball coach Jydor Locklear yesterday challenged the winners of the two other cage conferences in the county to see what team really is county champion.

Because of the segregated conference, there are three basketball teams who all proclaim to be the best in Robeson.

Pembroke's Eagles have won the County Indian Basketball conference. The Littlefield Hornets of Lumberton have won the Robeson County League, the white association.

Maxton's R. B. Dean team won the Negro county championship in the NC High School Athletic Conference Lumberton Center Tournament. The Maxton and Littlefield teams, of course, are presently playing in two district tournaments.

Coach Locklear at PHS said yesterday, "We know we've got the best team in the county" and said his team would be willing to take on both the others.

Principal Oxendine said he would "be willing to take part in" such a tournament. Principal D.C. McBee at Maxton told *The Lumbee* last night. "We would like to see such a tournament." His team is starting in district playoffs tomorrow night.

"In the event, there is further investigation, I'm sure we would be glad to go along in a playoff," said McBee.

Principal George Taylor at Littlefield said last night, "I personally have no objections at all."

However, he pointed out, the rules of the association to which Littlefield School belongs forbids cross-conference playing of this nature.

Y. H. Allen, county school superintendent, said last night. "The schools who are members of the state association are limited to two tournaments a year." (Pembroke High School is not a member of the state association, although applications have been made.

"In other words, Littlefield has played in one tournament, the regular, and is starting a second tournament, the state." Allen explained.

He said such rules are made up by the NC Athletic Association and endorsed by the State Board of Education.

When asked about the possibilities of an "informal" tournament among the county champions, Allen said, "It is a matter of decision for the Athletic Association.

The executive secretary of the Athletic Association is L. J. Perry of Chapel Hill and as of yesterday had not been contacted to discuss the possibilities of a special ruling for the county.

Thus it looks like that unless special arrangements can be made between the schools themselves or unless there is a special ruling, no one will know which team is really the best in the county.

PINEY GROVE SCHOOL

Photo courtesy of Robeson County Indian Education Resource Center

Piney Grove School circa 1934

The year of 1923 marked the beginning of Piney Grove School. In July, the Robeson County Board of Education purchased from W.S. Britt a five acre plot of land for the sum of $500.00. On this land a modern wood school facility was constructed. The school consisted of six classrooms, an auditorium, and a principal's office. The 6,560 square foot facility accommodated grades seven and eight and served 50 students.

The construction of this facility was the culmination of years of hard work by dedicated community leaders such as Maggie Locklear, James Dial, Willis Locklear, Riley Locklear, and Lloyd Lowery. Maggie Locklear has the distinction of being the first female to serve on a school committee in Robeson County, having been appointed September 20, 1923.

1941-42 was the last year high school students attended Piney Grove School. High school students were assigned to Magnolia High School. The principal at Piney Grove School during consolidation was Charles Luther Moore. Albert Hunt was assigned as principal to lead the Piney Grove Elementary School.

As the community developed, and with increased enrollment, there was a need for a more comprehensive education structure. In 1956, a modern brick building was constructed. The 9,440 square foot building consisted of six classrooms for grades one through eight.

In 1964, the Robeson County Board of Education purchased 11.91 acres of land from Evander Britt. This land joined the school property, and increased the campus to a total of 16.91 acres. Time has proven this to be a wise decision, one that exemplified considerable foresight, because the school was to experience much growth the following years.

Because of increased enrollment, an addition to the existing building was made in 1965. A grammar grade wing was constructed that included six classrooms, a cafeteria, and an auditorium that can serve as a gymnasium. With this addition, the total building space is 19,385 square foot. With the modern brick building in place, and enough space to accommodate the student enrollment, the wooden building used since 1923 was later razed.

In 1977, a new media center was constructed. The media center was connected to the grammar wing by a breezeway. The center was named in honor of James H. Brewington, who was principal at Piney Grove School from 1959 to 1978. Grady Locklear followed Brewington as principal.

In the school year 1983-84, the school district lines were changed, resulting in an increase in student enrollment. To have space for the increase and not have new construction, students in grades seven and eight were transferred to Magnolia School. Piney Grove School became a Pre-K through six.

For the 1999-2000 school year, Piney Grove School had an enrollment of 581 students. The racial composition was as follows: 404 American Indian (70%), 74 White (13%), 49 Black (8%), 39 Hispanic (7%), and 15 other (2%). The campus has a well-defined playground and a picnic area. The campus facilities are frequently used by members of the community for picnics, parties, barbecues, and class reunions. There is a regulation size baseball/football field, complete with a chain-link fence, dugouts, and concession stand maintained by patrons of the community. The Parent Teacher Organization provided funds to pave the parking lot. The parking lot has 50 marked spaces.

Interscholastic Athletic Program

Little is known about the interscholastic athletic program at Piney Grove High School. *The Robesonian*, Lumberton, NC, provides information of Piney Grove High School participating in the Robeson County Indian High School Athletic Conference post season basketball tournament. Marvin Lowry of Pembroke, NC, told of playing on the boys basketball team at Piney Grove High School in 1941-42. The family moved to the Prospect High School attendance district after that school year.

Photo courtesy of Bernice Brooks Lowry

"The college gym opened in 1940. This was during the Depression years, and parents of athletes did not have money to buy special tennis shoes required for play on the college gym floor. The new gym was the first facility where Indian athletes could play basketball indoors. Playing indoors was quite an adjustment for the players and coaches. The high school teams practiced and played on dirt courts at their respective schools. They continued to practice and play on dirt courts long after the college gym opened. Some teams had uniforms. When playing the game, most of the players played in the clothes they wore to school. Some players wore tennis shoes, others wore whatever they had. Some did not wear shoes during the game. When the teams played at the college gym, it was common for players to borrow tennis shoes from some one in the community where the player lived. Most time the shoes did not fit. The player would pack paper or rags in the shoes for a tight fit."

Marvin Lowry
Piney Grove and Prospect High Schools

PROSPECT SCHOOL

Photo courtesy of Robeson County Indian Education Resource Center

A Prospect High School building, circa 1935

One of the most important aspects of Prospect School is its community setting. Family surnames are often a hint a person is from Prospect. Bryant, Bullard, Chavis, Collins, Cummings, Dial, Flanagan, Goins, Harris, Jones, Jacobs, Locklear, Lowry, Maynor, Moore, Oxendine, and Sanderson are classics. The school and community have always been carefully intertwined for the benefit of both groups. The school and community have continued to grow for the past 123 years and continues to grow today. Prospect School is located five miles northwest of Pembroke, North Carolina. Church, religion, and education were the foundation for the early settlement of the Prospect Community. In 1876 community citizens built the first Prospect School. The log building was located where the old church sanctuary is today and served as a school and a place of worship for American Indians. The building was destroyed by fire in 1895. W.L. Moore was the first principal and teacher at Prospect School. Mary Catherine Oxendine (Tudy) Moore, wife of W.L. Moore, was the first Cherokee Indian female school teacher in Robeson County. Foster Sampson would later join Moore as a teacher.

Records indicate there were two schools for American Indians in Smith Township: Old Prospect and White Oak. Later four schools were created: Hickory Grove, China Grove, Purcell, and Biddy. These schools eventually closed, and the students were assigned to Prospect School.

At the turn of the century, the patrons of the Prospect community felt a need to separate the school and church from the same building. In the early 1900's, a two story building was constructed for a school. This building was located where the new church sanctuary, education building, and cemetery are now situated. Students from grades one through seven attended the school. From 1916-20 Plummer Lowry was the principal at Prospect School. Teachers were: Bertha Hunt, Mary Ellen Moore, and Gaston Locklear.

J.W. Smith of the Prospect community served as principal from 1920 to 1924. Teachers at the school during these years were: Mary Eliza Sampson, Susie Lowry, Colon Oxendine, P.M. Locklear, Mary Jane Oxendine and Emma Bullard.

During the 1923-24 school year another school building was constructed. The two-story building was moved to a location on the same site, near the canal. Thomas (Tom) Oxendine was the principal. Teachers were: Noah H. Dial, Charles Hadden Moore, Lacy Maynor, Elizabeth Oxendine, Emma Lowry, and Annie Bell Jacobs.

Carrie Moore Dial, a long time resident of the Prospect Community, tells that Tom Oxendine would ride his bicycle to and from school the years he was principal at Prospect School. Later, Oxendine set up residence in the bottom floor of the two story building and resided there until he left Prospect School.

In 1926, the parents and patrons of the Prospect community wanted their own high school. Students from Prospect traveled to Pembroke Normal School for their high school education. Leading the effort to establish a high school in the community was Charles Hadden Moore. Carrying a petition from citizens, the community leader met with the Robeson County Board of Education and requested the Board's approval of a school in the Prospect community. The Board approved the establishment of the community school under the condition that the administrator and teacher meet all requirements for state certification.

In 1926, a new building was constructed for the proposed high school. A.B. Riley served as the school's first principal. The Asheville, North Carolina native had previously taught at neighboring Pembroke Normal School. Moore recruited Susie S. Jordan, a certified teacher on leave from Pembroke Normal School. Jordan, who had taken leave to care for her ill mother, accepted the position and resided with the Moore family during the three years she taught at Prospect School. Jordan's

mother would join her at the Moore residence the last year she taught at the rural school. When opened, the school enrolled students completing the eighth grade at Oxendine Elementary School. Early teachers, in addition to Jordan, were: Clement Bullard, Noah H. Dial, Lacy Maynor, Charles Hadden Moore, Losha Lowry, and Roscoe Locklear. C.E. Locklear also served as principal during the school's formative years. Gaston Locklear, Bascom Blue, Wiley Thompson, French Bryant, and L.W. Moore served as school board of trustees.

The first high school classes began in the school year 1929-30. Riley would serve as high school principal until the first class graduated in 1932. Members of the first high school graduating class were: Lettie May Brooks, Marlee Jacobs, Callie Mae Jacobs, Jessie Bell Locklear, Lester Locklear, Nancy Ann Locklear, Carrie M. Moore, Andrew Locklear, David Locklear, Tommie Bryant, Therrel Locklear, and Jackie Locklear.

Prospect School consisted of grades 1-11 until 1945, when the twelfth grade was added. It remained a high school until school year 1983-84, when Prospect and Red Springs High School students were assigned to West Robeson High School (now Purnell Swett High School).

In 2000, the Pre-K through eighth grade enrollment at Prospect School was 850. The racial make-up of student body was predominately American Indian at 96%, white 2.4%, African American 1.5%, and Hispanic 1%.

The late Carrie Moore Dial contributed to this history.

Photo courtesy of Carrie Moore Dial

1925-26 PROSPECT HIGH SCHOOL BASKETBALL TEAM

FIRST ROW: Leola Locklear, Bert Goins Sampson, Coach Lacy Maynor, Bee Locklear, Tressie Locklear.

SECOND ROW: Susanna Locklear Oxendine, Edith Lowery, Emma Lowery, Annie G. Bullard, Elizabeth Oxendine Maynor, Martha Bullard.

Interscholastic Athletic Program

Interscholastic athletics have been an integral part of Prospect School and the community. Student athletes from both Prospect and Oxendine schools contributed to the success of the program. The boys basketball teams won the Robeson County Indian High School Tournament in 1941, 48, 49, 50, and 65. They played for the tournament championship in 1940, 44, 46, and 53. The girls were tournament champions in 1949. They played for the championship in 1948, and 57.

Coaches for the teams were: Curtis Moore, Nash Locklear, Conrad Oxendine, Mary Sanderson, Marvin Lowry, Reese Locklear, William Cancel Chavis, Sara Bullard Locklear, Pauline Bullard Locklear, Lucy Oxendine Thomas, Joe Swinson, and William Stanton.

BASKETBALL AT PROSPECT

This article was taken from the 1950 Prospect School Tomahawk Yearbook.

Photo courtesy of Mary Sanderson

Mary Sanderson

The 1949-50 Girls' Basketball team was one of the strongest ever produced at Prospect High School. The girls were under the direction of Mrs. Mary L. Sanderson. The girls would be congratulated for the fine work they did during the season. The team of next year will miss quite a few of the girls that have been doing such fine work. We are hoping to have girls to take their places and looking for a successful '51. They were rewarded with a banquet given by the teachers and a wiener roast at White Lake, NC, given by the principal, Mr. C.S. Lowry.

Prospect High School has had one of the strongest boys' teams it has ever had. Basketball is the favorite sport at Prospect High School, and furnished the fans with thrills throughout the season. The boys were under the direction of Coach Conrad Oxendine. They have won the County-Wide Tournament for three consecutive years. Graduation claims the two co-captains, James Earl Locklear and William Cancel Chavis, who will be greatly missed on the team in the years to come.

Prospect High School made a great showing in the Basketball Tournament. In the first night of the tournament, Prospect High girls defeated Pembroke High by a score of 23-21, but Magnolia High won over them in the third night, which threw Prospect out of the tournament. Magnolia High School Girls were an undefeated team for the year 1949-50. Prospect girls gave them a great game. It had been predicted that Prospect would be defeated by a score of at least 20 points, but the score was 16-38.

The boys defeated Pembroke High which put them in the finals. In the final game, the Prospect boys defeated Fairmont High. The boys were also given a banquet by the teachers and a wiener roast at White Lake, NC by Mr. C.S. Lowry.

Everyone is proud of the basketball teams of Prospect High.

The 1954 Tomahawk Yearbook, Prospect High School

1954 PROSPECT HIGH SCHOOL BOYS BASKETBALL TEAM

LEFT TO RIGHT: Bobby Locklear, Bobby Dean Locklear, James Collins, Ezra Locklear, Brantley Locklear, James Harold Woods, Daniel Tucker Dial, Jr., Hudell Harris, Sam Locklear, Vernon Chavis, Newton Cummings, Jr., Conrad Oxendine, Coach.

1954 PROSPECT HIGH SCHOOL GIRLS BASKETBALL TEAM

LEFT TO RIGHT: Cheryl Lowry, Myrna Bryant, Agnes Locklear, Thelma Locklear, Lola Merle Bullard, Onita Chavis, Lucille Locklear, Dorothy Sanderson, Betty Jane Locklear, Annie Pearl Revels, Annie Jarvie Lowry, Lilly Bullard, Sherrill Locklear, Myrtle Locklear, Alice Dale Dial.

REAR, LEFT TO RIGHT: Virginia Callahan, manager, Lucy Oxendine Thomas, coach, Betty Ann Chavis, manager.

1954 PROSPECT HIGH SCHOOL CHEERLEADERS

Joyce Dial, Fannie Jacobs, Betty Lou Locklear, Carrie Mabel Hunt.

"As a player, I recall the dressingroom being cold. But conditions would change when we came onto the gym floor for warm-up. The greeting from the cheerleaders and the cheers from the fans removed whatever coldness the body had. The smell of popcorn and peanuts alerted me of the environment we were in. The gym was full; the fans had come to see something special, to see their local teams play."

Mike Flanagan, Prospect High School Class of 1965

Prospect High School Boys 1965 Tournament Championship

Photo by Carmel Locklear

In 1965, Prospect High School boy basketball players formed one of local basketball's most remarkable Indian teams. The school, located in western rural Robeson County, had the smallest student enrollment of the four Indian schools entering the tournament that year. Students assigned to the school came from the Prospect and Oxendine communities. The basketball players were an intriguing and talented group of young Indian men, possessing championship craftiness and determination. Because these high school students had played basketball together since ninth grade, their instincts for one another's moves were intuitive. They were led by Hilbert Swinson, their coach who was nicknamed "Joe."

The team's leading scorer, Burlie Locklear, was arguably the premiere shooter in the conference. The shooter was masterful from the outside. Big Mike Flanagan, center, controlled the boards and was dominant on defense. He was good at scoring most of his points from close in. Purcell Locklear, a talented forward, complemented the team with his rebounding and defensive skills. Duo guards were Wyvis Oxendine and Talford Dial. Oxendine, a slashing penetrator, kept the defense off-balance with his scoring and passing. Dial ran the offense from the point position. He was an exceptional passer and ball handler. The team's additional strength was drawn from its bench.

The Prospect High School basketball players came into the tournament focused. A year earlier in 1964, the team was upset in tournament play by Magnolia High School. This time they were determined to prove their worth. Having advanced to the title game, they would be playing the talented Pembroke High School team, their neighbors four miles away. Pembroke High School had a size advantage and was coming into the conference play undefeated.

That fateful night Prospect upset Pembroke 53-50 and delighted many spectators from the Prospect and Oxendine communities. The tournament championship became the first for the Prospect boys team since 1949. Mike Flanagan, Burlie Locklear, and Talford Dial were placed on the all-tournament team. Coach Swinson gave his players enough structure to keep them organized; yet allowed them enough freedom to maximize their skills and create a thousand thrills for the overflow crowd who looked on in both glee and disbelief that night.

1967-68

Prospect High School's Varsity Basketball Squad defeated Magnolia Tuesday night for their seventh victory. After the game the team was presented blazers by the school. The blazers are for use during basketball season and school functions. The tally shows Chavis, 22 points, Brewer 5, Boutselis 18, J. Locklear 6, M. Locklear 10, A. Locklear 7, Brooks 2.

Photos courtesy of Ronnie Chavis

Lanette and Ronnie Chavis

FRONT ROW: George Warriax, Carlton Dial, Arvin Locklear, James Locklear, and Earl Brooks.

BACK ROW: William Stanton, Bobby Oxendine, Ronnie Chavis, Kirk Bullard, Aaron Brewer, Sherman Locklear, Chris Boutselis, Merris Locklear, and William C. Chavis.

Ronnie and Lanette Chavis were members of the Prospect Cats Basketball Team and Cheerleading Squad 1966-1970. Weekly sports stories in *The Robesonian* would often read ...Leading scorer for the Prospect Cats was Ronnie Chavis with a score of 21, 27, or maybe even 35. Lanette enjoyed cheering her big brother to victory. Ronnie is now the Athletic Director for the Public Schools of Robeson County. Lanette has worked closely with him for 25 years as a pre-K-8th grade physical education teacher.

These siblings are the niece and nephew of the late Coach William Cancel Chavis.

"The players represented the community; the patrons of the community shared a common bond with the players. Although they were not related by birth, the community adopted them as their children. Like a family."

James Moore, historian
Prospect High School

UNION CHAPEL SCHOOL

Union Chapel School is located in the northern part of Robeson County, North Carolina, about 11 miles from Lumberton and five miles north of Pembroke at the intersection of rural State Roads 1515 and 1513. A rural farming community, Union Chapel families are diversifying the method by which they make a livelihood. While some families still rely on farming as their main source of income, many others are working in educational, professional, and industrial fields.

Religion plays an important part in the lives of the people within this community. Churches of many denominations serve the area.

The history of Union Chapel School closely parallels the history of education for American Indians in Robeson and the state of North Carolina. American Indians were denied public education, except in rare cases, prior to legislative action by the North Carolina General Assembly in 1885. Enacted into law during this session was a provision to establish separate schools and school districts for people of different races. The County and City Boards of Education were mandated to carry out the law.

Union Chapel School was a direct result of the 1885 legislation. It was a member of the Burnt Swamp District and was a one-room school erected on .7 acres of land purchased from a local church. This building was situated on the site where the school gymnasium is now located.

At its December 4, 1916, meeting, the Robeson County Board of Education approved the building of a new Union Chapel School. Additional land consisting of .21 acres was purchased to construct the new school. The new school, a wooden two-story structure, had four classrooms down-stairs and three classrooms and an auditorium upstairs, the classrooms were described as being "very spacious," and the hallways as "being

huge." Students in grades one through eleven attended the school. A former student described the school as the most beautiful school in Robeson County.

Fire destroyed this well-designed building in 1933. During the site preparation and construction of a new school, a home that was used as a resident by the school principal and teachers was used for instruction. A country store owned by a local patron was converted into use for classrooms.

In 1935 a modern brick school was constructed on the original site. Renovations and additions have been made to this building on several occasions.

The first of these additions was the construction of four classrooms in 1950. A special project was completed in 1952 which demonstrated the strong support of the people of the community. Through fund raisings by the Parent Teacher Association and free labor by a local patron, a cafeteria was constructed at the school at no cost to the County Board of Education. In 1976 the former gymnasium was reconstructed into a functional and spacious media center.

In 1951 the high school students were assigned to Pembroke High School. This change left Union Chapel as an elementary school with grades one through eight.

Photo: Robeson County Indian Education Resource Center Archival Collection
Union Chapel School circa 1950.

During its years as a high school, Union Chapel School provided competitive interscholastics athletics for both boys and girls. The girls basketball team, coached by Theodore Maynor, won the Robeson County Indian High Conference Tournament in 1948 and 1950. The team lost to Prospect in the tournament championship in 1949.

Delton Lowry was the boys coach. Union Chapel boys teams, though competitive, did not win the post season conference basketball tournament. Forace Oxendine, Sr. was the star athlete for the boys team. Oxendine, who grew up in the shadows of the school campus, was gifted in basketball and baseball. He would go on and excel in basketball and baseball at Pembroke State College. Oxendine played baseball as a professional, advancing to the triple-A level. He was a teacher and coach at Hawkeye High School, Raeford, North Carolina.

Photo from Union Chapel School Archival Collection

Union Chapel Girls Basketball Team and their coach, Brewster Chavis, circa 1949

Bernice Dial	Ruth Brewington
Mary Jane Locklear	Ellen Deese
Loshia (last name unknown)	Sylvia Lowry
Velma Baker	Janice Lowry
Hazel Hammonds	Rose Oxendine
Geraldene Locklear	Mabel Doris Jones
Betty Lowry	Vashti Locklear
Mary Frances Chavis	Shelby Locklear
Edith Locklear	Annie Bell Chavis
Frances Locklear	Eudora Sampson
Clara Chavis	Kathryn Brewington

Teammates of Jennie Baker Smith

"When I was in the 6th grade, we moved from Pembroke to Union Chapel School. I started playing basketball. Brewster Chavis was our coach. He always picked me up to go play basketball. We had games in the gym at Pembroke College gym. I don't remember us ever losing a game.

I came back to Pembroke High School in the 8th grade. Mr. Joe Sampson was my teacher and our basketball coach. He was the best teacher and coach we ever had. After he moved to Ohio Mr. Fred Lowry became our coach. When we had a game away from home, the teachers would drive their cars. When we graduated in 1956 we had trophies from every game we played. I would go without supper in order to go play ball.

After high school, Mr. Eugene Chavis got a team together. We won all those games too. After he went fishing and died, we never had anyone to take his place. So that made me very sad, because that was the end of my basketball days."

Jennie Baker Smith

"COACH" THEODORE MAYNOR HONORED

PEMBROKE – Said Mrs. Fannie Lou Oxendine, "I catch myself now telling my children some of the things Mr. Theodore told me when I was in school at Union Chapel High School. He was just a wonderful man, he taught you more than what was in books. He taught a lot about life too. I guess he would be sort of like a counselor in school these days, although there was no such thing when we were in school."

It was sort of a surprise. It was a special moment for sure. Many of the students and basketball players who won the Robeson County Indian Girl's High School Championship in 1948 attended the meeting of the Pembroke Kiwanis last Tuesday night.

They presented a plaque of appreciation to Mr. Theodore Maynor who coached them to that championship.

Although Union Chapel was later consolidated with Pembroke High School it has not diminished the joy of that special championship in 1948.

Mr. Maynor responded at the meeting, "I've been trying to get these girls together for fifteen years. We were really happy in those days. We really enjoyed life back then and we still enjoy it today. Today it is so meaningful to live a Christian life."

Mr. Theodore can remember that championship game like it was yesterday. "I remember we took a time out to set up a play and we won by 1 point."

Mr. Maynor introduced each player present. Two of his team members were Adriene Locklear and Mazalene Dusan, both daughters of Pembroke Kiwanian, John L. Carter.

Team Captain Fannie Lou Oxendine presents a plaque of appreciation to Coach Theodore Maynor on behalf of the 1948 Union Chapel School Champions.

Photo: *The Carolina Indian Voice*

Mrs. Hartley (Fannie Lou) Oxendine was the team captain and she gave the response. She remembered how he taught them how to play the game of life. Said Mrs. Oxendine, "I can remember how you took us as an uncoordinated group and brought us to a championship. After 30 years we still love and appreciate you."

She remembered that Mrs. Theodore Maynor was their greatest fan and that Janie, their daughter, was sort of the team mascot.

Mr. Theodore Maynor, now approaching his 70th birthday and still an active Pembroke Kiwanis member, said, "Now I know why Elizabeth (his wife) wanted me to wear my suit and this red vest..."

President Ed Teet presided at the meeting. A special Christmas moment, too, was the appearance of Mr. Monroe Chavis to play the piano for the group's singing. He was a student of Mr. Ira Pate Lowry thirty years ago.

__The Carolina Indian Voice,__ Pembroke, NC
April, 1978

1947-48 UNION CHAPEL HIGH SCHOOL GIRLS CHAMPS

BOTTOM ROW: Betty J. Carter, Ludahalia Locklear, Sarah Sadie Oxendine, Sally Locklear, Effie Jane Locklear, Etta B. Locklear.

SECOND ROW: Pat Demery, Magdalene Chavis, Fannie Lou Maynor, Clella Locklear, Mary Sue Locklear, Iona Oxendine.

THIRD ROW: Coach Theodore Maynor.

1949-50 UNION CHAPEL HIGH SCHOOL GIRLS CHAMPS

BOTTOM ROW: Mazalene Carter, Adriene Carter, Ludahalia Locklear, Mary Sue Locklear, Calpurnia Bullard, Vashtie Oxendine.

SECOND ROW: Lucy Oxendine, Clella Locklear, Nellie Locklear, Barbara Lowry, Verona Oxendine, Nora Oxendine.

THIRD ROW: Coach Theodore Maynor.

Photo by Tim Brayboy

Fairgrove High School

The gymnasium at Fairgrove High School located in rural Fairmont, North Carolina, was part of the new consolidated school construction completed for the 1952-53 school year. The consolidated school was built to accommodate the high school students from Fairmont Indian and Green Grove High Schools.

The gymnasium was constructed as a multi-purpose facility. Included in the design were: a crown roof, a regulation basketball court 84 by 50 feet, wood basketball backboards, dressing and shower rooms for both gender, and a stage. The gym floor had a cement base covered with vinyl tile squares. Metal folding chairs were used for seating. The gymnasium was used for student assemblies, school plays, graduations, and several other functions.

Today, the inside features in the gymnasium have changed. The floor is wood, the backboards are made of glass, and the folding metal chairs have been removed and replaced with pull out bleachers.

> "Before gymnasiums were constructed at the Indian high schools, teams played on dirt courts at the high school campus. The courts were marked with lime. For equity, each team would provide a person to officiate the game."
>
> **Albert Hunt,** coach and school principal

Magnolia High School

Photo by Tim Brayboy

Magnolia High School located in rural Lumberton, North Carolina, was the last Indian high school in Robeson County to have a gymnasium. In 1955, the new gymnasium, an elementary building and a library were added to the campus.

The design of the gymnasium was like the one designed at Fairgrove High School. The facility had a regulation basketball court 84 by 50 feet, built on a cement base covered with vinyl squares; wood basketball backboards, fold up bleachers on each side of the gymnasium, modern dressing and shower rooms for both boys and girls. A stage was constructed at one end of the building.

In addition to sporting events, the multi-purpose facility is used for student assemblies, graduation, school socials, and community events.

Today, the gymnasium has a wood floor, glass backboards, and office space for athletic coaches.

Pembroke High School

Photo by Tim Brayboy

The Adrian B. McRae Gymnasium in Pembroke, North Carolina, located on the campus of the former Pembroke High School.

The gymnasium is named for Adrian B. McRae who was a member of the Robeson County Board of Education. The gymnasium was part of new construction on the Pembroke High School campus that included several classrooms, a band and music wing, and vocation education laboratories. The new buildings opened the 1952-53 school year.

The gymnasium had a regulation basketball court 84 by 50 feet. The court had a cement base covered with vinyl tile squares, glass backboards, a seating capacity of an estimated 600 with fold up bleachers on each side of the court, also fold up bleachers in each end zone. Featured were modern shower and dressing rooms for each gender. Additionally the brick building contained an office for coaches, and public restrooms. It had a crown roof.

The gymnasium was the site of the 1953 and the 1960 Robeson County Indian High School Athletic Conference Basketball tournament. Today, the McRae gymnasium sits on its original site. It is no longer in use. Because of neglect, the facility is in dire need of repair.

Prospect High School

Photo courtesy of Holly Floyd Locklear, Sr.

The gymnasium at Prospect High School located in rural route Maxton, North Carolina, was constructed during the 1952-53 school year. It was part of the bond money the county citizens had approved for school construction.

The gymnasium opened the 1952-53 school year. The multi-purpose facility included: a cement base floor with a basketball court 84 by 50 feet covered with vinyl tile squares, metal fan shaped basketball backboards, a stage located on the middle side of the building, and a cafeteria at one end of the gym floor. Metal folding chairs were used for seating. There were no dressing and shower rooms. The gymnasium was used for school assemblies. A cafeteria with portable tables was set up to serve school lunch. Graduation exercises, school socials and community functions were held in the gym.

Today, the inside features in the gymnasium have changed. The floor is wood, the backboards are made of glass, the folding metal chairs are no longer used, the chairs have been replaced with fold up bleachers. The cafeteria has been relocated. Dressing and shower rooms have been constructed in the space where the cafeteria was located.

"The gymnasiums were cozy. All seats were front row, ideal for fans to view the action up close. You had to be careful when shooting a fast break lay up; the end walls were very close."

Burlie Locklear, Prospect High School
Class of 1965

"Only a few people had automobile transportation during World War II. Fans would come to the games by automobiles, by horse and buggy, by mule and wagon, on horse back, and by walking."

James Moore, historian, Prospect Community

COACHES AND PLAYERS

Post-World War II Effects on High School Athletics

World War II would strike a major blow to high school athletics in the United States. The resounding blow was especially felt by Indian high school athletes in Robeson County, North Carolina. Many of-age men and women were drafted into military service during the war years; thus leaving 15,16, and 17-year old students to make up the interscholastic athletic teams. Subsequently, post-war sports participation increased at war's end in 1946. Returning war veterans, eager to complete their interrupted high school education, along with currently-enrolled students created a unique melting pot on respective high school teams.

"In 1948, I was in school at age 16 and played with and against guys who were 20 and 21-years old," says a former student. "They could tell some good war stories...quite an educational experience for us," he comments. "These guys had been through hell in the war and could be very intimidating. Those war veterans were great players for us back then," he continues.

The student-age situation caught local Boards of Education off-guard, because they had not prepared regulations to deal with over-age students participating in school athletics. Stories were told about war veterans who were not enrolled in school playing school athletics under assumed names. This type of practice usually occurred when a team played athletic contests against other schools outside the local geographic area. The issue of war veterans' participation, along with the practice of non-student participation, raised concern among local Boards of Education, school superintendents, principals, coaches, players, and parents who felt a need for regulating interscholastic athletic participation. All concerned parties endorsed the establishment of a set of uniform standards governing interscholastic athletic participation in the public schools of North Carolina.

In 1952, three major interscholastic athletic organizations administered high school sports. The primary purpose of these voluntary agencies was to administer interscholastic athletics within the geographic area of their respective jurisdiction. These athletic organizations were:

- *The North Carolina High School Athletic Association* with headquarters in Chapel Hill, which was founded in 1913. Operating with a full-time executive secretary and a support staff, this association administers interscholastic athletic rules and regulations to white high schools. Membership to the association is voluntary.

- *The Western North Carolina High School Activities Association*, founded in 1929, has headquarters in Winston-Salem. This association is divided into four conferences and has a full-time executive secretary, who serves schools located in the western and Piedmont sections of the state. It administers interscholastic athletic rules and regulations to approximately 40 member schools, which all have white enrollment. Membership to this association is voluntary.

- *The North Carolina High School Athletic Conference*, a Negro organization with a history that dates back to the 1920's, has headquarters in Rocky Mount. The commissioner serves only part-time to all Negro high schools. The conference, under the commissioner, trains and certifies Negro athletic game officials.

Because membership in these associations was voluntary, not all North Carolina public schools were members. The reasons are clear: some schools were already organized in local athletic conferences and saw no reason to become a member of a state association. School administrators wanted to be totally responsible for the operation of their athletic teams. The schools could play in other tournaments that were more prestigious than those of an association affiliate. The North Carolina High School Association was known to have issued invitations to schools to play in their state tournament. Once a school accepted the invitation, they became a member of the North Carolina High School Athletic Association only for the relative sport that sport season.

Because these high school athletic associations and conferences were organized to administer interscholastic athletics for members, the Indian schools in Robeson County were organized to play among themselves. However, Indian schools did play schools with white enrollment outside the boundaries of Robeson County.

Realizing the need for acceptable standards for the operation of sound statewide athletic programs, North Carolina's superintendent of public instruction appointed a committee of county and city school superintendents, principals, and coaches and directed them to devise and recommend minimum regulations for consideration by the North Carolina State Board of Education. The regulations considered were those in use by the North Carolina High School Athletic Association. The standards, "Regulations Governing Athletics," were adopted by the North Carolina State Board of Education on June 5, 1952. These regulations have been considered as minimum standards to each local school administrative unit and athletic association/conference to abide by

or surpass its efforts to maintain the highest possible standards relative to its interscholastic athletic program. The adopted minimum regulations dealt primarily with player eligibility. i.e. residence, class attendance, academic achievement, medical examination and age verification. Age verification was an issue because of the abuse previously mentioned. Age restriction was for the protection of the athlete -- protection from negative factors whenever possible. Without restrictions, there would be great danger to athletes who participate in contact sports. Without a maximum age restriction, the door would be left open for individuals to compete in interscholastic athletics at an age equivalent to that of the average college athlete. Further, the "Age Rule" treats all students equally regardless of race, religion, national origin, gender, gifted, or handicapped. It encourages athletes to complete four years of high school between ages of 15-18, and reduces the opportunity to hold students back(red shirt). The "Age Rule" tends to reduce the opportunity for mis-matches in competition. For example, a 15-year-old ninth or tenth grade student could be competing against a student going on age 20, 21,etc., as was the case with World War II veterans. The North Carolina State Board of Education allowed school administrative units and athletic associations/conferences to make exceptions to the adopted regulations under certain circumstances not the fault of the athlete. However, there are no exceptions allowed to the age rule. The age rule shall be enforced according to the State Board of Education's set of athletic eligibility regulations.

Note: "Red Shirt" means repeat grade.

Boys Basketball

This page appeared in the 1946 Pembroke State College yearbook, *The Indianhead*. All members of the "college" team played basketball in the Indian High School.

Basketball at Pembroke State College started its post-war climb this year and promises much in the future. The team this year started as almost a complete veteran team; but as the season progressed the freshmen and the returning veterans, who had played in past years, changed the complexion of the team. Competition for places on the team became keen for the first time in four years. Next year's basketball team should show more promise than this team, as all who were playing at the close of the season, with the exception of Danford Dial and those who will be entering the Armed Services will be here to answer the starting whistle next year.

The regular season was very successful, from the won-and-lost point of view, as the team developed a habit of winning games in the last minute or two. The team won seven of its regular season games, most of them by narrow margins.

	Score		Score
Pembroke	39	Hamlet All-Stars	20
Pembroke	26	Gardner-Webb	24
Pembroke	26	Gardner-Webb	19
Pembroke	34	Campbell Junior College	32
Pembroke	32	Hamlet All-Stars	28
Pembroke	21	Ivanhoe All-Stars	27
Pembroke	31	Ivanhoe All-Stars	28
Pembroke	38	Campbell Junior College	35

FRONT ROW: James Howard Locklear, Horace Howington, Robert Lee McGirt, Clyde Locklear, Johnny Lee Locklear, Danford Dial.

BACK ROW: Gurney Sampson, Vincent Lowry, Wilton Chavis, Wilson Chavis, A.G. Spaulding, Grady Oxendine.

JAMES HOWARD LOCKLEAR, SR.

Every now and again, you will find a person who has his own ideas and is content doing things on his own terms. A person with the confidence he will succeed because he possessed the attitude and work ethics to be successful. James Howard Locklear, Sr. best describes this person. His ideas would lead him to a successful career as an athletic coach.

Locklear grew up on a farm in the Prospect Community in western Robeson County. His parents were Asa and Susie Locklear. He was one of four sons and three daughters of this family unit. He was a standout student athlete at Prospect High School from 1942-45. He participated in varsity basketball and baseball at Prospect High School. In 1944, his junior year in high school, Locklear was the leader of the Prospect High School team that advanced to the Robeson County Indian High School basketball tournament championship game. Prospect was defeated by Pembroke before an overflow crowd at the Pembroke State College Gymnasium. In 1945, he was selected to the All-Tournament team of the Robeson County Indian High School basketball. The All Tournament team was selected on the basis of general excellence in all games.

After graduating from high school in the spring of 1945 – like most young men his age and because of World War II – Locklear was subject to be drafted into military service. While waiting to hear from the draft, he enrolled at Pembroke State College, Pembroke, NC, the fall semester. He participated on the varsity basketball and baseball teams at Pembroke State. At the end of the spring semester, Locklear was drafted into military service. From 1946-49, he served in the United States Air Force. In 1946, James Howard married Marie Collins whom he met through a friend. Marie graduated from Union Chapel High School where she was an outstanding softball player. James Howard and Marie are the parents of three daughters and one son. James

Howard Locklear, Jr. was an excellent high school athlete, and was a successful coach at South Robeson High School, Rowland, NC. Today, he is the Athletic Director at Purnell Swett High School, Pembroke, NC. His three daughters have successful careers. Susie graduated from the University of North Carolina at Pembroke with a degree in Elementary Education. She taught school for more than 30 years and retired from the profession. Carolyn has undergraduate and graduate degrees from UNC-Pembroke and is Principal of an Elementary school in St. Pauls, North Carolina. Brenda was an Administrative Assistant in the Financial Aids office at UNC-Pembroke. She has retired from the University.

James Howard Locklear, Sr. participated in basketball and baseball while serving in the US Air Force. During this time he played with, and against, good players. Many of these players had played in college. He was taught good skills and fundamentals in baseball by good coaches. This teaching was valuable in developing his knowledge of playing the game. Locklear had his first experience playing golf while in the military. This was a sport foreign to American Indians, because it was not available to them in the area they lived. Today many American Indians are enjoying playing golf as a sport and for recreation.

After his release from the military Locklear returned home to the Prospect community. He worked on the family farm for a year. In 1950, the United States became involved in the Korean War, and Locklear returned to military service. At the end of the Korean War, he was released from the military and returned home.

In 1953, eight years after graduating from high school, with a wife and children, Locklear re-enrolled at Pembroke State College. In 1955, he graduated from the school with a BS degree in Elementary Education.

Short in stature, the five-six Locklear was a dynamic athlete. Using his skills learned in high school and

Photo: 1955 Pembroke State College yearbook, *The Indianhead*

**1954-55 PEMBROKE STATE COLLEGE MENS
BASKETBALL TEAM**

KNEELING, LEFT TO RIGHT: Clarence Woods, Gerald Butler, William Hammonds, Ralph Hunt, Pete Jacobs, **James Howard Locklear**.

STANDING, LEFT TO RIGHT: Coach Belus V. Smawley, Bruce Jones, Reece Warwick, Joe Williams, James F. "Buddy" Bell, Kenneth Maynor, Forace Oxendine, Levi Hunt, Jr., team manager.

perfected in the military, he became one of the best athletes to play sports at Pembroke State College, excelling in basketball and baseball. He was selected to the University of North Carolina-Pembroke Athletic Hall of Fame in 1986.

While a student athlete at Pembroke State College, Locklear teamed with the late Forace Oxendine to make the best duo of athletes in the school's history. The two athletes developed a strong trusting friendship that would last way past their playing days and into their professional lives. Oxendine's positions were center and forward on the basketball team. He was good at rebounding the ball and getting a quick outlet pass to Locklear streaking down the court for the patented fast break the team was noted for. Both players were good defenders.

It was on the baseball diamond where the two players performed best. Locklear, as a slick fielding short stop, covered a lot of ground from his position. He had good hands and a strong throwing arm. For a small man he had a lot of power as a hitter. Mostly a singles hitter, he could also hit the long ball. He had

excellent speed, leading the team in stolen bases. Locklear was a versatile player who played several defensive positions. He played the catcher position whenever the flame throwing Oxendine pitched. The two players made history in the spring of 1955. Playing against the nearby Ft. Bragg Army Base team the first night game on the college baseball field with James Howard Locklear as his catcher, Forace Oxendine struck out 23 batters in a nine inning game. The strikeouts are still a school record. The Ft. Bragg team managed two hits off Oxendine in his record performance.

James Howard Locklear, Sr. and Forace Oxendine played several years of semi-professional baseball together after their college playing days. They would become teachers and athletic coaches.

Teacher and Athletic Coach

In 1955, Locklear began his teaching career at Oxendine Elementary School, a school located in Northwestern Robeson County. He left Oxendine School to take a teaching position at John Mosby Academy in Front Royal, Virginia. In 1964, he returned to Robeson County to teach at Ashpole Elementary School. In 1968, he accepted an Elementary Education teaching position at Prospect High School. He was also assigned positions as athletic director, head basketball and baseball coach at Prospect High School. He credits Danford Dial, Sr., Principal, at Prospect High School for giving him the opportunity to coach high school sports. "Mr. Danford was a fine school administrator, and demanded excellence from his teachers and coaches. He was very supportive of his staff and was especially supportive of me and the athletic teams", Locklear said. Locklear began a football program at Prospect and served as head coach of this sport. In more than a decade directing and coaching at Prospect High School he developed a sports program of excellence. During his teaching at Prospect High School, Locklear attended UNC-Pembroke to complete enough credits for certification in Health and Physical Education. After the certification he moved from elementary teacher to high school physical education.

The rapid development of the school's football team came as a surprise. Locklear with little experience coaching this sport sought help. This help came from Mike Olsen, Professor in the Health and Physical Education Department at near by UNC-Pembroke and Leroy Vaughn who coached at Maxton High School. Olsen provided information for the defense and Coach Vaughn provided information for the offense. Soon the football teams became one of the best 1A teams in the state. The football teams qualified for the NC High School Athletic Association playoffs several seasons. The farthest advancement was the state western semi-final game at Robbinsville. The game was played in the cold and snow at the smoky mountain school. Locklear remembers the site and conditions. "Being from the eastern part of the state we were not accustomed to playing in the cold and snow. Even in these conditions our team was playing well. We were behind 7-0 at half time. Our best running back was injured (hip pointer) and did not play. "Because we did not have our star running back, our offense was not the same, our defense was on the field a long time, and in the second half finally wore down. I want to give credit to the Robbinsville High School team, because they were a state championship quality team."

The boys basketball teams advanced to the state playoffs every year. The teams went several years where they won 20 or more games, the most wins in a season were 26. Locklear credits Laverne McInnis, basketball coach, Orrum High School with getting him involved in attending coaching clinics. "He arranged for me to attend clinics, he would take me with him. Coach McInnis was instrumental in elevating my basketball knowledge. He was my mentor, during our times together riding to and from clinics we would talk basketball. I learned the nuts and bolts of coaching from him. He was always helpful. He knew a lot about coaching basketball and shared a lot of his knowledge with me." McInnis and Bill Templeton of Red Springs High School lent their support for the American Indian High Schools in Robeson County while they were being considered for admission into the NC High School Athletic Association. With these

coaches' support and the support of the local Board of Education, the schools were accepted for full membership beginning the 1968-69 school year.

The baseball teams at Prospect were very successful. The teams won several conference championships. Prospect advanced to the 1A state championship on two different occasions. Loosing to Lucama High School once and to Jamesville High School once.

In 1979, Locklear left Prospect to become head football coach at 3A Pembroke High School. He directed the football program for one year. From 1980 to 1983, he served as Athletic Director and head basketball coach at Pembroke High School. At the beginning of the 1983-84 school year Pembroke, Prospect, and Maxton High Schools consolidated to become West Robeson High School.

With the consolidation of the schools, Locklear left coaching and took a position in the schools system's central administrative office. He was assigned to be an assistant to the Driver Education Coordinator. He retired from public school education in 1985.

Indeed, Locklear left his mark on athletics, not only in Robeson County but across North Carolina. He developed an athletic program at Prospect High School second to none in terms of football, basketball and baseball success. Prospect has had its fair share of athletes come through its doors. But the person who pulled everything together and called the shots was Locklear.

And he truly did things his way. Locklear was not in the coaching business for popularity. And he certainly had his share of critics and people who did not agree with his style of coaching or the strategies and decisions he employed. He was demanding and expected his players to give of themselves just as he did. He gave the Prospect School his best and expected his players to do the same for themselves and the program they represented. At times he was misunderstood. He had a tough outer shell but is a very good person who took pride in his players, his program and his school. He had his ideas as how the game was to be coached. He was a winner and still is. He did things his way.

FORACE OXENDINE, SR. (1928-1965)

MOST ATHLETIC
Forace Oxendine and Narva Lowry (Maynor)
Photo: 1955 Pembroke State College Yearbook
The Indianhead

Forace Oxendine, Sr. was born in Robeson County, North Carolina. He was the oldest of eight children born to the late Mr. and Mrs. Chesley Oxendine, Sr. Forace was married to Deola Dial. They were the parents of two children, Forace Jr. and Audrey.

Forace grew up in the Union Chapel community, located five miles north of Pembroke, North Carolina. The family residence was across the road from Union Chapel School. He graduated from Union Chapel High School. While in high school, Forace played on the school basketball and baseball teams. In basketball he was the team leader in both offense and defense. He

was selected to the 1946 Robeson County Indian High School all Tournament boys basketball team.

He received a BS degree in Health and Physical Education from Pembroke State College. The popular athlete was selected class president his senior year at Pembroke State College. He was a versatile student athlete, excelling in basketball, baseball, and tennis. He was selected by his peers as Senior Superlative "Most Athletic." In 1981, Forace was selected to the University of North Carolina-Pembroke Athletic Hall of Fame for baseball. He served two years in the U.S. Army.

On May 6, 1955, Forace accomplished a feat yet to be surpassed or equalled by a Pembroke State College baseball player. The 6'1" 180lbs fireball righthander, pitching for the college baseball team against an all-star team from nearby Ft. Bragg Army Base, struck out 23 batters in the nine inning game. The memorable event took place as the local college team was playing its first night game on its new lighted field. The game was witnessed by many local fans, including the Honorable Thad Eure, Secretary of State, (North Carolina), who pulled the switch to turn on the lights. The Pembroke catcher, James Howard Locklear, Sr., did a masterful job holding onto the pitcher's pitches. Those fans who were at the game, and living today, still talk about this marvelous record setting performance.

After graduating from college, Forace signed a professional baseball contract. He played professional for several years, advancing to the Triple-A level. This advancement was the farthest for an American Indian baseball player from Robeson County at that time. Gene Locklear and Dwight Lowry later advanced to major league baseball. After his professional career ended, Forace played semi-professional baseball for the local Pembroke team.

In 1961, Forace accepted a teacher/coach position at Hawkeye High School, Raeford, North Carolina. During his tenure at Hawkeye High School, he was lauded by the students and peers as an outstanding teacher. He reorganized the interscholastic athletic program to include a junior varsity program for both boys and girls. Under his guidance, Hawkeye became the dominant team in the newly formed Tri County Indian Athletic Conference. Forace used his talent and knowledge to develop good student athletes. One student, Durant Cooper, whom Forace mentored, signed a professional baseball contract with the Chicago White Sox organization. Cooper played several seasons of professional baseball, advancing to triple-A level.

Forace was more than a teacher/coach to the student athletes at Hawkeye, he was a father figure as well. Most of the American Indian athletes came from low level socio-economic homes. They could not afford athletic shoes, clothes, baseball gloves, and other athletic equipment. Forace provided his own finances to pay for these needed items. Additionally, he provided transportation for the athletes that needed a way home. These young people revered him as their hero. Forace could relate well to his students because he too had over come many barriers and obstacles in his lifetime. He had a deep love for these students, the school, and the community.

January 31, 1965 became a dark day for the Hawkeye School community. The popular teacher/coach died from a shooting accident. His death came just days before the conference post season basketball tournament. His assistant coach, Hartman Brewington, would coach the boys and girls teams for the tournament.

The untimely death of Forace brought sadness to all those who knew him, because a giant in the field of athletics had fallen. The legacy of Forace remains, and his memory will forever be a motivating force for those who loved him. The late Earl Hughes Oxendine, principal, Hawkeye School at the time of his death said, "The community needed a man with his reputation, skills, and fame. He was the best natural athlete that I have ever known, good in every sport and could beat you in every one of them."

Della Oxendine-Locklear, sister of Forace Oxendine, contributed to this piece.

Photo: Union Chapel School Archival Collection

UNION CHAPEL HIGH SCHOOL BOYS BASKETBALL TEAM, circa 1948

FRONT ROW, LEFT TO RIGHT: Welton Wilkins Jr., George E. Oxendine, **Forace B. Oxendine**, Captain, Rufus Locklear, Jr.

BACK ROW: Ernest Oxendine, Robert Burnette, James Ertle Deese, John Ander Oxendine, Cleveland Locklear, Earl Jones.

Fairgrove High School Basketball
Coached by Ralph Hunt

Winning the Robeson County Indian High Schools' basketball tournament championship back in the 1950's and 60's was not easy. But, Fairgrove High School's string of successes under Coach Ralph Hunt during the decade from 1956 to 1966 has to be among the most-remarkable accomplishments in Robeson County Indian High Schools basketball history. Fairgrove High School won tournament titles in 1957, 1958, 1959, 1962, 1963, and 1964.

During the majority of these seasons, Hunt's teams had talent-advantage over the rest of the teams. And rarely does the most-talented team fail to win a championship. The consummate coach and his players were the epitome of selfless performance. Of course, there were super players such as: Horace Hunt, Gerald Ransom, Bonson Locklear, Earl and Levon Sealey, Bruce Oxendine, Jesse Freeman, Wilbert Strong, Ardeen and Larece Hunt. Even the best of the Fairgrove players performed with equal intensity on both defense and offense. Most of Hunt's players were exceptional passers and ball handlers. His teams were the most fluid and organized. Their success was reflected in coaching and the execution of team concept.

Ralph Hunt was an outstanding athlete while a student at Pembroke State College. After graduation from college, he accepted the coaching position at Fairgrove High School, succeeding Leon Hunt who had coached the Fairgrove boys to the 1955 Robeson County Indian High Schools basketball tournament title. After a successful coaching career, Hunt served as principal of Fairgrove High School. Upon leaving the education profession, he served on the Robeson County Board of Education.

Photo: 1963 Fairgrove High School Yearbook, *The Fairgrovian*

1963 FAIRGROVE HIGH SCHOOL BOYS TOURNAMENT CHAMPIONSHIP TEAM

LEFT TO RIGHT: Bobby Lewis, Larece Hunt, Jesse Freeman, John Marvin Carter, Fairley Jacobs, Ardeen Hunt, Bobby Mitchell, Alford Hunt, Jr., Montford Sanderson, Jimmy Cummings, James O. Oxendine.
Coach Ralph Hunt (kneeling in front).

HORACE HUNT

by Tim Brayboy

Photo: 1963 Fairgrove
High School Yearbook,
The Fairgrovian

Horace Hunt

Horace Hunt has spent his adult life working to help others gain a higher ground. Born on November 28, 1938, Hunt grew up in the shadows of Green Grove Elementary School. He attended McDonald Elementary School in grades one through three and completed grades four through six at Green Grove Elementary School. In the seventh grade at Fairgrove School he began playing basketball. This writer played against Hunt throughout our high school years when he attended Fairgrove High School and I attended Pembroke High School. Whenever our basketball teams met, I was assigned to guard him.

Hunt played guard position for Fairgrove's boys basketball team. It was a challenge to defend his playing skills. He possessed a lightning fast step, could run, pass, shoot, score, defend and played with a magnitude of game intelligence. Both his body and mouth were in perpetual motion when he was on the basketball court. Hunt was the very first "trash talker" I played against. The talented player used the talking to motivate himself, as well as his opponent. He and I recognized this kind of talking to be a method that could be used to evoke a maximum performance from both of us.

The four years Hunt and I played high school basketball our respective schools each won the season ending tournament twice. Fairgrove High School won in years 1955 and 1957. Pembroke High School won in years 1954 and 1956. Hunt was selected the "Most Valuable Player" in the 1956 tournament. The Pembroke American

Legion presented a trophy for the selection. Hunt credits his late beloved friend and high school basketball coach Ralph Hunt for guidance in leading him on the path to better gains.

"Coach Ralph Hunt was the best friend I ever had. He was my mentor," the former athlete comments.

Hunt was graduated from Fairgrove High School in spring 1957. He enrolled at Pembroke State Collegethe following fall. While a college student, he participated in varsity basketball and baseball for two years. He excelled in baseball, playing centerfield for the college team.

His coach Richard Lauffer says of his star baseball player, "Horace was the best defensive outfielder ever to play for me."

During Hunt's sophomore year in college, his father's health began to decline. As the school year drew to a close, the young college student chose to halt his studies in order to aid his family during a financial crisis. Hunt took a summer job working for a steel company in Philadelphia, Pennsylvania in order to help his family with living expenses. He remembers that the pay was good and for the first time ever, he had money. Hunt says the work and money were so good that he decided to keep the job and not to return to college. He was employed less than a year with the company before being drafted into the United States Army where he served from 1960 to 1963. Most of his military tour was spent in Germany where he was assigned to a ballistic missile company. While playing basketball as a recreation sport for his Army company team Hunt was notified through a bulletin to try out for the Army Base basketball team. He tried out and was selected. He learned from a team player that the Army Base had a baseball team. Hunt participated in baseball tryouts and was selected as a member of the team. For the following two years he played both basketball and baseball for his Army Base teams. The teams competed against other military posts throughout Europe. Hunt's baseball team won the European championship the two years he played. The talented Indian athlete was selected to the All-European team both years.

After completion of his military service, Hunt returned to Philadelphia for a short period. Having spent his stay there, he returned to his native Robeson County where he sought employment. He was employed seven years with a hosiery manufacturer in Lumberton, North Carolina before accepting employment with the North Carolina Division of Vocational Rehabilitation Services. In the agency's Department of Health and Human Services Hunt's primary job is to assist people with disabilities in finding employment.

Married and residing in Lumberton, Hunt is active in community and citizen affairs. He is the father of two sons.

Reflecting on his high school and college athletic play experiences he remembers, "They were the most fun times in my life." Of his beloved high school coach, the late Ralph Hunt, he comments, "Not only was he a good coach, he was my friend, a father figure, and the best person I have ever been associated with."

Hunt credits two other persons as impacting positively on his life during the two years he attended Pembroke State College.

"Dr. Herbert Oxendine and Mr. Tom Oxendine, Sr. supported me with encouragement and gave me financial help," he reflects. "These two men were awful good to me. They provided me meals and expense money when the college team traveled to away games." Hunt says he will never forget the kind acts shown him by the two caring men.

"It all goes back to who we are and what we do in helping others gain a higher ground," the former two-sport star athlete adds.

1957 FAIRGROVE HIGH SCHOOL BOYS TOURNAMENT CHAMPIONSHIP TEAM

LEFT TO RIGHT: Gary Sampson, Delton Oxendine, Calvin Hammonds, Gerald Ransom, Thomas Oxendine, Earl Sealey, Pernell Locklear, **James Horace Hunt**, Carl Bradford, Charles Hunt, Tommie Strickland. Coach Ralph Hunt, Manager Edward Lowery.

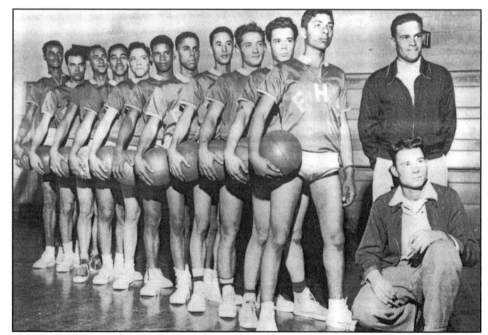

Photo: 1957 Fairgrove High School Yearbook, The Fairgrovian

Jydor Locklear was born in rural Pembroke, North Carolina. His parents were Willard Lee and Lillie Mae Locklear. On August 14, 1960, he married Joy Brayboy of Pembroke. Three daughters were born to the couple: Cindy Kay, Karen Ann, and Sharon Joy. Jydor Locklear was a leader as a player and as a athletic coach at Pembroke High School.

Player

Pembroke High School was home to some of Robeson County's finest student athletes. In the early 1950's, no basketball player in the Robeson County Indian high schools was a match for Jydor Locklear in terms of quality, ability, and diversity. Regarding athletic skills and techniques, Locklear may be as close to a Renaissance man as a athlete can be.

The versatile Locklear grew up five miles from the town of Pembroke. He became interested in sports at an early age. When he became eligible to play for his school basketball team, he immediately became an impact player. The young star's prowess was most-times misunderstood. His on-court demeanor, self-character, and style created a love-hate relationship from opposing players, coaches, and fans. He became one of those players who was an unlikely candidate to be voted most-popular.

But Locklear's fans recognized him as the riveting leader of the Pembroke High School boys basketball team – one of the best in Robeson County Indian high school history. The way Locklear played the game in the 1950's amazingly mirrors the way the game is played today. His repertoire included deft passes, excellent lead passes for assists, excellent ball handling, and a deadly jump shot. There was not a play he could not make; no opponent he could not agitate. He was perhaps the greatest clutch performer in the conference. Additionally he was an excellent defender.

Locklear was an outstanding baseball player. He played middle infield on the Pembroke High School team.

After graduating from high school, he played both sports at the varsity level at Pembroke State College from where he graduated in 1960. His first professional assignment was a teaching position at Pembroke Elementary School.

Coach

From 1960 until 1968, Locklear was a teacher and coach at Pembroke High School. During his years as a varsity basketball and baseball coach his teams won or shared the conference championship. His basketball teams won the conference post season tournament in both 1961 and 1966.

In 1967, Pembroke High School became the first Robeson County Indian high school to be accepted for membership in the North Carolina High School Athletic Association. In its first year as a member of the state Association, Pembroke High School boys basketball, coached by Locklear, was given a berth in the state playoffs. In a game played in Fayetteville, North Carolina, the Pembroke team defeated Hope Mills High Schools 102-48. Records are not available to show how far the team advanced.

Locklear left high school coaching at the end of the 1967-68 school year. He coached the Pembroke Junior High School boys basketball team for ten years. From 1979 until 1991, he taught at South Robeson High School where he had no coaching responsibilities. In June 1991, he retired from public school education, completing 32 years of teaching and coaching.

While out riding his bicycle in rural Pembroke on a Sunday afternoon in early September 1994, Locklear was fatally struck by a hit-and-run motorist. The driver of the vehicle was never apprehended; thus never prosecuted for the crime that claimed the life of the beloved teacher/coach.

His reputation for excellence as a player, teacher, and coach is well documented. But what is most-admired about Jydor Locklear is that he never forgot his humble rural roots and love for his family and the tribal community.

Photo courtesy of Kenneth R. Maynor

PEMBROKE HIGH SCHOOL 1952-53 BASKETBALL

FRONT ROW - Bundy Locklear, Harold Cummings, Ken Maynor, John H. Hunt, **Jydor Locklear.**

SECOND ROW - James Adams Oxendine, Freddie Mac Revels, Ray Oxendine, Bobby Jacobs.

THIRD ROW - Bob Lowry, Adna Lowry Jr., Joe Morgan (face hidden).

TOP ROW - Rod Locklear.

Robeson County Indian High School Conference and Tournament Champions; All-Tournament – Ken Maynor, **Jydor Locklear**, John H. Hunt; 1952-53 Record – 22 wins 2 loses; Conference Schools – Pembroke, Magnolia, Green Grove, Fairmont, Prospect; Outside Conference games (Wins) – Wadesboro, Candor, Gibson, Lilesville, Fort Bragg Squad Teams; (Losses) - Prospect, Lilesville (away).

Girls Basketball

Girls Basketball played a vital role in the Indian Interscholastic athletic program. Competition among teams and the players was outstanding and of high caliber. Many of the players later played at "the college," now UNC-Pembroke.

Photo: Pembroke High School Archival Collection

Photo: Pembroke High School Archival Collection

The photo to the right appeared in the 1946 Pembroke State College *The Indianhead*. All members of the Pembroke State College Team played in the Indian High School basketball conference.

FRONT ROW: Christine Roberts, Trudy Bullard, Retha Locklear, Loraine Burnette, Phoda Jacobs, Josephine Locklear.

BACK ROW: Debra Jacobs, Mary Martin, Clara Mae Oxendine, Clara Chavis, Agnes Hunt, Etta B. Revels.

ROSE OXENDINE HILL

Pembroke High School Basketball Player

Rose Oxendine Hill - Selected Most Athletic, *Senior Superlative*, in 1957 scored 53 points her last game at Pembroke High School.

Photo: 1957 Pembroke High School yearbook, *The Challenger*

As a child growing up in rural Robeson County, Rose Oxendine was athletically gifted. Recognizing the gift in his daughter, John W. Oxendine erected a basketball goal in the family's back yard so she could hone her basketball skills. Thereafter, anytime of the year –and whenever time allowed– Rose dribbled and shot a basketball. As a young girl growing up in the farming community of Union Chapel she untiringly worked at honing her basketball skills. During pick-up games with neighborhood children she would imagine herself playing in an actual game somewhere on a gleaming wooden basketball court before an overflow crowd. The young athlete's dedication to details during these countless pick-up games, coupled with her strong character, led her to stardom as a high school basketball player.

After completing Union Chapel Elementary School, Oxendine enrolled in Pembroke High School in 1953 from where she was graduated in 1957. Basketball was the only interscholastic athletic sport offered for girls in Robeson County Indian high schools during this period in time. The rules for girls basketball during this era allowed the game to be played by two teams of six players each: three forwards and three guards per team, on separate ends of the court. A player was restricted to two dribbles. Guards were not allowed to shoot the ball. Because of their positions on the courts, forwards did all the scoring.

Playing forward, Oxendine used her dribbling and shooting skills to become scoring leader in most games. In the ninth grade she became a "starter" on the varsity team. During the four years of her high school basketball play, she led the Pembroke High School girls team to four regular season championships and to three post-season tournament championships. The single tournament championship loss was to Magnolia High School in Oxendine's senior year.

Although Oxendine was an exemplary scorer, it was during her high school senior year that her shooting and scoring abilities were noticeable. Playing on an inexperienced team, she took it upon herself to be the team's offensive leader. Records are not available to support her game scores.

However, her high school coach once said, "She averaged 21.0 points per game." This may seem low compared to today's scoring, but game scores were historically low back then. From eye-witness accounts, Oxendine scored 54 points in the second-to-last regular season game her senior year, the most points ever scored by a girl in Robeson County Indian High School basketball. One week later, in her final career game,

Oxendine scored 53 points, ending the final chapter of perhaps the best female basketball player ever to play in Robeson County Indian high schools. Her peers selected her as the "Most Athletic" senior superlative. After graduating from Pembroke High School, Oxendine enlisted in the United States Air Force. She married an Air Force man and gave up her enlistment after giving two and one half years to military service. Two sons were born to the couple: John lives in Anchorage, Alaska. He is head coach of the mens Hockey team, University of Alaska at Anchorage. The other son, Richard, lives in Anchorage, Alaska.

Oxendine worked for the U.S. Indian Health Service in Anchorage, Alaska prior to retiring to her native Robeson County, North Carolina in 1996. Today, Rose Oxendine Hill is active in community affairs. She serves as a substitute teacher with the Public Schools of Robeson County. She attends sporting and social events at the University of North Carolina at Pembroke. The divorced mother keeps close contact with her two sons and is supportive of their careers. Oxendine's Lumbee Indian parents are John W. and Cordelia Oxendine of the Union Chapel community.

Photo: 1957 Pembroke High School yearbook, *The Challenger*

1957 PEMBROKE HIGH SCHOOL GIRLS BASKETBALL TEAM

BACK ROW: Kathryn Brewington, Deola Oxendine, Edna Berry, **Rose Oxendine**, Jeanette Ball, Heneritta Locklear, Shelvie J. Locklear.

FRONT ROW: Betty J. Locklear, Sylvia Lowry, Della Rae Oxendine, Joyce Baker, Lummie Jane Locklear.

PAULINE BULLARD LOCKLEAR

Photo of Pauline Bullard Locklear was taken from the 1956 Tomahawk, Prospect High School yearbook.

Pauline Bullard Locklear was born March 4, 1934 in the Prospect Community in Robeson County, North Carolina. The first of three children born to the late Ang and Annie Goins Bullard, Locklear was nine-years-old when her parents had their second child. Being the oldest child in the family, she began at an early age to work on the family-owned farm and took on duties normally performed by a man.

She says she plowed the black fields of her ancestral land with a mule. She also hoed tobacco, cotton, and corn as a child and labored inside tobacco barns, lifting sticks of strung, raw tobacco onto wood tiers where it would later be flue-cured.

"Farming was hard work," she exclaims. "Working hard was what people did in our Indian community, and those who did not work were frowned upon as being lazy and no good," she comments.

Locklear entered the first grade at Prospect Elementary School when she was five-years-old and went on to graduate from Prospect High School at age 16, in 1950. Academically and athletically gifted, she was valedictorian of her graduating class and played on a tournament championship basketball team in high school. The only member of her family to play high school sports, Locklear started all varsity games

her four years she played high school basketball. In 1949, she led Prospect High School to the championship game of the Robeson County Indian High School Basketball Tournament. Prospect defeated Union Chapel High School 19-14.

She remembers her high school basketball team members as being: Sara Neal Bullard, Harvelene Locklear, Annie Bell Jacobs, Hoyland Lowry, Sadie Mae Locklear, Mary Frances Chavis, Ellen Jane Bryant, Naomi Dial, Cleo Moore, Rosetta Oxendine, Mabel Moore, Lola Mearl Lowry, and Alice Ruth Collins. The girls basketball coach was Mary Sanderson.

Locklear says the support the team received from the Prospect community was exemplary. "Our school principal arranged for the boys and girls basketball teams to travel first class on their non-conference away games. When we traveled, we would ride in Trailway buses," Locklear says of the commercial buses used to transport the high school athletes. The all-Indian girls basketball team played against North Carolina high school teams in Star, West End, Aberdeen; and also played in McColl, South Carolina.

"We always had a large group from the community at the away games," she recalls.

Locklear says she and her fellow teammates got dressed in their game uniforms before leaving their respective homes before leaving on away games. Blue jeans and warm up jackets were worn over the uniforms.

"I was also a member of the cheerleading squad. When our game was over I would put on my jeans and join the cheerleaders in leading cheers for the boys team," Locklear comments. She speaks with glee of the season-ending trip to White Lake, a North Carolina water resort located approximately 50 miles from Prospect School in Robeson County.

"In late spring, when the weather was warm the coaches would take team members to White Lake for swimming and a cookout. This was another way the school and community gave their support."

Locklear graduated from Prospect High School in 1950. Her family were members at Prospect United Methodist Church. Her parents wanted her to go away to college, and Pfeiffer College, located in the village of Misenheimer, North Carolina seemed to be a practical choice because of its affiliation with the United Methodist Church. Locklear enrolled in the small junior college after graduation from high school. She says going away to college was her first experience in being away from home. There she quickly involved herself in studies and student activities. She was selected as a member of the college women's basketball team and participated on the team the two years she was a student at the school.

Locklear's roommate graduated from Pfeiffer College and invited Locklear to visit her homeland of Cuba. She accepted the invitation and spent 18 days in Cuba. "I would not take anything for this experience because the trip was something special for me during this time in my life," Locklear beams.

In the summer of 1952, Locklear married her former high school classmate -- and star basketball player -- James Earl Locklear. They moved to Detroit, Michigan, where he worked in the automobile industry. Six months later, the couple returned home to the Prospect Community where they awaited the birth of their first and only child, a son, Dexter Earl, who was born in late spring 1953. After the birth of her son, Locklear enrolled at Pembroke State College, Pembroke, North Carolina. In 1955 she received her college diploma, having majored in English. She also earned enough credits for a minor in Library Science and Social Studies.

Photo courtesy of Pauline Bullard Locklear

Pauline Bullard Locklear, 2001

The same year she accepted a teaching position at Prospect High School where she also served as coach for the school's varsity girls' basketball team. In 1957 her team advanced to the Robeson County Indian High School Basketball Tournament where they fell to Magnolia High School in the championship game.

In 1960, Locklear accepted a position as librarian at rural Hawkeye High School in Raeford, North Carolina. From 1975 to 1977, she was director of the Native American Museum at Pembroke State University. In the fall of 1977, Locklear accepted the position as librarian at Hoke County High School in the city of Raeford, North Carolina. In 1985, she retired from Hoke County High School with more than 30 years in public school education.

In retirement Locklear is actively involved in neighborhood and community affairs. She serves on numerous business and government boards as well as serves as township registrar for her local voting precinct. She has received numerous public service awards including Outstanding Indian Educator of the Year from Lumbee Regional Development Association and the prestigious National Lawrence O'Brien Award in 1998 for her outstanding achievement in grass roots volunteer work on behalf of the Democratic Party.

Of her life, Locklear reflects, "If I could live it over, I would not change a thing. My life has been just like I would have written it, chapter-by-chapter."

I am a person to take risks, and I am willing to suffer the consequences for my doings. When things happen that affect you, then deal with them. Be ready to make your commitment and stick to it," she advises.

"All of us did our best, and we had someone wonderful to guide and coach us. Mr. Marvin, who was our coach, was a very wonderful man. He always said funny things. At times we girls would fret him, but he would get over it. Then we all were okay. We had a wonderful time playing ball."

Byrtis Dial, Prospect High School, Class of 1959

Photo courtesy of Carrie Moore Dial

1959 PROSPECT HIGH SCHOOL GIRLS BASKETBALL TEAM

KNEELING - **Byrtis Dial** and Odessa Chavis, right.
STANDING, LEFT TO RIGHT: Andrea Locklear, Mildred Woods, Maggie Rose Locklear, Christine Hammonds, Jeannie Dale Locklear, Coach Marvin Lowry, Betty Clark, Annie Ruth Bullard, Dorothy Scott, Ceola Locklear.

KATRINA LOCKLEAR

Photo courtesy of Katrina Locklear

Katrina Locklear played basketball at both Fairmont Indian and Pembroke High Schools.

Katrina Locklear was born November 11, 1934, in Fairmont, North Carolina where she spent her early childhood. She worked on the family farm with her parents, the late Hardywell and Pearlie Mae Clark Locklear, and her siblings. All six of the Locklear children attended Fairmont Indian School and everyone of them played basketball for the school.

During the years Locklear attended Fairmont Indian High School, athletic eligibility regulations were not enforced. Being short of players for his girls basketball team, coach Albert Hunt invited Locklear to play when she was in the seventh grade. She was a starting guard for Fairmont High School her first year on the team. As a result of her early recruitment, Locklear played high school varsity basketball for five years. During this period the rules for girls basketball required six players: three forwards and three guards. Those in the forward position were the players allowed shot attempts. Those in guard positions tried to prevent the forwards from attempting basketball shots.

Locklear not only excelled as an athlete, she excelled in academics as well and was promoted from seventh to ninth grade where she continued to play on the varsity basketball team. At the end of ninth grade, Locklear moved with her family to a farm near Pembroke, North Carolina. The following school year she enrolled at Pembroke High School where she became a starting guard on the girls basketball team. She was assigned to guard the opponent's best forward. Because of her aggressive court play, Locklear's eye glasses were often ripped from her face. So as to prevent damage to her glasses, the basketball coach fitted her with a facial apparatus. The "cage" became her identifying trademark.

The 1951 season was an historical occasion for Pembroke High School boys and girls basketball teams that Tom Oxendine coached. With Oxendine at courtside, both teams won the annual tournament that year with Locklear leading the girls basketball team in defeating Magnolia High School 60-50 for the championship. According to former basketball coaches, the tournament was the first time ever an individual, serving both a boys and girls team, coached both teams to championships for a single high school in the same tournament year.

The Robesonian, Robeson County's daily newspaper, reported the annual basketball tournament in the March 22, 1951 edition. On page number 8, the paper writes, "This experience was Coach Oxendine's first and only high school coaching experience. He served as an aviator in World War II and served in the U.S. Navy Reserves."

Soon after the 1951 basketball season ended, Oxendine was called for military duty and served in the Korean War. After the war, Oxendine remained on active duty and subsequently retired after 20 years of service in the United States Navy. "We had a sports banquet for the championship teams before the end of the 1951 school year and Coach Oxendine arranged to get leave from his military assignment to be with us during the celebration," Locklear recalls.

After graduation from Pembroke High School, Locklear enrolled at Pembroke State College where she participated in sports for two years before suspending her studies to begin a family. She married Samuel R. Locklear on November 12, 1953.

"I wanted to be a full-time mother and be home with my children," Locklear says regarding her decision to leave the college classroom.

With her children all in school, Locklear re-entered Pembroke State College from where she earned her B.S. in Elementary Education in 1963. The same year she began her teaching career with Hoke County Schools where she served 14 years at Hawkeye School in rural Raeford, North Carolina. She then accepted a teaching position with the Lumberton City Schools where she served Carroll Middle School in Lumberton, North Carolina until her retirement in 1993. During her professional career, Locklear was appointed to the North Carolina Textbook Commission where she served 12 years.

After a 30-year teaching career, Locklear relishes a slower pace. She savors time working in her botanical garden at the home she shares with Samuel, her husband of 48 years. The couple, proprietors of Locklear & Son Funeral Home, raised four children in Pembroke, North Carolina.

She is active in the local chapter of Master Gardner, which serves to help homeowners and government agencies develop beautifully landscaped properties. As a certified master gardener few things delight her more than seeing the results of her labor blossom in a well-manicured lawn, landscaped with exotic flowers and a variety of plants, shrubs and trees.

"My interest and love of flowers and gardening started when my mother let me help with the flowers that adorned the family yard when I was a child," she remembers. "I can vividly remember the flowers my mother planted in the yard or displayed in containers. She let me help set them out and tend to them. I just fell in love with flowers," she explains.

Both Locklear and her husband are licensed pilots who enjoy flying. They attend Pembroke Gospel Chapel and are involved in church services and activities. She is active in the community where she serves as a member of the trustees at Southeastern Regional Medical Center in Lumberton. She is an active member of the Robeson County Retired School Personnel Association and also serves her alma mater as an advisory board member to the Givens Performing Arts Center. The Center is a part of the campus of the University of North Carolina at Pembroke, the school once known as Pembroke State College.

Photo: 1953 Pembroke State College yearbook, *The Indianhead*

1952-53 PEMBROKE STATE COLLEGE WOMENS BASKETBALL TEAM

These players were former participants in the Robeson County Indian High School basketball program.

LEFT TO RIGHT: Katie Lee Jones (Pembroke High School), **Katrina Locklear** (Fairmont & Pembroke High School), Arminda Locklear-Lowry (Prospect High School), Helen Bell (Magnolia High School), Bertha Locklear (Pembroke High School), Clarice Locklear (Green Grove High School), Betty Rae Hammonds (Magnolia High School) Bernice Brooks-Lowry (Pembroke High School).

LOUISE CHAVIS LOCKLEAR

Photo courtesy of Hayes Alan Locklear

Louise Chavis Locklear

Louise Chavis Locklear's face beams with excitement as she recalls the Magnolia High School girls team winning the championship game in the 1957 Robeson County Indian High School basketball tournament. Four teams participated in the tournament. Magnolia High School played Pembroke High School in the semifinals. Locklear played on the Magnolia team.

She replays the closing moments of the Pembroke and Magnolia game:

"We were behind by two points with only a few seconds remaining in the regulation. We were in control of the ball near our basket and our coach, Ned Sampson, called for a time-out. As we huddled Coach Sampson designed a play for the ball to be inbound. The teammate receiving the ball would pass it to me, and I was to drive hard to the basket, shoot and make the basket, draw a foul, and make the foul shot. When play resumed everything went as designed. I made the basket, was fouled, and we won 67-66."

She adds, "Both teams played so well. Rose Oxendine of Pembroke scored 53 points against us in this game. We could not stop her. We were fortunate to have the ball at the end." Locklear says the game was the most emotion-packed experience she ever had in any basketball game she ever played.

In the championship game the following night Locklear scored 20 points from the forward position to lead Magnolia High School to an easier defeat of Prospect High School, 57-35. Fellow teammate Patsy Ann Locklear scored 19 points, and Mattie Brewer added 19 more to the total for Magnolia High School. Other members of the Magnolia High School team were: Catherine McGirt, Alice Ree Locklear, Mabel Henderson, Ancie Dale Sampson, Ressie Carter, Lucy Jane Locklear, Olivia Emanuel, and Linda Gail Revels.

Locklear was one of nine children born to Buford and Atelia "Addie" Sampson Chavis. Her father was an auto mechanic; her mother a homemaker. Locklear received her early education at Piney Grove Elementary School. While a student at Magnolia High School she was involved in several school activities including memberships in the monogram club and student council. She graduated from Magnolia High School in 1958 and received the History Scholarship awarded annually by the Magnolia High School faculty to a student for scholarship excellence. Locklear enrolled at Pembroke State College in fall 1958. She used the scholarship money to help pay expenses for college.

Pembroke State College did not have intercollegiate athletics for women during the period Locklear attended the school. She did, however, participate in intramural basketball and was selected by the intramural director to an all-star team that played against local colleges and athletic clubs. She was graduated from Pembroke State College in 1962 with a degree in Business Education. The same year she married Hayes Locklear, Jr. and began her teaching career at Fairgrove High School in rural Fairmont, North Carolina. She later completed a one-year assignment to Pembroke Junior High School in Pembroke, North Carolina where she taught Physical Education. During the span of her professional career she taught Business Education at several schools for the Public Schools of Robeson County before retiring from the public school classroom in 1994.

Today, Locklear lives with her husband in the Union Chapel community, Robeson County. The couple has two adult sons, Hayes Alan Locklear, a Pembroke businessman, and Timothy Joel Locklear, a technician employed with DuPont Corporation in Fayetteville. In retirement, the grandmother of three stays very active.

She enjoys working with a variety of flowers, shrubs, and fruit trees that adorn the expansive grounds of the family's country home. She also works part-time in her son's full-service florist business in the town of Pembroke. She enjoys travel and vacations in the family's coastal home at Ocean Isle Beach. She has a collection of historical documents and memorabilia she plans to organize for safekeeping, and in the rush of her busy retirement life Locklear steals quiet time to read.

Photo by Elmer W. Hunt, Sr.

1957 MAGNOLIA HIGH SCHOOL GIRLS BASKETBALL TOURNAMENT CHAMPIONS

KNEELING, LEFT TO RIGHT: Olivia Emanuel, Linda Revels, Alice Ree Locklear, Mattie Brewer, **Louise Chavis,** Lucy Locklear, Lestine Locklear.

STANDING: Ancie Dale Sampson, Mabel Blanks, Ruth McNeill, Patsy Ann Locklear, Geraldine Spaulding, Catherine McGirt, Lucy Locklear and Mary Kate Jones. Ned Sampson was coach.

During school segregation, the educational process for American Indian students in the Cumberland County Schools was an arduous development for their parents. Because there was no high school in Cumberland County for American Indian students to attend, students completing elementary education attended Eastern Carolina High School, an all-Indian high school in adjoining Sampson County. This circumstance proved to be a hardship on students who were forced to travel as many as seventy round trip miles daily in order to get a high school education.

To accommodate the ever-growing American Indian population, and with strong support of County School Superintendent F. Douglas Byrd, Cumberland County appropriated funds for a new school. The new school was built in East Fayetteville, North Carolina, where the majority of the American Indians live.

Les Maxwell School, named for school board member, E.L. "Les" Maxwell of Stedman, NC, opened in school year 1956-57. With the opening of the new school, The American Indian students had a school they identified as their own. The majority of the faculty who served the school were Indian educators from adjoining Robeson County.

Interscholastic athletics played an important part in the education of the students and community at Les Maxwell School. The scope of this program was small. There were basketball and baseball for boys, and basketball for girls. Athletic facilities were limited. School construction did not include a gymnasium. The basketball teams practiced and played on a clay court. Inclement weather hindered use of the outside court, for both practice and play. Constant use of the clay court by local citizens often resulted in severe indentions in areas beneath the baskets. Repairing and smoothing

the site became a ritual for athletic coaches before each team practice. Some regulated games were played on the clay court. Lime was used to mark the boundaries. On occasions when the supply of lime was depleted, actual earth drawings were made to show boundaries for play. Some gestures of support for the athletics program came from the local business community. For instance, the posts supporting the wooden backboards were donated by electrical utilities companies. In 1963, the Cumberland County Schools paved the clay basketball court with asphalt. Other outdoor athletic facilities included a combination baseball/softball field.

Les Maxwell High School joined with Eastern Carolina High School in rural Clinton, NC and Hawkeye High School in rural Raeford, NC to form the Tri-County Indian High School Athletic Conference. In addition to playing conference schools, Les Maxwell played Prospect, Magnolia and Fairgrove High Schools in Robeson County.

Financial support for interscholastic athletics at Les Maxwell was very minimal. The beginning of the program found the school without funds to buy uniforms for the players. The Les Maxwell School community was rural, and Indian parents identified with the employment and socio-economic conditions of the period. They did not have money to buy uniforms for their children. In a display of unashamed determination, the boys wore blue jeans and tee shirts during regulation play. The girls wore dress shorts and tee shirts. The teams played several seasons in this type attire before uniforms were purchased.

During this period of racially segregated school systems, athletic coaches became more than instructors. They were like a good Samaritan, coming to the aid of their basketball teams. Their gestures of kindness shined brightest on road trips to play other schools. Coaches would arrange for the teams to eat at restaurants and would use their own money to pay for the meals.

In 1961, Tommy Dorsey Swett became basketball coach of the boys team at Les Maxwell. Swett played varsity basketball at Pembroke High School and Pembroke State College. This was his first coaching assignment. With a small student enrollment (student enrollment at Les Maxwell High School was 70 in grades 9 through 12), coach Swett involved a majority of the male students in the basketball program. Coach Swett, married with a family, had a home in Pembroke (Robeson County), a one-way commute of 40 miles. On away games, he and the other coaches, transported players back to campus. Once back to campus, players needing transportation home were given a free ride there by one or more of the coaches. After these "away" games, it was not uncommon for these coaches to arrive back to their respective Robeson County homes hours past midnight.

In 1965, Eastern Carolina High School in Sampson County closed, reducing membership of the Tri-County Indian High School Athletic Conference to two schools. Through Coach Swett's efforts, Les Maxwell and

Hawkeye High Schools joined with Fairgrove, Magnolia, Pembroke, and Prospect High Schools in Robeson County to form a new Tri-County Indian High School Athletic Conference. Les Maxwell's boys basketball team, coached by Swett, competed well in the conference. In 1967, playing Magnolia High School for the tournament championship, the team lost to the Magnolia team in overtime. This would be the last game Swett would coach for the Les Maxwell team. He had accepted a non-coaching position with the Public Schools of Robeson County.

Coach Swett leaving meant changes in the Cumberland County Indian school. The coaching staff had been together at the school since 1961, and had contributed immeasurably to the good of the east Fayetteville community. The Les Maxwell boys basketball team would play two more seasons under the leadership of a new coach. The school closed for high school students at the end of the 1968-69 school year. The students were assigned to school districts where their families lived. This major change in the social and academic fabric of the American Indian student and their parents created a lasting effect on their lives.

Photo: 1957 Pembroke High School yearbook, *The Challenger*

1957 PEMBROKE BOYS BASKETBALL TEAM

BACK ROW: Coach Delton Ray Locklear, Hartman Brewington, Paul Brooks, **Tommy Dorsey Swett,** Oceanus Lowry, Howard Sampson, Jr.

FRONT ROW: Lynwood Sampson, Timothy Brayboy, Reggie Strickland, Stacy Brayboy, Jeffery Maynor.

ALBERT HUNT

Public School Administrator and Basketball Coach

Albert Hunt

Albert Hunt, now retired from public education, is proud of his career and the schools and communities he served. A devout Christian, he was born July 7, 1918, in the community of Lowe, a tiny village located in the middle of Robeson County, North Carolina. Before Hunt was born, his father was called into military service during WWI. His mother with unborn child, left the family residence in Sellers, South Carolina to be near her parents pending the birth of her son, Albert. Hunt was subsequently born while his father was away at war.

Later, upon his release from the military, Hunt's father returned home, and his wife resumed living with him. In a mutual family agreement, young Hunt remained living with his maternal grandparents in Lowe; Hunt has fond memories of his years growing up on his grandparents' farm near the village. He remembers the large general store that was the anchor of the rural community. "You could buy food, clothes, farm and garden equipment, gasoline, kerosene, and about anything you wanted at the store," Hunt recalled.

In addition to the general store, the thriving village claimed a train depot, a warehouse, an automobile dealership, a cotton gin, and a U.S. post office. Several large, beautifully designed homes dotted the village and surrounding community.

Albert Hunt speaks with excitement as he recalls growing up in Lowe, a Robeson County Village. Hunt graduated from Pembroke State College. He earned a post graduate degree from George Peabody University in School Administration and Secondary Education. As a student at Pembroke State College he served as manager of the college athletic teams. When the college gymnasium opened in the fall of 1940, Hunt inquired about the operation procedure of the game clock. The company installing the clock provided operation instructions to the inquisitive student. Operating the game clock became another one of his duties as student manager. Later, he operated the game clock for the Indian High School Basketball Tournaments.

School Administrator

Albert Hunt served as principal of several schools in Robeson County. He served in school administration his entire career in public education. From 1943 to 1945, he served his first assignment as principal at Piney Grove School, following Charles Luther Moore. Piney Grove School, nestled in a pine grove in the farming community of Saddletree, served Indian students in grades 1-11. The school lost its high school status in 1943 when grades 8-11 were transferred to Magnolia High School, its neighbor five miles north. "Piney Grove School, a well designed and constructed school, perhaps the best school facility among the schools in the Robeson County Education System," Hunt said. The patrons financed a central heating system for the school. Welton Lowry would follow Hunt as principal of Piney Grove School.

In 1945, Hunt's next assignment was principal at Fairmont Indian High School. The school served students in graded 1-11. Few Indian High Schools had girls basketball teams in the early 1940s. Magnolia High School, coached by Eugene Chavis, had the first successful program during that time. Early into his tenure, Hunt was intent on building a girls basketball team at the isolated school located in the town of Fairmont. The visionary leader formed the first girls basketball team and became its coach, "out of necessity," Hunt said, "there was no one else to coach the team." The premier team had to overcome obstacles from the very beginning. The natural expanse of the primary agricultural and rural settings played into the early development of the girls basketball program.

Hunt explains, "The player's residences were so spread out, and they had no transportation to and from practice and games. I would often take them to my home on away games. My wife Cattie Mae would provide them meals and I would take them home after the games, often returning to my home in Pembroke most times after mid-night," Hunt said.

Because there were no indoor basketball facilities at the Indian high schools during this period, teams practiced and played on dirt courts at their respective school. During this time Hunt says he found support in an Orrum High School basketball coach who officiated many of the Fairmont Indian High School basketball games. A professional interest developed between the coach and Hunt. The Orrum coach invited Hunt to bring his girls basketball team to use his school's gymnasium for their practice sessions. Hunt accepted the invitation and on several occasions the Fairmont Indian High School girls basketball team practiced in the gymnasium on the all-white high school campus. During these practices, with the invitation of Hunt, the Orrum coach would provide coaching and developmental skills to the Fairmont Indian High School players. Many times the two coaches would exchange information about the offenses and defenses they used in games.

This information was most useful for the Fairmont Indian High School basketball coach. The friendship bonding the coaches transcended the racial prejudices that existed during the pre-Civil Rights era. The coaches' respective schools were separated by racial segregation, and because of this truth, neither basketball team could practice or play the other.

The Fairmont Indian High School boys basketball team was well established. The coach of the team was Carlie Oxendine. The team won the Robeson County Indian Basketball Tournament Championship in 1948.

Hunt remained principal of Fairmont Indian High School until 1952 when the school closed. He and the students were assigned to the new Fairgrove High School. Students from Green Grove were also assigned to the new school. Fairgrove gets its name from the two former schools. Hunt continued coaching the girls basketball team. Adna Lowry, who had coached at Fairmont Indian High School, was given the boys basketball team at the new consolidated school. A gymnasium was included in the construction of the new school. A stage with storage cabinets beneath the stage was constructed at one end of the gymnasium. B.E. Littlefield, who was Superintendent of the Robeson County Schools during this time, believed in multiple-use construction. Gymnasiums constructed at Prospect and Magnolia High Schools have the same design as Fairgrove. Pembroke High School was one of the first Indian High Schools in Robeson County to have a gymnasium.

Hunt served Fairgrove School for two years before being assigned to Oxendine Elementary School. He said his tenure at Oxendine School was one of the most satisfying assignments of his career. The community support of their school and not working in a high school made it easier he said. His next assignment was at Pembroke Elementary School. He served that school five years before being assigned as principal of the new Pembroke High School.

Hunt spent his last years in education working in the Robeson County Schools central office as assistant Superintendent for Federal Programs.

Much can be said of Albert Hunt's contribution for the betterment of the education and the interscholastic athletic programs in the Public Schools of Robeson County. In the 1940s, 50s, and 60s, he served on the committee that organized, administered, and supervised the Robeson County Indian High School Athletic Conference. He assisted in administering the post season basketball tournament, served as game clock operator and was on the all tournament selection committee. He was instrumental in using outside agencies to assign officials to officiate the Indian High School Basketball Tournament, eliminating local persons from officiating and problems associated with it. Later, he supported the Robeson County Indian High Schools for membership in the North Carolina High School Athletic Association.

Albert Hunt married Cattie Mae Locklear on May 27, 1944. The couple met while students at Pembroke State College. Cattie Mae, with a degree in Elementary Education, taught school for more than 30 years. They are the parents of two daughters, Dixie and Iris.

Photo: *Lumbee Tattler, Pembroke State College, 1941*

Albert Hunt

"You could buy food, clothes, farm and garden equipment, gasoline, kerosene, and about anything you wanted at the store."

Albert Hunt, remembering the general store in Lowe, the village where he spent his childhood.

Former Participants in Robeson County Indian High School Basketball Program

Photos and text appeared in the 1941 Lumbee Tattler, a Pembroke State College yearbook.

VERNON OXENDINE Center	**MILLARD SMITH** Guard	**JAMES A. JONES** Forward
EUGENE CHAVIS Forward	**ALBERT HUNT** Playing Manager	**JAMES MOORE** Guard
CARLTON CHAVIS Captain, Guard	**NASH LOCKLEAR** Forward	**THOMAS OXENDINE** Forward

The Pembroke College basketball team did not take all the glory of the season by winning so many games, but they showed improvement all the way through the season.

The teams played by the Pembroke College basketball were: Wingate Junior College, Pfeiffer Junior College, Red Springs All-Stars, Campbell College, Boiling Springs College, Sphinx Athletic Club of Charlotte, Textile College, Orrum All-Stars, Louisburg College, Kings Mountain Lions Club.

The best game of the season was the 31-29 defeat of Louisburg College. The game was nip and tuck all the way. After the second half had been underway three minutes, there was never over two points difference in the scores. A field goal could have decided the game for anyone until the last whistle went off for the end of the game.

The varsity squad had ten players which were as follows: James Sanderson, James A. Jones, Nash Locklear and Thomas Oxendine, forwards: Carlton Chavis, Eugene Chavis, James Hammonds, James Moore and Millard Smith, guards: Vernon Oxendine, center. Thomas Oxendine was high scorer for the year, and Captain Carlton Chavis was the outstanding guard.

Seniors on the basketball squad are: Nash Locklear, Eugene Chavis and Millard Smith.

MARVIN LOWRY

Marvin Lowry

An athlete, coach, former prisoner of war, sports official, parent of athletes, and member of the athletic hall of fame, he is all of these.

Marvin Lowry has been involved with a variety of sports as a player, a coach, a teacher, sports official, and a parent. He served his country in two major military wars. Lowry knows what is like to be at risk and fight for a cause. He lives through his words and deeds. He possesses the attitude of what we can do to help our neighbor and country, and says, "we are blessed to live where we live."

Staying involved has been his life. Lowry was born March 4, 1926, the third of the late Neal and Leola Lowry's eight children. Being one of the oldest children, it was expected that he assume the role of leadership and help the family. He grew up during the depression years of the 1930s and early 40s. In his early years, the family residence was near the outskirts of Lumberton in Robeson County. The Lowry children attended Piney Grove School.

Lowry was a star athlete at Piney Grove High School. His coach was Calvin Lowry. The principal at Piney Grove School at this time was Charles Luther Moore.

In 1941, the family moved to the Prospect Community in Robeson County. The same time high school students from Piney Grove School were assigned to Magnolia High School. Lowry participated in varsity football, basketball, and baseball at Prospect High School, excelling in all three sports. The 6-1, 170 lb. athlete, considered one of the best student athletes at the school, led Prospect High School boys basketball team to the 1944 Robeson County Indian High School Basketball tournament championship. The team lost to Pembroke High School in the final game. His coach at Prospect High School was Curtis Moore. The gifted athlete relates, "Times were hard for people during this post Depression period. Parents could not afford basketball shoes for their children. Players played in the shoes they wore to school. When we played the tournament at the college gym, players would check with citizens in the community that might have tennis shoes they could borrow for the tournament. I was unable to find any; I had a pair of rubber overshoes (galoshes) I wore during the tournament."

Lowry was drafted into the United States Army only weeks after graduating from Prospect High School in 1944. Soon after completing basic training, he was involved in World War II in Europe. He fought in France and Germany near the end of World War II, loading artillery shells in an M-4 tank. His unit was cleaning equipment preparing to ship out to Japan when the war ended in late 1945. Lowry was released from the military in 1946. Upon his return home he enrolled at Pembroke State College. While attending college he participated in varsity football, basketball, and baseball. His athletic performance was so recognized that he was selected to the University of North Carolina-Pembroke Athletic Hall of Fame.

During the time Lowry was enrolled in college, he was in the United States Army Reserves. While in his junior year in 1950, he was called back to active duty. Soon after returning to active duty, he was involved in the Korean War. By the time his unit reached the Asian

Peninsula, communist troops had entered the war and had American troops pinned near the China-Korea border. On February 10, 1931, Lowry's unit was camped in a valley observing communist troops marching along a ridge. The enemy attacked his unit after dark. As Lowry drove his M-4 tank trying to move away from the attack, a bazooka round fired by the enemy hit into the tanks battery box. The impact disabled the tank and partially blew Lowry out of the hatch. He grabbed the main barrel on the tanks turret and swung out.

In all the commotion, a bullet ripped through his thigh. In frigid cold, he ran into a rice patty for cover, but was captured. "Death is all I could think about," Lowry said. "I had a strong idea they were going to kill me." According to Lowry, several other U. S. Army soldiers were also captured during the assault. The enemy marched the captured away as they wondered about their fate. For two months, the enemy soldiers routinely moved them during the night so as not to be detected by their allies. The prisoners received little food and no medical attention. As the American forces shelled closer to their encampments in early April, Chinese officers became worried. "Two days we sat in a hut and listened to our forces firing on the other side of the mountain ridge. About three or four o'clock on the third day, a Chinese officer informed the prisoners they were being released. He gave us a half bag of rice and led us out to the main road," Lowry continued. Hampered by the bullet wound and dragging his injured leg, Marvin and the four released prisoners walked several miles when they met the 7th United States Calvary. After several months of medical care in a hospital, he was released and returned home.

Upon his return, Lowry re-enrolled at Pembroke State College. In 1954, he graduated with a degree in Elementary Education. He was employed as a teacher at Prospect School. He taught seventh and eighth grade math at Prospect School for 28 years. Years counted for military service, combined with his teaching years allowed Lowry to retire from public school education in 1983. In addition to his teaching duties at Prospect School, Lowry coached the varsity boys and girls basketball teams at Prospect High School. He also coached the varsity baseball team at Prospect High School for several years. Lowry did not coach losers. The student athletes who played sports for him did not always win of course. But they did not lose. From his perspective, athletes who gave their best always win regardless of the final score. "If they work hard as they can they are winners."

In the 1960's, Lowry played several seasons of semi-pro baseball in the Border Belt League. Teams represented in this league were from towns along the North-South Carolina border. After retiring from teaching, Lowry officiated high school basketball and baseball as a registered official with the North Carolina Athletic Officials Association.

Family of Athletes

Lowry was one of three brothers and one sister, Jarvie, who participated in interscholastic athletics at Prospect High School. Brothers Neal and Walter were all star players, excelling in basketball. A brother, Benford, did not participate in school athletics, but his children did. Narva, Janice, Sylvia, and Benford, Jr. were outstanding players for Pembroke High School.

Lowry and his wife, Bernice Brooks Lowry, met while attending Pembroke State College. They are the parents of four sons and a daughter. Like their father, the four sons played sports in high school and college.

The Lowry family interest in sports increased in 1980, when the Detroit Tigers Major League Baseball organization drafted a son, Dwight, out of the University of North Carolina at Chapel Hill. Dwight played several years of minor league baseball before making the major league roster in 1984. He played four years with Detroit in the major leagues. Dwight was a member of the 1984 Detroit Tigers World Series championship team. After retiring from major league baseball in 1989, Dwight was given a position as field manager in the Tiger organization. He was field manager in Fayetteville, North Carolina, before being assigned to their minor league team in Jamestown, New York. On July 10, 1997, after a home game, Dwight died of a heart attack at his residence in Jamestown.

Lowry calls his son's unexpected death his saddest moment. With the death of Dwight, Lowry's interests in sports dwindled. "I watch a little, but not like I did." Lowry's remaining family and his faith in God helped him through the period after Dwight's death. Today, apart from spending time with church functions, Lowry relaxes at home with Bernice, enjoying visits from the children and grandchildren. He and Bernice travel to the annual reunion of his former U. S. Army Unit, held at various locations in the United States.

Photo: 1953 Pembroke State College yearbook, *The Indianhead*

1953 PEMBROKE STATE COLLEGE MENS BASKETBALL TEAM

FRONT ROW LEFT TO RIGHT: Holland Jacobs, Ralph Hunt, Bill R. Locklear, William Hammonds, James Howard Locklear.
BACK ROW LEFT TO RIGHT: **Marvin Lowry**, Reece Warwick, Ned Sampson, Sam Locklear, Delton Ray Locklear.

WILL GOINS, JR.

Will Goins, Jr.

Talk basketball with someone who has been around Robeson County a while and they will tell you about the best American Indian high school players in the 1940s. Ralph Locklear, Howard Lee, and Freddie Revels were star players for Magnolia. Big Clifford Oxendine led Fairmont Indian High School to a championship. Cecil Hammonds and Aubrey Graham were outstanding at Green Grove. Garnett Lowry, Walter Bullard, and Ned Sampson were terrific at Pembroke. Marvin Lowry and James Howard Locklear, Sr. of Prospect and Forace Oxendine of Union Chapel were future Hall of Famers. There were plenty others that have not been mentioned and should be.

Then ask who was the best player? The player most mentioned is Will Goins, Jr. from Prospect High School. "Will Goins was the best basketball player ever to play in the Robeson County Indian High Schools; he could shoot, rebound, had good hands, and was a good defensive player," stated the late Danford Dial. Goins and Dial grew up in the same community. They played against each other on the practice courts at Prospect High School. James Moore, a local writer and a historian said, "Andrew Locklear, who was a three sports star at Prospect High in the 1930s was the best athlete ever in the American Indian high schools and Will Goins without question was the best basketball player ever."

As evidence of Goins' play, *The Robesonian*, Lumberton, NC, Monday, March 17, 1941, provides an account of the championship game of the Indian High School Basketball Tournament.

Pembroke, March 17, 1941, paced by Will Goins, tournament high scorer, Prospect High School Saturday night defeated Pembroke, defending champions, in the finals of the annual Indian Conference event here 31-29 in an over-time thriller. Seldom, if ever, has the Cherokee Indian Normal gymnasium scene of the second annual tournament seen a harder fought and more evenly contested game. The regular game ended 29 all, about midway of the three minute over-time period, Wayne Locklear of Prospect looped in a two pointer to provide the new champions with the needed points. Prospect entered the finals with a win over Piney Grove Thursday night and a close victory over an ever-threatening Magnolia outfit. Pembroke defeated Union Chapel in the opening game and top seeded Green Grove in the semi-finals.

Will Goins, who tallied a total of 53 points during the three nights event scored 12 points in leading the Prospectors. Three men, J.R. Locklear, James Sanderson, and William Earl Locklear led Pembroke's defeated effort with seven points each.

Will Goins, Jr. was born in June, 1923. He grew up on a farm in the Prospect community in western Robeson County. He was the last of seven children of the late Will "Willie" Goins and Mary Sampson Goins. Daughters from this family were Carrie, Annie, Bertha and Sally. The sons in the family were Tom Russell, Ernest and Will, Jr. Sports in the Goins family would have a carry-over to the next generation of children. Annie's daughter, Pauline, was an outstanding player at Prospect High School and later coached girls basketball at the school. Two sons of Ernest, Bobby and Jimmy, played at Prospect High

School. Bertha was the mother of three boys and three daughters. Five of her children played basketball at Pembroke High School. Two of the sons, Ned and Kent, were among the best to play high school basketball in the state of North Carolina. Their legacies are forever being discussed. Shelby Jane, a daughter, was one of the best ever in girls basketball.

Will Goins, Jr. was a self-made basketball player. He could be seen practicing before, during, and after school. Every chance he got he would be shooting the basketball. In games he would dominate. With his size at 6-4 200lbs, he controlled the boards on both ends of the court. Will scored most of his points from medium range and close to the basket.

Was Will Goins, Jr. the best basketball player ever in the Robeson County Indian High School Athletic Conference? The people you talk with that have followed basketball the last 65 years when asked will pause, mumble, and say, "I don't know anyone better."

Will graduated from Prospect High School in the spring of 1941. He had no intention of going to college. The United State was involved in World War II. Most young men were being drafted into military service. Will took a job working in the shipyard in Wilmington, North Carolina. He would stay in Wilmington during the week and come home on the weekend. After several paychecks, Will purchased a motorcycle. He could be seen riding his motorcycle around town and in the community during the weekends. "That was something, big Will on what I thought was the biggest motorcycle I ever saw," stated his nephew Ned Sampson.

The uncle and nephew spent lots of times together in their younger years growing up. Will was seven years older than Ned, but age did not prevent them from doing "boy things" together. Will taught Ned to ride his bicycle. The two would develop a close uncle/nephew bond that is still strong today.

Will worked in the shipyard less than a year. In 1942, he was drafted into the United States Army. After completing Basic Training, he was assigned to an Army base awaiting further orders. While serving at the base he had an opportunity to play basketball for the base team. His team won the tournament championship.

Soon after the basketball tournament, he was in combat in Europe. Will was involved in several combat missions, including The Battle of the Bulge that ended his combat involvement. The Battle of the Bulge was fought between the United States and its allies against Germany and its allies. The Battle took place in late 1944 and early 1945. It was Hitler's last desperate attempt to turn the tides of defeat and posed a stunning challenge to the Americans and its allies. After a hard and brave struggle America and its allies won the battle in early 1945. The fighting took place during the winter. Deep snow and bitter cold weather took its toll on both sides. Soldiers hovering in foxholes and snow banks during the sub-zero weather were the victims of frostbite.

Will suffered a severe case of frostbite. He was relieved of his combat duty and admitted to a hospital in England. His brother, Ernest, who was stationed in Europe, learned of Will's illness and visited him in the hospital. Ernest said when he saw Will, he had the worst-looking feet he had ever seen. "His feet were black; I felt for sure he would lose them."

The medical staff worked to save his feet, but the damage done would bother Will the rest of his life. "There is not a day they don't bother me," Will said of his feet.

Will was released from the Army and returned home to Robeson County. He was ready to give college a try. He enrolled at Pembroke State College. Ned enrolled at Pembroke State College the same time. The uncle and the nephew played together on the college football team. At the end of the football season Will dropped out of school. He said his feet hurt when he played. He could play linesman in football but did not have the movements and speed to play basketball. Will left Robeson County for Detroit, Michigan, joining the migration of other American Indians from the area looking for better job opportunities and a better life. He found employment with General Motors. Today, Will is retired from General Motors and he lives in South Lyon, Michigan with his wife, children and grandchildren.

John W. "Ned" Sampson

Athlete/Teacher/Coach

If you share Ned Sampson's broad view of sports, you understand why he has devoted a career to its teaching. "I see sports as a way to stay alive and enjoy human companionship," he said. Sampson, who lives in Pembroke, North Carolina, spent 34 years as a public school teacher and a school athletic coach. He directed and coached youth sports in the Pembroke area.

Except for serving a tour in the U.S. Air Force, Sampson has lived all his life in the town of Pembroke. He graduated from Pembroke High School in 1947 and Pembroke State College in 1953. He met his wife, Eva Brewington, when she was in nursing school. They were married February 6, 1954. They have four children. Ursula is an elementary education teacher in Cary. Kelvin is head coach of the mens' basketball team at Oklahoma University. Karen is a pharmacist in Charlotte, North Carolina, and Suzanne is a physical therapist in Savannah, Georgia.

Sampson's father, Cliff Sampson, owned and operated a grocery store and a movie theater in Pembroke. Cliff married Bertha Goins and they have six children. Ned, Cliff, Jr., Shelby, Norma, Kent, and Jane. The Sampson family home was located on the north side of the Seaboard Railroad, about four tenths of a mile east of the Pembroke State College campus.

An impressive set of hobbies keeps Sampson busy. He goes to the physical fitness center most days for exercise and attends athletic events at the local high schools and at the University of North Carolina-Pembroke. He and Eva travel to Norman Oklahoma and other sites to attend Kelvin's basketball games. When they are not at the games, they watch the games at their home on satellite television. They visit the other children and grand-children. Sampson is an active member of the Pembroke Lions Club. He is a long time member of the UNC-Pembroke Braves Club; a member of Purnell Swett High School booster club, and is a member of Berea Baptist Church Board of Deacons.

ATHLETE

Sampson began his early development as an athlete when the boys in town would get together for informal play. There was no organized sports program in the town of Pembroke at this time. The local boys would find a space, choose sides, and play whatever game they agreed on. Several from this group of boys were members of the local Boy Scout troop. Walter J. Pinchbeck was the scoutmaster. Pinchbeck was employed as a custodian at Pembroke Graded School. He would arrange for scout members to use the school's outdoor space for pick-up games. "Walter Pinchbeck did more for boys in the Pembroke area than any person I know," Sampson said. "Not only did he teach us about scouting activities, he also provided opportunities and taught us physical activities. He took us to Lumber River and taught us how to swim."

Sampson began to show his natural athletic skills during the "Scout" games. "Playing in the Scout games kindled me toward sports," he said. Pinchbeck and Sampson developed a trust between them that would provide the young scout opportunities to use the new college gym. By the time Sampson was in high school Pinchbeck had been employed as buildings and grounds supervisor at Pembroke State College. In an agreement between the two, Pinchbeck would allow Sampson use of the college gymnasium on Sunday afternoon provided he would not let anyone else in.

Photo: Pembroke State College Archival Collection

Ned Sampson performing during a Pembroke College game.

"There would be my friends, the boys that I played with in the scouts, banging on the gym door, climbing up to the windows yelling wanting in, I would keep shooting trying to ignore them, because if I let them in I would loose my privilege. I did not let them in," Sampson said. "During the time I was in high school and in college, Mr. Pinchbeck was good about letting me use the gym."

The way Sampson played basketball in high school and in college was appealing. He played with confidence, poise, and grace. He could be counted on to have a good game because he prepared himself for a good game. Sampson worked to be a great basketball player. He was an effective shooter, most times the ball going through the basket. The traits that made him a great basketball player also made him a good football and baseball player.

In 1942, the North Carolina State Board of Education adopted regulations requiring a student to complete 12 years of school in order to receive a diploma. The class of 1947, of which Sampson was a member, was the first class at Pembroke High School to complete four years of high school.

The Indian high schools only fielded varsity athletic teams during this time. Coaches selected members for their team from the upper classmen. It was seldom that a student from the ninth and tenth grades was selected. Sampson was first selected for the Pembroke High School basketball team when he was in the tenth grade. Dorsey V. Lowry coached the team when Sampson was in the tenth and eleventh grades. Joe Sampson coached during Sampson's twelfth grade senior year. "Mr. Joe Sampson was a great coach. He was a good teacher of fundamentals and taught basketball as a team sport. He had more influence on my development as a player than any other coach I played for," Sampson remembers.

Today, Sampson is the same person he was when he was a star athlete. He is a people person. He did not let the success he had as an athlete change his behavior or love for the local people that followed and supported him as a student athlete.

TEACHER AND COACH

After graduating from Pembroke State College in 1953, Ned Sampson began a lengthy teaching and coaching career at Magnolia High School, a school located about six miles north of Lumberton, North Carolina. He was a teacher and a coach at Magnolia until 1968. Several years he coached both the boys and girls basketball teams at Magnolia High School. He also coached the baseball team at Magnolia. In 1967, the Magnolia High School boys basketball team coached by Sampson won the last Tri-County Indian High School Athletic Conference tournament championship. The team defeated Les Maxwell High School by the score of 56-53 in overtime. American Indian communities would not likely know the significance of this last game between these two schools. This game ended a period of segregation for athletic teams from American Indian schools in North Carolina. Magnolia succeeded Pembroke High as tournament champion. Pembroke did not compete in this tournament; they were scheduled to play in the North Carolina High School Athletic Association district 2-A tournament at Fayetteville Senior High. Magnolia represented the Tri County Indian High School Athletic Conference in the North Carolina High School Athletic Association Class 1-A district tournament which was held at Campbell College, Buies Creek, North Carolina. Magnolia lost to Boone Trail High School from Mamers (Harnett County), North Carolina. This game was an historical moment for the Magnolia team. They were the first and last team from the American Indian athletic conference to play in the North Carolina High School Athletic Association state playoffs. Upon their acceptance into the North Carolina High School Athletic Association in 1968, the American Indian High Schools in Robeson County joined with Littlefield, Maxton, Parkton, Red Springs and Rowland high schools to form a new athletic conference.

Sampson left Magnolia at the end of the 1967-68 school year. From 1968-83, he was athletic director and boys varsity basketball coach at Pembroke High School.

Sampson was a big brother and a coach to his sisters, brothers and son. He spent many hours working one on one with his sister Shelby, teaching her the techniques of shooting. Shelby became one of the best forwards to play girls basketball in the Indian High Schools. He would take his younger brother Kent to his high school basketball practices. "Kent did not seem interested in playing basketball, when he was a young boy I would take him with me to Magnolia for team practices hoping to inspire his interests in playing," Sampson said. "When he was in the ninth grade I bought him a new pair of Converse shoes as an inspirational ploy." The ploy seem to work because Kent went on to have a terrific high school basketball career.

Ned and Eva's son Kelvin, was a three-sport star athlete at Pembroke High School. He played football, basketball and baseball. Kevin was selected All Conference in all three sports his senior year in high school. Ned was his coach for football and basketball. The sports connection between the father and son had an early beginning.

Kelvin says, "Some of my fondest memories were getting to go to practice with my dad on Saturdays. The manager was always my baby-sitter and the players were my entertainment... When I look back as a kid growing up in Pembroke, I feel lucky to have witnessed the teams, the coaches, the rivalries, and the players in the Robeson County Indian Basketball League. I wish every Native American kid could have lived that experience. I will never forget my mother getting four kids dressed and in the car for the ride to Magnolia High School to watch my dad's team play. The smell of the popcorn and peanuts in those little brown bags... the excitement, the fans, the cheerleaders - I loved everything about it!

"I have always encouraged kids all over the world to have a hero, to find somebody that inspires them to do great things. The players in the Indian Basketball League were my early heroes and my dad was my inspiration - and still is."

Sampson dedicated many years to the interscholastic athletic program in the public schools of Robeson County. Like all the other athletic coaches in the Indian Basketball Conference he gave his time working with student athletes and not receiving any supplemental salary. His wife, Eva, told of the many times after games the Sampson family would use their vehicle to take players home. Sometimes the trips would take them to the edge of Bladen County to the east and Hoke County to the northwest.

Sampson spent many years directing and coaching youth sports in the Pembroke area. Some highlights of his coaching youth sports: In the summer of 1953, he and Robert McGirt formed an American Indian all-star teener baseball team that played in the state tournament in Monroe, North Carolina. In 1956, he and Forace Oxendine coached the same group of players in the local American Legion Baseball League.

Ned Sampson is truly a model that any aspiring young athlete or young adult should follow. He is a class act and has made a difference for generations of young American Indian people in Robeson County.

"There would be my friends, the boys that I played with in the scouts, banging on the gym door, climbing up to the windows, yelling wanting in. I would keep shooting, trying to ignore them, because if I let them in I would lose my privilege. I did not let them in."

John W. "Ned" Sampson

Brothers Basketball Best

BY GENE WARREN
The Fayetteville Observer, January 26, 1969

Brothers Kent and Ned Sampson

The name Sampson towers like a Saturn moon rocket in the annals of basketball at Pembroke State College.

Seventeen years ago a Lumbee Indian named John W. (Ned) Sampson amazed even the likes of All-American Dick Groat of Duke. Groat took a group of his teammates and went on a post-season barn-storming trip in this part of the state.

Ned Sampson showed Groat a variety of shots that even he had seldom seen before. "He's one of the best I've seen," Groat was quoted as saying later in a newspaper article.

Ned, a 6'-2", 190-pound forward, averaged 24.3 points in '52 and tallied 40 points in a single game against Campbell in '51. This stood as the single-game school scoring record until Gordon Puskus broke it with 41 in '63.

Now Ned Sampson's younger brother, Kent, is knocking the bottom out of the hoop here at Pembroke State, Taller than his heralded brother at 6-7, Sampson jumps center and plays forward. Only a sophomore, Kent averaged 32 points a game for Pembroke High School and poured in 51 in one game for his high school record.

Shelved most of last season with a broken bone in his foot, Kent Sampson is hot now. In the last six Pembroke State games, he has blazed away for a 15.2 scoring average. His 25-point outburst against Wofford in the Hickory Jaycee Holiday Tournament tied for the team's individual season high.

Coach Lacey Gane is the first to hail Sampson's marksmanship. "Kent is a very good shooter," says Gane.

Kent Sampson believes he is improving because he is playing more than ever before at PSC. "I am a junior academically," says Kent. "Coach Gane held me out the first year. And last year I broke a bone in my foot when I scored 13 points and captured 12 rebounds against Mars Hill." This happened in the second Pembroke game – and Sampson was sidelined for six weeks. He was never the same afterwards.

When Sampson was an 11th grader at Pembroke High School, he received letters from Virginia Tech, N.C. State, The Citadel and Illinois. He was averaging 17 points a game. The next year his average soared to an astronomical 32 points per contest.

"During my junior and senior year at Pembroke High, we lost only one basketball game. In my senior year we were 25-0, beating such schools as Hamlet, Laurinburg, Rockingham, and Rohanen. We didn't take part in the North Carolina High School Athletic Association basketball playoffs because we weren't a member. Two years ago we were admitted to the association," said Sampson.

It was in his senior year in 1966 that Sampson poured in 51 points against Fairgrove for his school's record.

Why did he choose Pembroke State College over the other schools?

"It's right here at home," Kent said. "The college is a quarter of a mile from my house."

A year ago Kent married the former Celia Jane Hammonds of Lumberton. They now have a four-month-old son, Robert Shane.

Kent believes his older brother, Ned, who now coaches basketball at Pembroke Senior High School, could have played for any larger schools. "I remember seeing Ned score 55 points one night against a group of college all-stars," said Kent. "Ned was the best shooter I've ever seen. He could shoot 20-foot hook shots as well as players today can shoot 20-foot jumpers. He could use either hand equally well. He didn't want to go off to school, however. He liked it here and didn't want to leave."

Ned Sampson commented on this; "When I was playing, we met a Fort Bragg team which had Carl Braun who later saw action with the New York Knickerbockers and Boston Celtics. He told me he could get me a scholarship to Colgate if I wanted one. Another coach at Edwards Military Institute, now Southwood, said if I went to school there he could later get me in Carolina."

Ned decided to stay at Pembroke.

Does the older brother ever advise the younger brother?

"Ned goes to all of our games and loves to talk about basketball, but he doesn't like to give advice," said Kent.

Says Ned of his younger brother: "Kent has improved this year a lot. He is becoming more aggressive on the boards, mixing it up more. His game against Wilmington when he scored 21 points was the best one I've seen him play. No, I don't give Kent advice unless he wants help. Kent is quiet in that way."

Lloyd Noble Center • 2900 S. Jenkins • Norman, Oklahoma 73019-0660 • Office (405) 325-4732 • FAX (405) 325-7562

COACH KELVIN SAMPSON REMEMBERS...

My first heroes on the basketball court were not major college players or NBA stars, they were players like my Uncle Kent Sampson, Sam Oxendine, Harry Canady, Dexter Brewington, Jimmy Hammonds, Tim Locklear, Leon Maynor, Dexter Earl Locklear, Richard Oxendine, James Maynor, Chester Chavis, Durant Cooper, Ardeen Hunt, Larece Hunt and countless others. These were the stars of the Robeson County Indian Basketball League. Arguably, the best of his era was my father, John W. (Ned) Sampson. Not only was he a great Indian League player, but he later became the head basketball coach at Magnolia High School and Pembroke Senior High School.

In the past twenty-plus years, I have experienced first hand the Michigan/Michigan State, the Washington State/Washington and the Oklahoma/Oklahoma State rivalries. They all pale in comparison to the Pembroke High School vs. Prospect rivalry, or the Magnolia/Pembroke rivalry or even the Fairgrove-Les Maxwell rivalry. These games were not only hard fought and represented community pride, but they were also the "hi-lite" games of the year. There was no football, women sports were not as heavy on the scene yet and baseball was not as popular with the fans. Indian League basketball to Ned and Eva Sampson's son was "Big Time."

Some of my fondest memories were of getting to go to practice with my dad on Saturdays. The manager

Coach Kelvin Sampson, son of John W. "Ned" and Eva Brewington Sampson of Pembroke, is head basketball coach at Oklahoma University.

Photo courtesy of Kelvin Sampson

was always my baby-sitter and the players were my entertainment. "Mr. Ned," as his players called him, had this drill called "Bench Jump" that I became mesmerized with. Sam Oxendine was amazing in this drill. He could jump the "bench" 110 times in one minute. This year I will be entering my 18th year as a head basketball coach at the collegiate level and I still compare all of my players' bench jump counts to Sam Oxendine. When I was a youngster, Robeson County Indian League Basketball was all we had, and you know what? It was all we needed at the time.

When I look back as a kid growing up in Pembroke, N.C., I feel lucky to have witnessed the teams, the coaches, the rivalries, and the players in the Robeson County Indian Basketball League. I wish ever Native American kid could have lived that experience. I will never forget my mother getting her four kids dressed and in the car for the ride to Magnolia High School to watch my dad's team play. The smell of the popcorn and the peanuts in those little brown bags... the excitement, the fans, the cheerleaders – I loved everything about it.

I have always encouraged kids all over the world to have a hero, to find somebody that inspires them to do great things. The players in the Indian Basketball League were my early heroes and my dad was my inspiration – and still is.

"Some of my fondest memories were of getting to go to practice with my dad on Saturdays. The manager was always my baby-sitter and the players my entertainment... Robeson County Indian League Basketball was all we had, and you know what? It was all we needed at the time."

Kelvin Sampson

Photo courtesy of Kelvin Sampson

LESLIE "LES" LOCKLEAR

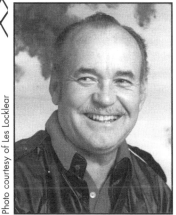

Photo courtesy of Les Locklear

Leslie "Les" Locklear

Leslie "Les" Locklear has a special knack for causing people to laugh. His humor can lift the depressed and calm the disgruntled. His voice rises as his body language and facial expression reflect the joy of times, places, and events he has witnessed during his everyday life.

"I want to make people happy because there is so much beauty in the world," he explains.

Life takes on a certain rhythm for Locklear in his retirement from a career as a public school teacher. He and his wife, Fannie, live in their comfortable home on Deep Branch Road outside Pembroke, North Carolina. He keeps busy maintaining the family property, taking care of a horse and several goats, and managing a small mobile park that he owns. He also sells pre-owned cars as a hobby.

Locklear grew up in the Barker Ten Mile community of Robeson County, North Carolina. The style of life then is markedly different from today's.

Born August 13, 1925, he was the eighth of nine children born to the late Jasper and Luvenia Emanual Locklear. His parents married in Claxton, Georgia where they farmed and worked in the turpentine forests. Six of the children were born before the couple relocated to their native Robeson County in the early 1920's. Three other children, including Les and two sisters, were born after the family moved back "home."

Locklear recalls the wrenching hardships of growing up in a sharecropper's family.

"The life of a sharecropper was a hard one. The family tenant house we lived in had no running water or indoor toilet." he remembers. "Our work was from sun-up to sundown and my brothers, sisters, and I often stayed out of school to work on the farm."

When he did go to school he attended Barker Ten Mile School, a wooden building that contained seven classrooms for students in grades 1-7.

Tom Oxendine,Sr. was school principal during the time Locklear attended the school. Oxendine organized a sports program so that the boys in the upper grades could participate in interschool play against the other Indian schools in Robeson County.

Young Locklear got his first taste of competitive sports while a student at Magnolia School, where he excelled in varsity basketball and baseball.

In 1943, World War II was raging. It was not uncommon for local high school boys to be called to military. As Locklear was about to enter the tenth grade, he received his draft notice. There was a hardship provision that allowed a deferment for sons to work in support of the family. Locklear used the provision and received a one-year military deferment.

In 1944, upon completing the tenth grade Locklear was drafted into military service. After completing basic and advanced training, he received orders for Germany and was assigned to the U.S. Army 70th Infantry Division. His Division fought along the Rhine River. After the war ended Locklear was assigned to the 3rd Infantry Division. In June 1946, Locklear was released from military service.

The following fall, at age 21, he resumed his high school career at Magnolia. He joined several war veterans that made up the school's student body. Because there were no school rules and regulations that prohibited older students from playing school sports, Locklear became one of two war veterans participating on the school's athletic teams. Eugene Chavis coached the boys and girls basketball teams during this time at Magnolia School.

Because there was no school gymnasium, the teams practiced and played on a dirt court located on the school campus. There were no team uniforms. The boys wore jeans and t-shirts, and some form of shorts and blouses were the court attire for girls. Shoes were not required for participants, and they wore whatever they owned; often times they played in their bare feet. Later, the patrons of Magnolia High School raised money to buy uniforms so the teams would have them to wear when they played their games in the gymnasium at Pembroke State College.

"The Magnolia boys basketball team usually consisted of seven-to-nine players. My senior year, we had eight," Locklear recalls. He says the starting players on the 1946 Magnolia High School boys basketball team were: Thural Locklear, Cecil Locklear, Hardy "Red" Bell, Versel Hunt, and himself. Pembroke State College basketball coach James Thomas Sampson attended athletic contests at local Indian high schools and observed Locklear as he played sports for Magnolia High School. Impressed by Locklear's athletic skills, Coach Sampson encouraged him to enroll at Pembroke State College in the fall of 1947. The coach arranged for him to move into the college dormitory and to have his meals in the school cafeteria. As a military veteran he qualified for financial assistance from the GI Bill which helped to pay for his college expenses.

"Had it not been for Coach Sampson's insistence, I never would have gone to college," Locklear comments.

During summer vacation days from school, Locklear lived in Detroit, Michigan, where he worked in automobile manufacturing in order to supplement his income. Locklear would return to his native Robeson County each fall to resume his college education. He was a three-sports star during his playing days at Pembroke State College. He played football, basketball and baseball.

"We did not have many players on the football team. The players played both ways," he says. "I played left end on offense, and when the other team had the ball, I played defensive end. From the opening kickoff a player remained in the game until the end; every play," he continues.

In 1982, Pembroke State University formally recognized Locklear's outstanding athletic performance by selecting him to the school's Athletic Hall of Fame.

In the summer of 1950, Locklear married Gladys Oxendine, his longtime college sweetheart, in Detroit, Michigan. In 1954, he received his college degree in Science Education from Pembroke State College and took a fulltime employment with Chrysler Motors in Detroit. He worked there in the automobile industry for two years before being recruited to his first teaching position by Union Chapel Elementary School principal Barto Clark. In 1956, Locklear's wife Gladys, fell ill and was admitted to a Lumberton, North Carolina hospital where she underwent surgery to have gallstones removed. Locklear says that after his wife's operation, she contracted a viral infection while in the hospital. Mrs. Locklear- -young, beautiful, and beloved- - died from medical complications within a few days of her surgery.

Locklear remained at Union Chapel Elementary School until the end of the school year 1960-61, when he accepted a transfer to Green Grove Elementary School.

In 1961, the 36-year old widower married Fannie Dial Chavis, the widow of Eugene Chavis. In the summer of 1959, Chavis drowned in Lumber River in Robeson County. He had been Locklear's high school coach at Magnolia School. Locklear ended his public school teaching career at Fairgrove School at the end of the 1987-88 school year.

Photo: Lumbee Regional Development Association Archival Collection

Lacy Maynor

Lacy W. Maynor, son of Mr. and Mrs. Luther V. Maynor, was born October 8, 1904. He attended school at Pembroke Graded and High School and the College at Pembroke, NC. After finishing college, he taught for sixteen years at Prospect High School. He served as president of the Lumbee Basketball Conference. He left the teaching profession and became the supervisor of the National Youth Administration (N.Y.A.) located at Red Bank, NC.

When the N.Y.A. closed in 1941, he accepted a position as dispatcher at the Laurinburg-Maxton Air Force Base Motor Pool. He worked in this position until the base was de-activated in 1946. From 1946-1955, he taught a Veteran's Course at Pembroke High School.

He served as the Judge of Recorders Court, Maxton District from 1956 to 1966. His last position was with the Robeson County Board of Education from 1966 until he became ill. Maynor had been a lifetime barber, farmer, and resident of Robeson County. Judge Maynor was an active Berea Baptist Church member. He participated in all aspects of church life – Deacon, Sunday School teacher, Training Union Director, choir member, and Building Committee chairman.

His love of community was shown by his work with the Robeson County Fair, the Burnt Swamp Singing Association, the Firemen's Relief Fund, the Pembroke Kiwanis, the Pembroke Chamber of Commerce, and the young Indian students of the schools of Robeson County.

Judge Maynor also was a respected member of the National American Indian Community. He traveled and spoke extensively to Indian tribes calling on them for unity and service to their people.

Judge Maynor loved, and gave freely of himself, to all manner of men. He saw good in all men and was willing to extend a helping hand to them. He spent a great part of his life helping build the churches, schools, and various communities among the Lumbee Indians.

His life was one of service to God, his community, people, and his family.

Photo courtesy of Mary Martin Deese

Frank Howard Epps (1904-1974)

Born in Person County, North Carolina, Epps served as principal of Magnolia School from 1933 to 1968. He was a member of Ten-Mile Center Baptist Church, where he served as Sunday school superintendent and deacon. Epps also served as moderator of the Burnt Swamp Baptist Association.

During his school administration, Epps was a leader in the organization, administration, and supervision of the interscholastic athletic programs for the Robeson County Indian High School Athletic Conference.

Elmer Theodore Lowry (1906-1986)

Born in the Hopewell Community, Robeson County, North Carolina, Lowry served as principal of Pembroke High School from 1940 to 1964. He was a member of Hopewell Methodist Church, where he served on several church boards.

During his school administration, Lowry was the leader in the organization, administration, and supervision of the interscholastic athletic programs for the Robeson County Indian High School Athletic Conference. He is credited for arranging *The Robesonian* writers to cover the post season Indian basketball tournaments.

Photo: 1953 Pembroke High School yearbook, *The Challenger*

Robeson County Indian High School Basketball Coaches

Lucy Oxendine Thomas
PROSPECT HIGH SCHOOL

Photo: 1967 *Fairgrovian*

Kenneth Ray Maynor
FAIRGROVE HIGH SCHOOL

Photo: 1967 *Fairgrovian*

James F. "Buddy" Bell
FAIRGROVE HIGH SCHOOL

Photo: 1964 *Fairgrovian*

James Sanford Hunt
FAIRGROVE HIGH SCHOOL

Photo: 1964 *Fairgrovian*

Conrad Oxendine
PROSPECT HIGH SCHOOL

Photo: 1954 *Tomahawk*

Robert McGirt
MAGNOLIA HIGH SCHOOL

Photo: 1946 *Indianhead*

Eugene Chavis
MAGNOLIA HIGH SCHOOL

Photo: 1941 *Lumbee Tattler*

Leon Hunt
FAIRGROVE HIGH SCHOOL

Photo: 1967 *Fairgrovian*

Hartman Brewington
HAWKEYE HIGH SCHOOL

Photo: 1962 *Indianhead*

THE TOURNAMENTS

THE TOURNAMENTS!

The following are accounts of tournament games played from 1939-1967 by the Indian high schools in both the Robeson County Indian High School Athletic Conference and the Tri-County Indian High School Athletic Conference.

The accounts were taken from the sports pages of *The Robesonian* and are herein reprinted by permission.

The Authors

Indian Cagers Organize Loop

Correspondence of *The Robesonian*

PEMBROKE, January 18 – The Lumbee Basketball Conference gets underway this week, and the following schools will be represented: Pembroke, Prospect, Fairmont, Magnolia and Green Grove. The coaches of the schools met before Christmas and completed the schedule. They are looking to a successful year.

The rules governing players are the same as those for football, that is, the rules of the conference issued last November. Each team is requested to send a list of its players to President Lacy Maynor as soon as possible. The visiting teams will furnish officials. Any team wanting information concerning the conference or schedule, write to Lacy Maynor, President, and he will he glad to supply it to you. The finals will be played off at Pembroke after the regular schedule has been completed.

Magnolia Basketball Schedule Announced

Coach Margolis Sanderson of Magnolia High School announces his Basketball schedule for 1939. He expects a successful year in spite of a limited number of players. The schedule:

January 19, Pembroke - home; January 24, Green Grove - away; January 26, Prospect - home; January 31, Fairmont - away; February 2, Green Grove - home; February 7, Open; February 9, Prospect - away; February 14, Pembroke - away; and February 16, Fairmont - home.

***The Robesonian*, Lumberton, NC**
Wednesday, January 18, 1939, Page 6

New Walls Rise On Pembroke Gym

New walls have been constructed on the gymnasium at Pembroke Normal School. Inspectors found the original walls not meeting standards thus instructing the contractor to tear them down and start over. An inspector has been assigned to closely monitor the laying of the bricks to see that the new walls meet state and federal construction standards. Griffith Construction Company of Rockingham, NC is the general contractor building the gymnasium.

EDITOR'S NOTE: Construction on the gymnasium at Pembroke Normal School was under way in January 1939. The use of the gym for basketball play could not have started until its completion which most likely been in 1940.

***The Robesonian*, Lumberton, NC**
January 27, 1939, Page 1

Prospect News

By James E. Moore

The Prospect High School Basketball team has still won five and tied one and lost one game this season. The star players for the Marathon Racers are: Isaac Locklear, Vernon Oxendine, Timothy Strickland, Will Goins, David Jackson, Lee D. Jones, James Moore, Lonnie Maynor, Clyde Locklear, Wayne Locklear, Purcell Jones, and Talmage Locklear. The team is coached by Curtis Moore. Prospect has played Green Grove, Fairmont, Magnolia, and Pembroke.

The Robesonian, Lumberton, NC
Friday, March 3, 1939, Page 7

Indian Cage Tourney Opens at Pembroke

PEMBROKE, March 13, 1940 – the Lumbee Indian High School Basketball Tournament will be held at Pembroke Cherokee Indian Normal School Gymnasium beginning Thursday. This will be the first high school tournament in the new Indian Normal Gym. Fairmont will play Green Grove and Pembroke will meet Piney Grove in the opening round games. Friday night Prospect will play the Fairmont-Green Grove winner and Magnolia will tangle with the Piney Grove - Pembroke winner. The finals will be staged Saturday night.

EDITOR'S NOTE: Results of the 1940 tournament championship winner were not found in *The Robesonian*. The March 12, 1941 *Robesonian* listed Pembroke the winner.

The Robesonian, Lumberton, NC
Wednesday, March 13, 1940, Page 6

Robeson Indian Basketball Tourney To Start Thursday

SEVEN HIGH SCHOOL TEAMS ARE ENTERED IN CAGE EVENT AT NORMAL.

Correspondence of *The Robesonian*

PEMBROKE, March 12, 1941 – The Robeson County Indian High School basketball tournament will be held in Cherokee Indian Normal Gymnasium March 13, 14 and 15, under sponsorship of the School Masters' club.

Defending champions are Pembroke High School. The tournament will open Thursday at 7 p.m. with a game between Union Chapel and Pembroke, followed at 8 o'clock by a contest between the Fairmont and Magnolia quints and at 9 o'clock by a tilt between Piney Grove and Prospect.

The Fairmont-Magnolia winners will take on the Piney Grove-Prospect winners Friday at 8 p.m., and Green Grove, which drew a bye, will play the winners of the Union Chapel-Pembroke game Friday at 9 p.m. The finals are set for Saturday at 8 p.m.

TEAM STANDINGS:

Standings of the teams, with figures representing games won and lost and percentage, in order, are:
1 - Green Grove, 11–1–917; **2 -** Prospect 11–1–917;
3 - Pembroke, 6–5–545; **4 -** Magnolia, 6–6–500;
5 - Fairmont, 3–7–300; **6 -** Union Chapel, 2–9–182;
7 - Piney Grove, 1–11–25.

Green Grove won a draw for No. 1 standing which put Prospect, with the same record, in second place on the card.

The Robesonian, Lumberton, NC
March 12, 1941, Page 3

Prospect Defeats Pembroke For Indian High School Tournament Title In Thrilling Game 31-29

GOINS IS HERO OF VICTORY OVER DEFENDING CHAMPION; HIGH SCORER

PEMBROKE, March 17, 1941 – paced by Will Goins, tournament high scorer, Prospect High School Saturday night defeated Pembroke, defending champions, in the finals of the annual Indian Conference event here 31-29 in an over-time thriller. Seldom if ever, has the Cherokee Indian Normal gymnasium, scene of the second annual tournament seen a harder fought and more evenly contested game. The regular game ended 29 all, about midway of the three minute over-time period Wayne Locklear of Prospect looped in a two pointer to provide the new champions with the needed point. Prospect entered the finals with a win over Piney Grove Thursday night and a close victory over an ever threatening Magnolia outfit. Pembroke defeated Union Chapel in the opening game and top seeded Green Grove in the semi-finals.

GOINS IS STAR

Will Goins, who tallied a total of 53 points during the three night event scored 12 points in leading the Prospecters. Three men, J. R. Locklear, James Sanderson, and William Earl Oxendine led Pembroke's defeated effort with seven points each.

Superintendent C. L. Green of the Robeson County Schools presented Prospect the championship trophy in ceremonies following the game.

Tom Cope and H. Hinnant of Red Springs, NC, were game officials during the tournament and M. Smith and E. Sampson were official scorer and timer respectively.

CHAMPIONSHIP GAME (OVER-TIME)

Prospect - 31		Pembroke - 29	
Will Goins	12	J.R. Locklear	7
Fred Locklear	0	Garnett Lowry	1
Wayne Locklear	2	James Sanderson	7
Lee D. Jones	3	Walter Bullard	5
David Jackson		Wm. E. Oxendine	7
Subs:			
Purcell Jones	0	Earl Oxendine	2
Talmage Locklear	8	Sampson	0
Lonnie Maynor	2		
Henry Moore	2		
Lawrence Locklear	2		

Prospect - Curtis Moore, Coach
Pembroke - Margolis Sanderson, Coach

The Robesonian, Lumberton, NC
Monday, March 17, 1941, Page 3

Photo courtesy of Will Goins, Jr.

Will Goins
Prospect High School

Indian High School Cage Tourney Gets Under Way As Favorites Win

Bob Taylor, Sports Editor

PROSPECT, PEMBROKE AND GREEN GROVE WIN ON OPENING NIGHT

PEMBROKE, February 5, – Robeson County Indian High School Basketball Tournament got underway here last nigt before a large crowd of howling fans. The tournament is being played in the Pembroke State College gym.

Three teams fought their way to the semi-finals, which will be run off here tonight, the first game pitting Magnolia, who won in the conference race and received a bye, against Green Grove, who took a 33-9 win over Union Chapel, the first set to start at 7:30.

In the opener of the three day event, Prospect High edged a win over Fairmont, 18-12. However, the game was a runaway more than the score indicates. Prospect was in possession of the ball most of the time but apparently could not hit the basket.

PEMBROKE WINS

The high scoring Pembroke Quint rompered to a 37-25 win over Piney Grove in the second game of the night. The Pembroke five has rolled up a total of 799 points in 20 games prior to the tourney. Garnett Lowry, rangy Pembroke center, who scored over 60 points in a single game during conference play, had a total of 374 points in 17 games before the opening of the meet here. This is an average of 22 points per game. The Pembroke High team had 564 points scored against them. This give the Pembroke Club an average just a shade under 40 points each game to 28 for opponents.

Lowry was the runner-up in the scoring for his club last night, accounting for 13 while Walter Bullard chopped in 16. Green Grove, who ended the season,

cut short because of lack of transportation, in second spot, rolled over a decidedly weaker Union Chapel Five, 33-9. Jones led Green Grove with 12, Archie Oxendine had 4 for Union Chapel.

Admission price are set at .15 cents for students and .25 cents for adults. A tournament pass for the three night affair is .40 cents.

The finals will be played Friday night at 8 o'clock. A consolation game between the two teams eliminated in the semi-finals will be played at 7 o'clock on the final night. George Powell and Joe Langley of Lumberton who matriculated at Appalachian State Teacher College, are the officials. Powell had this to say about last night's play, "those boys are the cleanest bunch of high school players I have ever seen." This was evident in a tabulation of fouls committed in the three games, with a total of 58 fouls called during tournament play. Each club that takes the floor has plenty of vocal support.

The Robesonian, Lumberton, NC
Thursday, February 5, 1942, Page 3

Grovers Upset Magnolia As Pembroke Wins In Semi-Finals Of Indian Meet

Bob Taylor, Sports Editor

GREEN GROVE CLUB TOPS MAGNOLIA; PEMBROKE ROUTS PROSPECT; FINALS TONIGHT

PEMBROKE, February 6 – Pembroke and Green Grove will meet tonight in the finals of the Robeson County Indian High School Basketball Tournament being played in the Pembroke State College Gymnasium. The Green Grove pulled a whale of an upset in the opening game here last night in the semi-finals, topping the highly favored Magnolia Quintet, 18-12.

Magnolia which won out in the conference play was expected to "walk over" the Grove team but could not get started. Both clubs opened slowly and Magnolia led at the end of the first quarter, 2-1. Each club dropped in a field goal in the second period and Magnolia was ahead at half time 5-3.

Third quarter play was more active, Green Grove spurting for 3 while Magnolia was getting 1. Green Grove out scored the Magnolia time again in the final "chukker" and won going away, 18-12. Charlie Chavis topped the winners' attack with 7 makers. Howard Revels was high man for Magnolia with 7.

BULLARD GETS 16

In the Prospect - Pembroke setto, Prospect jumped into the lead with the first score of the game. The Pembroke Club was "cold" during the first quarter and was on the short end of a 13-4 score at the quarter. In the last four minutes of play of the first half, Walter Bullard, Pembroke forward, sank three successive field goals, followed by two by Garnett Lowry and Pembroke edged in the lead as the half ended, 16-13.

From here on, the game was termed a "rout," Pembroke never was seriously in danger. Bullard dropped in 8 field goals for 16 points to lead Pembroke Quints, while Lowry was runner-up, managing 12.

Fred Locklear and Marvin Lowry were top scorers for Prospect, each with 6. Magnolia and Prospect will meet in the consolation contest which starts at 7 o'clock. The finals start at 8 o'clock. A trophy will be awarded to the winning club tonight.

One of the highlights of the tourney is the high school spirit the teams' supporters have. From the opening whistle until the final second, these loyal fans back their respective clubs with resounding cheers.

Last nights' crowd was estimated by school officials to be the largest on hand in the Pembroke gym for a cage game. Officials for both games were Joe Langley and George Powell.

The Robesonian, Lumberton, NC
Friday, February 6, 1942, Page 3

Pembroke Edges Grovers For Indian Tourney Championship
Bob Taylor, Sports Editor

PEMBROKE TAKES 27-21 DECISION OVER GREEN GROVE; PROSPECT WINS CONSOLATION GAME

PEMBROKE, February 9 – Pembroke emerged champion of the Robeson County Indian High School Basketball Tournament here Friday night taking a 27-21 win over Green Grove in the finals of the three night affair held in the Pembroke State Gymnasium. Prospect edged a 25-20 decision over Magnolia in a consolation game played prior to the championship event. Green Grove jumped into the lead early in the opening period gaining a 6-0 handicap before Pembroke came up with a field goal, the score tanding at 6-2. The Grovers added a free throw but Garnett Lowry high scoring Pembroke center, came back with a two-pointer to set the score at 7-4. At the end of the first period, Green led 11-9.

The crowd in the over flowing gym was tense, as were the players as the second quarter play began. Only 8 points were rung up in the quarter, Pembroke getting 6 to edge ahead at half-time 15-13.

The Pembroke Boy Scouts gave impressive flag ceremonies between the halves. As the second half opened, Garnett Lowry dropped in a crip for the Pembroke Five and Charlie Chavis made good on an "up and over" shot for Green Grove, Pembroke leading 17-15. Chavis came up with another score and Pembroke was in the lead by only one point, the score standing at 19-18. At this point of the game, Pembroke put on a spurt and out scored the Groves 8-3 as the game ended 27-21. The presentation of the trophy to the Pembroke team was made by Horace Cummings, Indian County farm agent, and was accepted by Earl Oxendine, Pembroke's captain.

The Prospect team was also presented a trophy at this time, a football award going to the winners in County football. The Prospect - Magnolia setto opened very slowly, and it was tied up at 3 all as the opening quarter ended. Prospect led at half time 8-6. The score was tied four time during the last half. Prospect pulled away in the final quarter after the score has stood at 18-18, for the same time. Prospect wound up with a 25-20 win.

Green Grove gained the finals with a pair of victories, coming at the hands of Union Chapel and Magnolia, who was rated as favorites to cap the meet. Pembroke marched into the final night via wins over Piney Grove and Prospect. The box scores:

CONSOLATION GAME

Magnolia	FG	FT	TP
Revels, J.	3	0	6
Emanuel	0	0	0
McGirt, Robert	2	0	4
Revels, Howard	1	1	3
Haggans, Willie	2	1	5
Hunt, Vereace	1	0	2
Carter, Harley	0	0	0
TOTALS	9	2	20

Prospect	FG	FT	TP
Lowry, Marvin	3	0	6
Dial, Jim	0	0	0
Locklear, Fred	4	1	9
Jones, Purcell	0	0	0
Locklear, Walter	4	2	10
Collins, Ledford	0	0	0
Moore, Henry	0	0	0
Locklear, Lawrence	0	0	0
Locklear, Talmage	0	0	0
Maynor, Lonnie	0	0	0
TOTALS	11	3	25

CHAMPIONSHIP GAME

Green Grove	FG	FT	TP
Chavis, Charlie	4	1	9
Jones. L.	2	0	4
Carter, E.	1	0	2
Swett, L. S	0	0	0
Swett, R.C	0	2	2
Rogers, Isred	1	0	2
Hammond, William	0	0	0
Hunt, Rucious	0	0	0
Spaulding, A.G.	0	0	0
Hunt, L.	1	0	2
TOTALS	9	3	21

Pembroke	FG	FT	TP
Bullard, Walter	2	0	4
Oxendine, Earl	1	0	2
Lowry, Garnett	6	2	14
Martin, Dick	1	3	5
Blue, Brantley	0	0	0
Chavis	1	0	2
Smith, Henry	0	0	0
Godwin, Fred	0	0	0
Jacobs	0	0	0
Lowry, Henry Ford	0	0	0
TOTALS	11	5	27

The Robesonian, Lumberton, NC
Monday, February 9, 1942, Page 3

Prospect Basketball Squad To Give Party

Pembroke, March 19, 1942 – The Basketball Squad of Prospect High School will give a party this Thursday evening to celebrate the conclusion of the basketball season in the Home Economics building. Members of the faculty have been invited.

The Robesonian, Lumberton, NC
Thursday, March 19, 1942, Page 3

EDITOR'S NOTE: No information of the 1943 Robeson County Indian High Schools Basketball Tournament was found in *The Robesonian.*

Indian High School Tournament, March 9-11, 1944

PEMBROKE, February 29 – Plans are in readiness for a basketball tournament among six Indian high schools to be held in the gymnasium of Pembroke State College March 9, 10, and 11 at 8:00 p.m.

On the night of March 9 the first game will be played between Fairmont and Green Grove, the second between Union Chapel and Magnolia. Winners of the former game will play Prospect and the winner of the latter will play Pembroke on the 10th. Winners in these two games will play in the finals March 11, with the losing teams having preliminary games that night.

Trophies will be awarded the winners of the tournament and of high point score.

Officials for the tournament have been named as follows: Earl Thompson, doorkeeper, Albert Hunt, scorekeeper, Miss Vonda Wicker, timekeeper.

Free admission will be given to all high school principals, with a small fee charged to all others. Everyone is invited to attend.

PAIRING

March 9   Fairmont vs. Green Grove
Union Chapel vs. Magnolia

March 10   Prospect vs. Winner of Fairmont - Green Grove
Pembroke vs. Winner of Union Chapel - Magnolia

March 11   Championship

***The Robesonian*, Lumberton, NC
Tuesday, February 29, 1944, Page 4**

News Letter From Pembroke State College For Indians

A basketball tournament for boys teams from local high schools was held in the College gymnasium March 9-11, 1944. The following schools were represented: Fairmont, Green Grove, Union Chapel, Magnolia, Prospect and Pembroke. The winners were Pembroke after a hard struggle with Prospect. In a preliminary to this final game, Magnolia defeated Fairmont. A trophy was presented to the winning Pembrokers.

***The Robesonian*, Lumberton, NC
Tuesday, March 21, 1944, Page 3**

Fairmont Wins School Tourney

GREEN GROVE RUNNER-UP IN CLOSE CONTEST AMONG INDIAN HIGH SCHOOLS.

PEMBROKE – The 3-day basketball tournament to determine the championship among the Indian High Schools of Robeson County was won Saturday night by Fairmont after a close contest with Green Grove by the score of 22-16. Fairmont won its way into the finals by a victory over Pembroke on Friday night 30-19. The other finalist, Green Grove, played see saw battle, 17-15, on Friday night nosed out Prospect, 23-20. On Saturday night the finalists found themselves almost deadlocked at half time, Fairmont leading, 11-10. In the third quarter Fairmont scored six points and shut out its opponents, thus acquiring a commanding lead which it maintained until the end despite Green Grove's rally in the last quarter. Captain Clifford Oxendine, playing at forward for Fairmont, was high scorer with nine points, closely followed by Cecil Hammonds of Green Grove, with 9. Vardell Ransom of Fairmont scored 7, J. Hunt, 3, Hardywell Locklear, Jr., 2. For Green Grove, Earl Scott made 4, Oscar Oxendine, 2, Ray Chavis, 1.

At the conclusion of the tournament, which was held in the Pembroke State College gymnasium, Dr. R.D. Wellons, President of the College, presented the trophy to the winning Fairmont team, and announced the all tournament team selected on the basis of general excellence in all the games. Judges Harold W. Kennedy, Paul L. Hollister and Albert Hunt chose the following five: Cecil Hammonds of Green Grove, Clifford Oxendine of Fairmont, James Howard Locklear of Prospect, Aubrey Graham of Green Grove, Curtis Lowry of Pembroke.

Pembroke high school played three games. On Thursday it defeated Union Chapel, 36-16. On Friday it lost to Fairmont, and on Saturday the two rivals, Prospect and Pembroke clashed in a staggering battle which was staged in a preliminary to the final games. Prospect lead at half time, 16-10, but in the second half Pembroke found itself and won out, 24-19.

Officiating at the games was a high order. The play was fast at all times, but was never permitted to get out of control of the referee and umpire. For the first two nights, Lt. R. Novothy and Sgt. Irwin Benjamin were the officials, and on Saturday Lt. Novothy worked with Cpl. Bandock. All three are from the Maxton-Laurinburg Air Base.

The Tournament Committee was composed of Dean Clifton Oxendine, Dr. Kennedy and Miss Vonda Wicker of the college. In charge of finances was Elmer Lowry, Principal of Pembroke High School. The score-keepers were Albert Hunt and Clyde Locklear. The team coaches were: Carlie Oxendine, Fairmont; Joe Sampson, Green Grove; Eugene Chavis, Magnolia; Dorsey V. Lowry, Pembroke; Nash Locklear, Prospect; and Delton Lowry, Union Chapel.

The Robesonian, Lumberton, NC
Wednesday, March 7, 1945

Basketball Tourney At Pembroke College

BY PHONE TO *ROBESONIAN*

PEMBROKE – The first game in the high school basketball tournament series held at Pembroke State College, March 7-9, when Magnolia played Fairmont Thursday night, was won by Fairmont with a score of 35-17. The winning team from this match plays Prospect tonight, Friday at 8 o'clock.

The game between Green Grove and Union Chapel Thursday night was won by Green Grove with a score of 31-20, with the winning team from this game playing Pembroke tonight, Friday at 7:30 p.m.

Clifford Oxendine scored highest for Fairmont and Earl Locklear for Magnolia, while Cecil Hammonds made the most for Green Grove and Forace Oxendine for Union Chapel.

In addition to the boys championship game Saturday night, the Magnolia girls play Pembroke girls at 7:30 p.m.

The Robesonian, Lumberton, NC
Friday, March 8, 1946, Page 8

Photo: Glenn Swain, *The Robesonian*

Cecil Hammonds
Green Grove High School, selected to the all tournament team.

Green Grove Wins 1946 Indian Cage H. S. Championship

PEMBROKE – In a game of keen competition and cheering spectators, Green Grove won the 1946 Robeson Indian High School Basketball Championship Saturday night at Pembroke State College, matching Prospect with a final score of 33-16. Green Grove got an early lead and maintained this lead throughout the game; the score was 15-4 at half and 23-8 at third quarter. Kenneth Brooks and Cecil Hammonds scored highest for Green Grove, and Dook Locklear and Glenn Jacobs for Prospect.

These two teams entered the finals after emerging as victors in the semi-finals Thursday night, Green Grove winning in a hard fought battle with Pembroke by a score of 42-31 and Prospect over Magnolia by 48-15. Ned Sampson and Joe Oxendine scored highest for Pembroke with 10 points each, while Aubrey Graham made 25 and Cecil Hammonds made 9 points for Green Grove and Dook Locklear 18 for Prospect.

Before the conference finals Friday night, Pembroke girls clashed with Magnolia girls, with a score of 21-12 in favor of Magnolia.

After the games Dr. R. D. Wellons, President of Pembroke State College, presented the trophy to the winning team. He also commended the two referees, Herbert Oxendine and Willard Locklear, for their excellent services during the tournament. The following were selected as the tournament team: Aubrey Graham and Junior Locklear - Green Grove; Dook Locklear - Prospect; Forace Oxendine - Union Chapel; and Hardywell Locklear, Jr. - Fairmont. They won miniature basketball trophy charms.

Fairmont forfeited the game Thursday night because an ineligible player was used.

The Robesonian, **Lumberton, NC**
Tuesday, March 12, 1946, Page 6

Six Schools Enter Pembroke School Tournament, March 5-7

PEMBROKE BOYS, MAGNOLIA GIRLS FAVORED

PEMBROKE, March 3, 1947 – Six schools will participate in the Robeson County Indian High School Basketball Tournament at Pembroke State College gymnasium March 6, 7, and 8.

The Pembroke High School Boys and the Magnolia High School Girls are favorites in the early tournament prognostication but anything can happen and probably will. The tournament committee is urging the fans to turn out and support their favorite teams.

EDITOR'S NOTE: No information was found in *The Robesonian* who won championships in this tournament.

The Robesonian, **Lumberton, NC**
Monday, March 3, 1947, Page 6

PSC Cagers Win From HS Champs

PEMBROKE, March 10 – Both the boys and girls teams of Pembroke State College defeated the high school champions in games played at the College gymnasium Tuesday night. The PSC girls defeated the Union Chapel girls by a 20-13 count, and the PSC boys defeated Prospect 53-35.

Dook Locklear was high scorer for the evening when he racked up 16 points for Prospect. Horace Howington led the college quintet with 12, and Elizabeth Berry was high scorer in the college girls game.

The Robesonian, **Lumberton, NC**
Friday, March 12, 1948

Prospect To Play McColl High Team

PEMBROKE – Prospect Indian High School Basketball teams and the McColl, S.C., High teams will clash in a double header at the Pembroke State College gymnasium next Tuesday night, starting at 7:30 o'clock with the girls game.

The Prospect teams will be out for revenge in these games since McColl swept a double bill between the clubs last Tuesday. The McColl boys won by the narrow margin of 34 to 30.

In other games this season Prospect has won over Fairmont, Green Grove, Pembroke and Magnolia. Against Star the boys won and the girls lost, while against Aberdeen, Prospect lost both games. The schedule for the reminder of the season consists of Gibson at Gibson on Jan. 28, Union Chapel at P.S.C. on Feb. 1, Pembroke at P.S.C. on Feb. 15, and West End at West End on Feb. 18.

Conrad Oxendine is coach of the boys team assisted by Adolph Dial, and Mrs. Mary Sanderson is coach of the Prospect girls team. Players on the boys team are Reese Locklear, Dook Locklear, Wiley Oxendine, James Earl Locklear, Neal A. Lowry Jr. and Charles "Bill" Moore.

Players on the girls team are Arminda Locklear, Harvelene Locklear, Sara Neal Bullard, Rose Dial, Rosetta Locklear, Pauline Bullard and Verdie Locklear.

The Robesonian,
Lumberton, NC
Friday, Jan. 21, 1949

Photo courtesy of Sara Neal Bullard Locklear

Sara Neal Bullard
Prospect High School

Pembroke State College Athletic Club Sponsors Tournament For Indian Schools From the Pembroke State College News

PEMBROKE – A high school basketball tournament was held last weekend with both teams from Prospect High School chalking up final victories.

Prospect girls defeated Union Chapel 19-14 and Prospect boys won over Pembroke 27-15.

The schools competing were Green Grove, Magnolia, Union Chapel, Pembroke and Prospect.

***The Robesonian,* Lumberton, NC**
Wednesday, March 23, 1949

Prospect, Union Chapel Teams Win In County Indian Tourney

PEMBROKE– Prospect boys and Union Chapel girls came up as champions of the Indian High School Basketball Tournament which ended Saturday. The winning teams were presented with trophies. Runners up were Fairmont boys and Magnolia girls.

The tournament was played in the Pembroke State College gymnasium. Schools participating were Pembroke, Prospect, Fairmont, Magnolia, Union Chapel and Green Grove.

An all-tournament team was selected from the competing teams, and members were presented with individual trophies.

For the boys tournament team the following players were selected: Judson Hammonds of Magnolia, James Earl Locklear of Prospect, Sanford Hunt of Fairmont, James Ertle Deese of Union Chapel, Eugene Jacobs of Pembroke.

Tournament team girls selected were: forwards, Vashti Oxendine, Union Chapel; Mary Sue Locklear,

Union Chapel; Elsie Ree Bell, Magnolia; guards: Sadie Oxendine, Fairmont; Ludalia Locklear, Union Chapel; Rosa Mae Locklear, Magnolia.

An Elementary School Tournament will be staged in the P.S.C. gymnasium this week, beginning Wednesday. The finals will be played Saturday night by boys teams and girls teams.

Trophies will be awarded to winning teams. An all tournament team will be chosen, the members of which will receive individual trophies. Grades eight on down from the Indian elementary schools in the county will participate.

The Robesonian, Lumberton, NC
Tuesday, March 21, 1950, Page 2

Pembroke Wins Both Trophies In Annual Tournament Games

Before a capacity crowd Coach Tom Oxendine's Pembroke High School Conference winning girls and boys defeated Magnolia and Fairmont to win both trophies in the annual Robeson County Indian High School Basketball Tournament finals held at the Pembroke State College gymnasium Saturday night.

SATURDAY NIGHT

The Pembroke-Magnolia girls score was 60-50, while the Pembroke boys took a 38-19 count over Fairmont.

Janice Jones, Pembroke's sophomore forward and tournament high scorer with an average of 32 points per game, and co-captain Mary Sue Locklear led the team with 30-22 points, respectively.

Pembroke took an early 16-10 lead in the first quarter which Magnolia overcame by a half-time score of 28-25. In the second half Pembroke rallied and won a decisive 60-50 victory.

Narva Lowry, Pembroke's sophomore forward's expert ball handling set up the majority of the second half scores. Outstanding defensive players for Pembroke were: Katrina Locklear, Jeanie Brewington, and Geneauga Oxendine. Owido Locklear and Pauline Sutton were high scorers for the loser, with 18 and 17 points.

Van Benson Locklear, boys tournament high scorer, sported the Blue Devils to an easy 38-19 victory. The Devils held Fairmont scoreless the first quarter and were never headed. Lynwood Locklear, Gerald Maynor, Denford Oxendine, and John C. Locklear all contributed heavily to the Pembroke victory by their control ball tactics.

Sanford Hunt and Ralph Hunt scored six points each for the loser.

The Robesonian, Lumberton, NC
Thursday, March 22, 1951, Page 8

Local Tournament

In the Pembroke State College gymnasium, the Indian elementary schools are staging a basketball tournament, The high schools will participate in a tournament the weekends of the 14th and 15th and the 21st, and 22nd.

The Robesonian, Lumberton, NC
Thursday, March 6, 1952, Page 15

Photo: UNC-Pembroke archives

Gerald Maynor
Pembroke High School

Eight Indian Teams Square Off

DERBY CONTINUES UNTIL SATURDAY AT PEMBROKE GYM

PEMBROKE – The Indian High School Basketball Tournament will begin this evening at 7:30 o'clock in the gymnasium of Pembroke State College, when the Magnolia girls and the Fairgrove girls meet.

The tournament will begin tonight and run through Saturday evening, with two games being played each evening, at 7:30 and 8:30 o'clock. Taking part in the tournament, with both boys and girls teams, are Pembroke, Magnolia, Fairgrove and Prospect.

The Friday games will see the Pembroke and Prospect girls playing at 7:30 o'clock; the Pembroke and Fairgrove boys will clash at 8:30 o'clock.

The finals will be played Saturday evening.

The Pembroke girls are considered the top teams; they have lost only to Fairgrove. Two players are over six feet tall, Shelby Jane Sampson and Frances Locklear. The Fairgrove girls are second, on the record, with Magnolia giving them a good run for the place. Prospect is at the bottom with only two conference wins.

The Pembroke boys also lead the group on the basis of conference play: Prospect and Magnolia are in the running for second and third places; Fairgrove is on the bottom.

The players will be considered eligible under the rules set up by the North Carolina High School Athletic Association. The referees will come from the Fort Bragg agency.

The Robesonian, Lumberton, NC
Tuesday, March 4, 1954, Page 6

Pembroke, Prospect Meet Tonight — Fairgrove, Magnolia Advance to Indian Finals

PEMBROKE – The Fairgrove girls and the Magnolia boys won places for themselves in the finals of the Indian High School Basketball Tournament which is being played at the Pembroke State College gymnasium through tomorrow night.

In the first game, the Fairgrove girls, coached by Albert C. Hunt, defeated Magnolia girls, coached by Ned Sampson, by a score of 50 to 45. The game started off evenly with Fairgrove leading 8 to 6 at the end of the first quarter; at the end of the half, it was 18 to 16, still in favor of Fairgrove. In the third quarter Fairgrove took a decisive lead, scoring 19 points to the opponents' 12. Magnolia's comeback in the last quarter was not quite good enough for a win; they made 17 points while holding Fairgrove to 13. The final score was 50 for Fairgrove, 45 for Magnolia.

High scorer for Fairgrove was Laura Lee Hunt, 24 points; Geraldine Hunt had 15 points. Mary Lois Lowry with 19 points led the Magnolia girls; second was Dorothy Jacobs with 18 points.

In the boys game Magnolia stomped all over Prospect with a 56 to 28 score. Magnolia took the lead in the first quarter, never lost it, and in each quarter outscored the opponents, coached by Conrad Oxendine. Magnolia's score by quarters was 11, 14, 16, 15 for 56; Prospect's score was 10, 8, 6, 4 for 28.

Magnolia produced a group of players who seemed out to beat each other in the scoring department: Willie Fay Sampson, 13; Howard Sampson, Jr., 12; Gerald Butler, 11; Stacy Locklear, 9. Highscorers for Prospect were Bobby Locklear and James H. Woods with 9 points each.

Tonight the Pembroke girls open the session with a game with the Prospect girls; the Pembroke boys will meet the Fairgrove boys in the second game.

The finals will be played tomorrow evening.

The Robesonian, Lumberton, NC
Friday, March 5, 1954, Page 7

Pembroke Teams Win Finals

PEMBROKE CAGERS KNOCK MAGNOLIA, FAIRGROVE OUT

Pembroke's boys and girls are Indian Basketball Champions for another year in Robeson County.

The two Pembroke schools eliminated final opposition for the title Saturday night at the Pembroke State College gym when they beat Fairgrove, 64-41, and overcame the Magnolia boys, 81-48.

Friday night the two teams whipped Prospect and Fairgrove to earn the right to advance to the Saturday night playoffs. The Pembroke girls thoroughly thrashed Prospect, 62-33, and the Pembroke boys outscored the Fairgrove boys, 78-44.

In Saturday night's finals, the Pembroke girls were never headed although the Fairgrove girls put up a good first half. At the end of the first period Pembroke led, 18-16 and increased the margin to 33-28 at half-time.

Scoring 18 points in the third quarter to Fairgrove's 5, the Pembroke girls broke to the wire with a comfortable lead. Final score, 64-41.

Pembroke's Shelby Jane Sampson led in the high scoring department with a 38 point average, followed by Frances Locklear, who got 17. Vashti Locklear got seven.

Fairgrove's Laura Lee Hunt got 32 points with Arberdale Sanderson getting four.

Magnolia made a real battle out of it but fell completely apart in the final quarter to fall before the Pembroke cagers. With Magnolia in a one point lead at the end of the first quarter, the Pembroke boys tied the game up 28-28 at half-time and held on until the end of the third quarter, when the score was still locked at 45-45.

But in the final quarter Pembroke caught fire for 36 points and held the Magnolia boys to a mere nine. That was the ballgame.

Pembroke's John H. Hunt got 19 points but fell behind Ray Oxendine's 33 for night's scoring honors. Bob Jacobs got 13.

Magnolia's Stacy Locklear got 21 for the losers with Howard Sampson, Jr. getting 14.

The Robesonian, Lumberton, NC
Monday, March 8, 1954, Page 9

PEMBROKE'S GIRLS won the annual Robeson Indian Tourney and the Fairgrove boys beat Magnolia 44-43 to wrap up the boys division in a Saturday night finals at the Pembroke State College gym.

Fairgrove High School Boys Basketball Team, 1955 Champions	**Pembroke High School Girls Basketball Team, 1955 Champions**
Leon Hunt, Coach	Fred Lowry, Coach
Kendall Hunt	Shelby Jane Sampson
Jimmy Smith	Dorothy Swett
Earl Strickland	Frances Locklear
James Hunt	Vashti Locklear
Javie Locklear	Janice Lowry
Willie Hunt	Ellen Deese
Gene Brayboy	Rose Oxendine
C. L. Locklear	Ruth Brewington
Carson Mitchell	Kathryn Brewington
Lenwood Hunt	Nancy Louise Locklear
Jamie Locklear	Jennie Baker
Bowman Hunt	Eudora Sampson
Pernell Locklear	

The Robesonian, Lumberton, NC
Monday, February 28, 1955, Page 7

Robeson Indian Cage Tourney Gets Underway

PEMBROKE - The annual Basketball Tournament of the Indian Schools of Robeson County began last night at the gymnasium of Pembroke State College. There will be games tonight and the championship bracket will be played tomorrow night with a girls game at 7:30 o'clock and boys tussle at 8:30 o'clock.

In last night's contests, the Pembroke girls defeated the Prospect girls, 52 to 30 to enter the finals. They will meet the winner of tonight's contest between the Magnolia girls and the Fairgrove girls, set for 7:30 o'clock.

In the second game last night, the Fairgrove boys defeated the Magnolia boys, 48 to 45, to win a place in the Saturday's finals. They will face the winner of tonight's game between Prospect and Pembroke, set for 8:30 o'clock. In the boys game, Chad Hunt of Fairgrove, got confused in the first quarter and after a magnificent drive down the court, in which he contested the ball with all-comers, he dropped a beautiful shot into Magnolia's basket, giving the opponents two points.

GIRLS GAME

Prospect	8	8	8	16	40
Pembroke	19	9	14	11	52

High Scorers:

Pembroke: Frances Locklear 18; Shelby Jane Sampson 12; Rose Oxendine 9.

Prospect: Alice Dial 15.

BOYS GAME

Magnolia	12	8	13	12	45
Fairgrove	14	7	16	11	48

High Scorers:

Fairgrove: Horace Hunt 26; Gerald Ransom 10; Pernell Locklear 10; Chad Hunt 10.

Magnolia: Furman Brewer 23.

The Robesonian, Lumberton, NC
Friday March 2, 1956, Page 11

Pembroke Teams Make Sweep Of Indian Tourney

PEMBROKE - Teams of the Pembroke High school made a clean sweep Saturday evening to take championships in both the girls and boys divisions of the Robeson County Basketball Tournament for Indian Schools.

The Pembroke girls, had tough sledding to defeat the Fairgrove girls in an overtime game ending with a score of 64 to 62 for the Pembroke team. The regular game ended with a 59-59 tie. Fairgrove made its way into the finals by defeating Magnolia on Friday evening. The six first team members of Pembroke are all seniors.

The Pembroke boys edged the Fairgrove boys by a 45-42 score to claim the championship. Pembroke had won its finals' place by defeating Prospect Friday evening.

In post-game festivities Adolph Dial presented trophies to the winners and runners-up in the tournament.

Accepting the championship trophy for the Pembroke girls were Frances Locklear and Shelby Jane Sampson; for the boys, Bob and Adna Lowry. Claiming runners-up trophies for Fairgrove were Wyvette Jacobs, and Martha Ray Hunt for the girls and Horace Hunt for the boys.

Horace Hunt claimed a trophy for himself when he received a "Most Valuable Player" award, donated by the Pembroke American Legion, from Bruce Jones, Legion Commander.

GIRLS GAME

Pembroke	20	10	4	25	5	64
Fairgrove	12	12	18	17	3	62

High Scorers:

Pembroke: Frances Locklear 33; Shelby Jane Sampson 25; Rose Oxendine 6.

Fairgrove: Laura Lee Hunt 32; Wyvette Jacobs 23; Dorothy Hunt 7.

BOYS GAME

Pembroke	15	5	12	13	45
Fairgrove	8	8	13	13	42

High scorers:

Pembroke: Randall Chavis 11; Reginald Strickland 10; Venus Brooks, Jr. 14.

Fairgrove: Horace Hunt 12; Gerald Ransom 15; Bonson Locklear 7.

The Robesonian, Lumberton, NC
Monday, March 5, 1956, Page 8

Magnolia, Pembroke Cagers Advance To Finals Saturday

PEMBROKE - The Magnolia girls and Pembroke boys moved in to the finals of the Robeson County Basketball Tournament of Indian Schools as they racked up victories in last night over the Pembroke girls and the Prospect boys respectively.

The girls game was not only the curtain-raiser for the double-header, it was the thrill provider too, with Magnolia winning in the closing seconds with a shot from the free throw line, 67 to 66. So close to the end of the game did the successful free throw come, that the girls went off the field to the cheers of their partisans, and were called back for five more seconds of play to make it all official.

The high scorer for both teams, however, was Rose Oxendine of Pembroke who racked up a whopping total of 53 points. Mattie Brewer of Magnolia scored a good 31 points for the victors.

In the boys game Pembroke led all the way in a game that provided few thrills. Taking a lead of 22 to 13 at the first quarter, the Pembroke boys built up the score in each quarter and only in the last round did Prospect hold them to even terms, 10 to 10. Pembroke's high scorer was Howard Sampson, Jr. 23; Prospect's James Alton Revel, had 15.

In tonight's games the Fairgrove girls will meet Prospect girls in the first game at seven o'clock; the Magnolia boys and the Fairgrove boys will clash at 8:30 o'clock.

The Finals tomorrow night will see the Magnolia girls meeting the victor of the Fairgrove-Prospect contest at seven o'clock. The Pembroke boys will play the winner of the Magnolia-Fairgrove duel at 8:30 o'clock. All games are played in the Pembroke State College gym.

GIRLS GAME

Magnolia	16	19	11	21	67
Pembroke	15	18	15	18	66

Magnolia		**Pembroke**	
Louise Chavis	14	Rose Oxendine	53
Mattie Brewer	31	Edna Berry	9
Patsy Locklear	22	Henrietta Locklear	4
Lucy Locklear		Joyce Baker	
Geraldine Spaulding		Della Oxendine	
Alice Ree Locklear		Sylvia Lowry	

BOYS GAME

Pembroke	22	19	17	10	68
Prospect	13	11	7	10	41

Pembroke		**Prospect**	
Howard Sampson	23	James Alton Revels	15
Tim Brayboy	3	Randall Chavis	10
Paul Brooks	12	Carlton Cummings	0
Tommy Swett	15	J.R. Cummings	8
Oceanus Lowry	5	H, Locklear	0
Sub:		Jack D. Clark	8

The Robesonian, Lumberton, NC
Friday, March 1, 1957, Page 7

Magnolia, Fairgrove Schools Win Indian Cage Tournament

The Magnolia girls and the Fairgrove boys had large shiny new trophies in their trophy cases today after winning the Robeson County Basketball Championships for Indian Schools at the Pembroke State College gymnasium Saturday night.

Magnolia's girl champions dropped Prospect by a wide 57-35 score in the opening game, and Fairgrove coped the nightcap by 50-39. The overflow crowd of spectators which witnessed the final night of action was so large that they spilled out on to the playing court to be halted for almost a quarter of an hour while space could be made to accommodate them.

At the conclusion of the night's program, Dr. Walter J. Gale, President of Pembroke State College, presented the championship and runner-up trophies to the girls teams, and Young Allen, Assistant Superintendent of Education in Robeson County Schools presented the boys awards.

Byrtis Dial of Prospect topped the game's scoring with 21 points but all three of Magnolia's forwards were close behind with Louise Chavis getting 20, Patsy Locklear 19, and Mattie Brewer 18.

Fairgrove had to come from behind 26-18 at the half to win their county title over Pembroke, and big scoring sprees in each the third and fourth periods netted them their victory.

The Pembroke team grabbed a 14-6 lead in the initial quarter, and they held their margin even though each team scored the same number of points in the second period. In the third quarter Fairgrove went to town and rammed 17 points through the basket while holding Pembroke to 6, and then they added 15 more in the final stanza.

Gerald Ransom and Bonson Locklear each with 16 points toppled the winners' scoring, and they were also high for the game. Horace Hunt trailed with 14 points for Fairgrove. High scorers for Pembroke were Paul Brooks with 15 and Howard Sampson, Jr. and Tommy D. Swett with 10 each.

The Fairgrove team was coached by Ralph Hunt, and Pembroke was tutored by Delton R. Locklear.

GIRLS GAME

Magnolia	13	18	7	19	57
Prospect	8	8	10	9	35

Prospect		Magnolia	
Byrtis Dial	21	Louise Chavis	20
Alice Dial	7	Mattie Brewer	18
Annie Ruth Bullard		Patsy Locklear	19
Myrtle Locklear		Alice Ree Locklear	
Shirley Locklear		Geraldine Spaulding	
Dorothy Scott		Lucy Locklear	

BOYS GAME

Fairgrove	6	12	17	15	50
Pembroke	14	12	6	7	39

Fairgrove		Pembroke	
Horace Hunt	14	Howard Sampson	10
Pernell Locklear		Paul Brooks	15
Gerald Ransom	16	Tommy D. Swett	10
Gary Sampson	4	Tim Brayboy	2
Bonson Locklear	16	Oceanus Lowry	

Fairgrove High School 1957 Boys Basketball Champions

Ralph Hunt, Coach

Pernell Locklear

Horace Hunt

Charles R. Hunt

Tommie Strickland

Thomas Oxendine

Earl Sealey

Calvin Hammonds

Chad H. Hunt

Crafton Chavis

Gary Sampson

Bonson Locklear

Gerald Ransom

Pembroke High School 1957 Boys Runner Up

Delton R. Locklear, Coach

Howard Sampson, Jr.

Tim Brayboy

Sam Brooks

Tommy Dorsey Swett

Oceanus Lowry

Reginald Strickland

Jeff Maynor

Paul Brooks

Hartman Brewington

Lynwood Sampson

Jerry Revels

Howard Brooks

Stacy Brayboy

The Robesonian, Lumberton, NC
Monday, March 4, 1957, Page 7

Pembroke And Fairgrove Win Indian Cage Championships

Pembroke - Fairgrove high school's boys basketball team and Pembroke's girls were the 1958 champions of the Indian Schools today following their victories in the county tournament at Pembroke State College gymnasium Saturday night.

Fairgrove repeats as champion of the county, while Pembroke replaces Magnolia as the queens of the rectanglar court. Fairgrove downed Pembroke, 63-36 for the boys title, and Pembroke defeated the Fairgrove girls, 45-39.

In the opening game Pembroke had to come from behind 31-30, at the end of the third period to secure its win with a 15 point scoring rally in the final quarter while holding Fairgrove to just eight points.

Fairgrove, behind the scoring arm of Brenda Ransom, worked itself into an 11-8 lead at the end of the first period, but Pembroke edged ahead 21-19 by intermission.

Coach Delton Ray Locklear's Pembroke girls were led in scoring by Henrietta Locklear, with 17 points, and Patsy Locklear with 16 markers. Brenda Ransom paced Fairgrove with 25 points.

The victory for Fairgrove in the boys contest allowed the county champs to remain undefeated for the 1957-58 season. Coach Ralph Hunt's crew took an early lead in the game, and led by comfortable margins at the end of each quarter.

Bonson Locklear was the scoring leader for the winners with 16 points, while Tommy Strickland came into the game as a substitute and scored 15.

Championship trophies were presented at the conclusion of the games by Judge Lacy Maynor. Other members of the basketball committee which secured the awards were Frank Epps and Adolph Dial.

Pembroke 45, Fairgrove 39

GIRLS GAME

Pembroke	8	13	9	15	45
Fairgrove	11	8	12	8	39

Pembroke		**Fairgrove**	
Edna Berry	12	Brenda Ransom	25
Henrietta Locklear	17	Vashti Jacobs	3
Patsy Locklear	16	Janice Sealey	7
Jeanette Bell		M. Hunt	
Joan Lowry		Treva Hunt	
Vashti Chavis		Vanena Hunt	

Pembroke Subs: Deola Oxendine
Fairgrove Subs: Doris Locklear

Fairgrove 63, Pembroke 36

BOYS GAME

Pembroke	5	10	8	13	36
Fairgrove	13	15	23	12	63

Pembroke		Fairgrove	
Jerry Revel	7	Charles Hunt	6
William Brant Lowry	2	Chad Hunt	
Hartman Brewington	4	Gerald Ransom	13
Leverne Oxendine	8	Bonson Locklear	16
Lynwood Sampson	4	Earl Sealey	7

Pembroke Subs: Bobby Jacobs 4, Jimmy Lowry, Walter Oxendine, Howard Brooks 4.

Fairgrove Subs: Tommy Oxendine 15, Tommy Strickland 2, James R. Sanderson, Franklin Hunt, Calvin Hammond 2, Stanton Lewis.

Fairgrove High School 1958 Boys Basketball Champions

Ralph Hunt, Coach
Thomas Oxendine
Calvin Hammonds
Bruce Oxendine
Tommy Strickland
Charles Hunt
Chad Hunt
Franklin Hunt
Bonson Locklear
Earl Sealey
Stanton Lewis
Gerald Ransom
James R. Sanderson

Pembroke High School 1958 Boys Basketball Team

Delton Ray Locklear, Coach
Jerry Revels
William Brant Lowry
Hartman Brewington
Lynwood Sampson
Bobby Jacobs
Walter Oxendine
Howard Brooks
Leverne Oxendine
Jimmy Lowry
Billy Ray Locklear

Fairgrove High School 1958 High School Runner Up

Ralph Hunt, Coach
Brenda Ransom
Vashti Jacobs
Janice Sealey
M. Hunt
Treva Hunt
Vanena Hunt
Doris Locklear
Clara Locklear

Pembroke High School 1958 Girls Basketball Champions

Delton Ray Locklear, Coach
Barbara Ann Locklear
Vashti Chavis
Joan Lowry
Sylvia Lowry
Norma Jean Sampson
Betty Joyce Locklear
Deola Oxendine
Henrietta Locklear
Mary Edna Berry
Patsy Locklear
Jeanette Bell

The Robesonian, Lumberton, NC
Monday, March 3, 1958, Page 8

Pembroke Girls Win; Fairgrove Takes 3rd Crown

PEMBROKE - Pembroke's girls and Fairgrove's boys defending champions of the Robeson County Basketball Tournament for Indian Schools - successfully protected their thrones here Saturday night with decisive victories.

Pembroke, which reached the girls finals by smashing Prospect, 66-54, in a preliminary game earlier in the week, rompered to a 59-45 win over Fairgrove's sextelle. Fairgrove had gone into the final round with a 48-36 win over Magnolia.

Fairgrove's boys, working with uncanny precision in the latter stages of the game, tucked away its third straight championship when it upended Pembroke's quintet, 52-32. The domination of Coach Ralph Hunt's Fairgrove team began in 1957 when it turned back Pembroke in the finals.

Sparked by the sharp shooting of Gerald Ransom and the terrific backboard play of forward Thomas Oxendine, Fairgrove drove to a 26-19 lead at intermission. During the last two quarters the Champion rammed 26 more points through the basket, 17 of them in the final period, to accomplish its smashing victory.

Fairgrove held the lead during most of the first half, but a Pembroke rally tied the score at 17-17 with two minutes to go in the half. A free throw and four field goals by Fairgrove in the remaining minutes broke Pembroke's back and handed the winners a 26-19 margin at the halfway point.

Fairgrove went into the finals with a 57-53 win over Magnolia, while Pembroke blasted Prospect 43-26.

Top scorer of the evening was Gerald Ransom who accounted for 21 of Fairgrove's points. Thomas Oxendine also had 13 points in addition to his numerous rebounds, William Brant Lowry paced Pembroke with 10 points, while Howard Brooks had nine and Hartman Brewington had eight.

In the first game of the evening Edna Berry and Patsy Locklear scored almost all of Pembroke's points to lead the Pembroke win. Berry had 32 and Locklear 24. Brenda Ransom, Clara Locklear, and Treva Hunt had 10 each for Fairgrove, but their team's scoring was led by Janice Sealy with 15 points.

Pembroke led 39-15 at the half, but during the second part of the game Fairgrove outscored the winners, 30-10.

Pembroke 59, Fairgrove 45

GIRLS GAME

Pembroke	20	19	10	10	59
Fairgrove	8	7	14	16	45

Pembroke		Fairgrove	
Edna Berry	32	Brenda Ransom	10
Patsy Locklear	24	Clara Locklear	10
Henrietta Locklear		Janice Sealy	15
Jeanette Bell		Treva Hunt	
Bellene Brooks		Geraldine Spaulding	

Pembroke Subs: Norma Jean Sampson 1, Barbara Ann Locklear, Deola Oxendine, Betty Joyce Locklear.
Fairgrove Sub: Doris Locklear.

Fairgrove, 52, Pembroke 32

BOYS GAME

Pembroke	10	9	4	9	32
Fairgrove	13	13	9	17	52

Pembroke		Fairgrove	
William Brant Lowry	10	Thomas Oxendine	13
Howard Brooks	9	Chad Hunt	8
Hartman Brewington	8	Charles Hunt	10
Lynwood Sampson	4	Gerald Ransom	12
Walter Oxendine		James R. Sanderson	

Pembroke Sub: Leverne Oxendine 1, and Bobby Jacobs
Fairgrove Sub: Bruce Oxendine.

**The Robesonian, Lumberton, NC
Monday, March 9, 1959, Page 5**

Pembroke Cops Tournament

WALTER OXENDINE, BILL LOWRY SET EAGLES' WINNING PACE

By Bill Norment, *Robesonian* Sports

PEMBROKE - Walter Oxendine and William Brant Lowry combined to pump in 35 points for the Eagles of Pembroke High School here Saturday night to lead the Eagles to a 52-41 victory over Magnolia in the championship round of the Robeson County Indian High School Tournament. The Tournament was held at the Pembroke High School gymnasium.

Walter Oxendine led both teams with 18 points, but he was followed closely by William Brant Lowry who collected 17 points. Pembroke gained its entrance to the tourney finals by downing Fairgrove in the preliminary game. Magnolia beat Prospect in its preliminary.

The hard fought battle was played on even terms in the first half, but excessive fouling in the second half got Magnolia in hot water and the Eagles burst the contest wide open from the free throw line.

Pembroke and Magnolia were deadlocked 21-21 about 30 seconds before the end of the half, but a free throw by Walter Oxendine gave the Eagles a 22-21 lead at intermission. The half ended with both teams leaping for a rebound under the Magnolia goal.

Magnolia came back strong in the second half and piled up a 27-25 advantage with five minutes to play in the third quarter. Pembroke Coach Jim Cook then directed his players into a close man-to-man defense and Pembroke started climbing.

During the next three minutes the Eagles pumped 10 straight points through the basket while holding Magnolia scoreless for a 37-35 lead. With one minute to play in the period Pembroke made it 12 straight points for a comfortable 37-27 lead.

Pembroke's play was steady during the fourth period, and Magnolia's anxiety to get possession of the ball sent Eagle players to the foul line on numerous occasions, adding to their headway.

Leverne Oxendine, who scored only one point for Pembroke, proved his worth in other ways in the championship game by riding both backboards of rebounds.

Top scorer of the game for Magnolia was James Swett with 13 points. He was the only Magnolia player to score in the double digits.

In the opening game Saturday night Fairgrove and Prospect met for the consolation championship with Fairgrove taking a 55-32 decision. Bruce Oxendine and James R. Sanderson set the pace for the winners with 11 points each. Claude Moore of Prospect was high for the game with 13 points.

Pembroke	10	12	15	15	52
Magnolia	11	10	6	14	41

Pembroke		**Magnolia**	
William B. Lowry	17	James K. Swett	13
Leverne Oxendine	1	Wendell Lowery	6
Bobby Jacobs	12	Carnell Oxendine	11
Walter Oxendine	18	Jerry Baker	7
Steve Jones	4	Gerald Locklear	3

Pembroke subs: Billy Ray Locklear and Benford Hardin.

Magnolia subs: Billy Fields, James Harris 2, Welford Clark, Freddie Revels, W. Locklear.

Walter Oxendine
Pembroke High School

Photo: 1961 Pembroke State College Yearbook, *The Indianhead*

Pembroke High School 1960 Boys Basketball Champions

Jim Cook, Coach

William B. Lowry

Bemus Blue

Holland Locklear

Leverne Oxendine

Billy Ray Locklear

Bobby Jacobs

Jimmy Ray Locklear

Walter Oxendine

Benford Hardin

Steve Jones

Gervais Oxendine

Magnolia High School 1960 Basketball Boys Runners-Up

Ned Sampson, Coach

James Swett

Wendell Lowery

Carnell Oxendine

Jerry Baker

Gerald Locklear

Billy Fields

James Harris

Welford Clark

Freddie Revels

W. Locklear

The Robesonian, Lumberton, NC
Monday, February 29, 1960, Page 7

Jerry Baker
Magnolia High School

Wendell Lowery
Magnolia High School

Indian Playoffs Open Here At Armory

The Robeson County Indian Basketball Tournament begins three nights of games here this evening in the first round of the annual playoff for the county championship.

This year the event has been switched from the Pembroke gymnasium to the Lumberton Armory. Overflow crowds beyond Pembroke's capacity was a prime factor in the move.

Four teams - Pembroke, Magnolia, Fairgrove, and Prospect play a doubleheader each night. The playoff is of the "Round Robin" style, and the team with the best record on the final night will be declared the champion.

A girls game between Magnolia and Fairgrove schools will precede the boys game Saturday night. Magnolia and Fairgrove were the only schools to field girls team in the county this year.

Championship trophies will be presented to each the winning boys and girls teams, according to league officials. Awards will also be made Saturday night to runner-up teams.

Tonight's opening round sends Pembroke against Prospect in the first game and Magnolia against Fairgrove in the second game. Friday night it will be Magnolia vs. Prospect and Pembroke vs. Fairgrove, and Saturday it will be Fairgrove vs. Prospect and Pembroke vs. Magnolia.

Pembroke High is defending champion of the tournament, and they also boast the best record 9-1 in the playoffs this year.

The Robesonian, Lumberton, NC
Thursday, March 2, 1961, Page 6

Prospect, Magnolia Lose

PEMBROKE, FAIRGROVE WIN OPENING TOURNAMENT GAMES

By Walter Oxendine, Special Correspondent

The 1961 Robeson County Indian Basketball Tournament got under way here at the Lumberton Armory Thursday night with Pembroke High defeating Prospect High 62-24, and Fairgrove High upsetting Magnolia High 42-41.

In the first game, Pembroke downed Prospect 62-24 with Steve Jones setting the pace for Pembroke with 12 points. He was followed by Curley Locklear with 10 points. Ronald Brewer was high for Prospect with 9.

In the first quarter, Prospect failed to score by trying to work the ball for a good shot, whereas, Pembroke racked up 16 points to give them a 16-0 lead at the end of the first quarter.

The second quarter was a little different. Ronald Brewer of Prospect hit four straight field goals, and Prospect cut the lead to 13 points, but Pembroke played steady ball and at half time had a 16-11 lead.

Pembroke started fast breaking in the third quarter and added points to their lead as the game played out.

In the second game of the evening, Fairgrove upset Magnolia 42-41. James Hunt collected 11 points, Jesse Freeman 12, and Gary Sanderson 13, to lead the Fairgrove victory. Gerald Locklear was high for Magnolia with 11 points.

Both teams played a hard game until the final horn, but Fairgrove's shooting from outside the circle gave them the winning edge.

At the end of the first quarter, Fairgrove had an 8-7 lead, but Magnolia bounced back to obtain a 30-16 lead at intermission.

The game was tied five times during the game. When the second half started, Magnolia started finding the range and racked up the 11 point lead with about four minutes left in the third quarter. Coach Ralph Hunt of Fairgrove then directed his players to begin shooting from outside and before Magnolia could stop them, they had narrowed the margin to 6 points at the end of the quarter.

At the beginning of the fourth quarter, both teams were hitting but near the end of the period Fairgrove used its outside shooting and a final free throw by James Hunt to clinch the thrilling 42-41 victory.

Tonight's schedule sends Magnolia against Prospect, and Pembroke against Fairgrove. Saturday it will be the Fairgrove boys against Prospect, and Pembroke against Magnolia. The Fairgrove and Magnolia girls play a preliminary game Saturday night.

Starting lineup for Magnolia: Wendell Lowery 10, Ray Chavis 7, Carnell Oxendine 8, Gerald Locklear 11, and Jerry Baker 5. Magnolia subs: Freddie Revels, W. Locklear, and Billy Fields. Magnolia coach is Ned Sampson.

Starting lineup for Pembroke: Curley Locklear 10, Gervais Oxendine 8; Jimmy Ray Locklear 8; Steve Jones 12, and Benford Hardin 7. Pembroke subs: Bemus Blue 2; J. P. "Rooster" Smith 5; Johnny Sampson, 2; Bruce Swett; Ed Chavis 2; Jerry Lowry 2; and Dennis Clark 4. Pembroke coach is Jydor Locklear.

Starting lineup for Prospect: Ronald Brewer 9; Sherwood Locklear 4; Claude Moore 2; Harleywell Oxendine, and Freddie Oxendine. Prospect subs: Harold Harris 5; Ronald Strickland, Truman Lowry 4; James Flanagan, P.R. Bullard, James W. Brewer, and James "Dick" Locklear, Truman Oxendine and Clement Bullard, Jr.. Prospect coach is Reese Locklear.

The Robesonian, Lumberton, NC
Friday, March 3, 1961, Page 7

Pembroke Boys, Fairgrove Girls Win

PEMBROKE TOPS MAGNOLIA FOR BOYS CROWN

By Walter Oxendine, Special Correspondent

Fairgrove girls and Pembroke boys are the winners of the 1961 Robeson County Indian Basketball Tournament for the second straight year. Fairgrove won its crown by defeating Magnolia 68-38 and Pembroke copped its championship with a 49-43 win over Magnolia here at the Lumberton Armory Saturday night.

Pembroke went into the tournament with an advantage based on the best record in season play. Magnolia was second in the standing, Fairgrove third, and Prospect fourth. Pembroke, taking advantage of its prestige, downed Magnolia with Curley Locklear popping in 19 points. His 19 points was the highest for both teams, but he was followed closely by Carnell Oxendine of Magnolia who collected 18 points.

Pembroke was the defending champion and Magnolia was the defending runner-up.

Pembroke's Steve Jones started the scoring for both teams on a field goal from out front. Magnolia came down and Carnell Oxendine hit to establish the first tie of the game. After this tie, Magnolia tied the game twice more and Pembroke also tied it twice.

During the first quarter and about six minutes of the second quarter, the lead changed back and forth, but Curley Locklear's shooting from the side gave Pembroke a 32-25 lead at half time. The half ended with a scramble for the ball under the Magnolia basket.

When the second half began, Magnolia shifted into a man-to-man defense. After a free throw by Wendell Lowry and three field goals by Carnell Oxendine, the game was tied for the fourth time. A field goal by Steve Jones and a free throw by Gervais Oxendine gave Pembroke a three point lead.

Magnolia's Carnell Oxendine came through with a three point play and the game was tied again. Curley Locklear of Pembroke broke the 35-35 tie and Pembroke began to roll and held the lead until the game ended.

At the end of the third quarter, Pembroke had a 39-36 lead. Both teams played steady during the fourth quarter except in the last three minutes. Pembroke set up a freeze play to protect its lead, and Magnolia started its close man-to-man defense to try to over come Pembroke's lead, but they committed costly fouls and Pembroke hit on free throws to maintain the slim lead which they held until the final horn blew.

Curley Locklear
Pembroke High School

Photo: 1962 Pembroke State College Yearbook, *The Indianhead*

Gervais Oxendine
Pembroke High School

Photo: 1964 Pembroke State College Yearbook, *The Indianhead*

Fairgrove Girls Win

Fairgrove girls won their second straight championship behind the high scoring of Janice Sealey, who scored 35 points as they downed Magnolia 68-38 in the first game of the evening.

Magnolia played a hard game, but they were unable to stop the scoring of Sealey, who was helped in the scoring by Brenda Ransom with 15 points and Dorothy Lewis with 14. Janette Hunt had a good night for Magnolia as she scored 21 points.

In the first quarter Fairgrove started using their advantage of height and experience as they racked up a number of points and continued to do so until the game ended.

At the end of the first half, Fairgrove had a comfortable 40-20 lead. Magnolia failed to even closely overcome the lead and Fairgrove went on to clinch their championship.

Magnolia was awarded the runner-up trophy in the girls division.

The second game of the evening matched Fairgrove boys against Prospect boys is which Fairgrove won 50-37. Gary Sanderson scored 15 for Fairgrove and Leon Harris had 9 for Prospect.

During the first three quarters it looked like Prospect would give Fairgrove a rough game until the finish, but Fairgrove got hot in the last quarter to walk away with the victory.

Fairgrove was awarded the runner-up trophy in the round-robin tournament because they defeated Magnolia and Prospect but lost to Pembroke for the second best record.

In the game played Friday night, Magnolia defeated Prospect and Pembroke defeated Fairgrove.

Starting lineup for Pembroke: Curley Locklear 19, Gervais Oxendine 7, Jimmy Ray Locklear 6, Steve Jones 8, and Benford Hardin 5. Pembroke subs: Bemus Blue, 4.

Starting lineup for Magnolia: Wendell Lowry 5, Ray Chavis 6, Carnell Oxendine 18, Gerald Locklear 8, and Jerry Baker 6. Magnolia subs: Billy Fields.

Starting lineup Fairgrove girls: Guards - Brenda Ransom 15, Janice Sealey 35, and Dorothy Lewis 14. Forwards - R. Locklear, L. Mitchell, and L. Oxendine. Fairgrove subs: Guards - P. Hunt, F. Chavis 2, and E. Hunt 2. Forwards - A. Hunt, V. Brooks, and V. Chavis.

Starting lineup for Magnolia girls: Guards - Letha Brewer 15, J. Hunt 21, and C. Knight 2. Forwards - L. Chavis, L. F. Chavis, and E. Bell. Forwards - B. Jacobs.

Starting lineup for Fairgrove: Jesse Freeman 12, James E. Hunt 5, Montford Sanderson 6, and Wilbert Strong 11. Fairgrove subs: P. Hunt 1, James H. Oxendine, A. Cummings, and G. Jones.

Starting lineup for Prospect: Sherwood Locklear 7, Clement Bullard,Jr, Leon Harris 9, Claude Moore 7, and Harleywell Oxendine 4. Prospect subs: P. R. Bullard, Freddie Oxendine 4, and Truman Lowry 6.

**The Robesonian, Lumberton, NC
Friday, March 3, 1961, Page 7**

Inter-Area Cage Tourney Is On

PEMBROKE - A basketball tournament involving East Carolina High School, Clinton: Les Maxwell, Fayetteville: and Hawk Eye High School, Raeford, will be played this weekend.

Friday night's games, beginning at 7:30 o'clock will be played in the gym at East Carolina High School, Clinton: Saturday's beginning at 7:30 o'clock at Haw Eye High School, Raeford.

Coaches for the teams are: Hawk Eye, Forace Oxendine, Les Maxwell, Tommy D. Swett; East Carolina: Furman Brewer.

In games last week, the Pembroke State College All-Star boys lost to Hawk Eye boys, but the College All-Star girls lost.

The Robesonian, Lumberton, NC
Friday, February 23, 1962, Page 7

AT RECREATION CENTER

Robeson Indians Tourney Starts

The Robeson County Indian Conference basketball tournament opens here at the Lumberton Recreation Center tonight for a three-day run. This year's playoff will have junior varsity and varsity teams playing, but there will not be any girls team in action.

Pembroke's jayvees meet Fairgrove tonight at 7 p.m. in the opening game, and the Magnolia and Fairgrove varsity teams battle in the nightcaps. Two more games are on tap for Friday. Prospect and Magnolia clash in the junior varsity tilt, and the Pembroke and Prospect varsities play.

Winners of the junior varsity games tonight and Friday will play for the jayvee championship Saturday evening. Varsity teams will follow the same pattern. Pembroke is defending champion of the tournament, after having made a clean sweep of the 1961 event. Pembroke is coached by Jydor Locklear.

The Robesonian, Lumberton, NC
Thursday, March 15, 1962, Page 9

Fairgrove, Pembroke Teams Win Indian Tourney Openers

By Walter Oxendine, Special Correspondent

Fairgrove's varsity downed Magnolia's varsity by a score of 38-15 and Pembroke's jayvees defeated Fairgrove's jayvees 43-25 in the first games of the Robeson County Indian Tournament at the Lumberton Recreation Center Thursday night.

There was much action by both teams in the varsity game, but Fairgrove produced more effort which enabled them to win by a margin of 24 points.

Wilbert Strong and James E. Hunt combined to score 21 points to lead Fairgrove's scoring, with Strong collecting 11 and Hunt 10. Grady Harris was high man for Magnolia with 4 points.

Neither team scored during the first four minutes, but a steal by James H. Oxendine and a fast break with Oxendine scoring on the play started the scoring. Magnolia came down and Grady Harris scored a jumper from the free throw line, but Fairgrove could not be stopped as they continued to add to their total.

Magnolia tried different plays most of the time and were unable to do much scoring, while Fairgrove free-lanced and ran the...

SECOND GAME

In the first game of the evening, Pembroke's jayvees handed Fairgrove's jayvees a 43-25 loss.

Ray Brayboy of Pembroke led both teams in scoring with a total of 17 points. He was followed by Jimmie Cummings of Fairgrove who collected 8.

The first few minutes of the game was played on even terms, then Brayboy got two lay-ups and Pembroke began to climb. At half time the score was 20-10 in favor of Pembroke.

During the first half both teams played a zone defense, but in the third quarter, Fairgrove started a man for man defense and managed to cut Pembroke's lead from 20 to 13, but when the final horn blew, Pembroke had worked back up to a 18 point lead.

Tonight at the Recreation Center Prospect's jayvees play Magnolia's jayvees at 7 p.m. and Pembroke's varsity goes against Prospect's varsity in the nightcap.

The Robesonian, Lumberton, NC
Friday, May 16, 1962, Page 8

Fairgrove Takes Robeson Indian Meet

CHAMPIONS END 2-YEAR REIGN BY PEMBROKE

By Walter Oxendine, Special Correspondent

Fairgrove High School now reigns as the new champs of the Robeson County High Schools by defeating the defending Pembroke champs 45-39 in the final game of the Robeson County Indian Tournament Saturday night at the Lumberton Recreation Center.

The Pembroke jayvees retained their jayvee crown by downing the Prospect jayvees 38-27.

There was a packed crowd of over 1,000 on hand to see Pembroke and Fairgrove play one of the most exciting and thrilling games in the history of the tournament.

From the beginning to the final horn, there was much action and tenseness by both teams, but the extra steam put on in the last quarter by Fairgrove helped them to obtain their 1961-62 championship.

Each member of the starting five for Fairgrove scored seven or more points of the final total except one of them. James E. Hunt led their scoring with 12 points and was followed by team-mates Ardeen Hunt and James H. Oxendine with 9 each.

Johnny Sampson of Pembroke was high scorer for both teams with a total of 13 points. He was followed by teammate Bruce Swett who added 12.

Fairgrove began the scoring on a jump shot by Wilbert Strong and they managed to keep the lead throughout most of the game, but Pembroke played hard and tied the game four times.

The score at the end of the first quarter was 11-10 in favor of Fairgrove, and when the first half ended they led by a score of 25-23.

The first half ended with Pembroke taking possession of the ball after Fairgrove had held it with 26 seconds to go for one shot.

When the third quarter started Pembroke got hot and managed to obtain a 34-33 lead when the quarter ended.

In the fourth period the odds changed. The Fairgrove defense held Pembroke to 5 points while scoring 12 themselves. Pembroke had a chance to cut Fairgrove's lead from the free throw line, but failed to do so when they missed on their last three free throws, and Fairgrove made their last three which insured their victory.

Pembroke gained the right to enter the finals against Fairgrove, which defeated Magnolia Thursday night, by beating Prospect 56-43 in a well played game Friday night.

Jerry Deese of Pembroke and Ronald Brewer of Prospect captured scoring honors with 15 points each in that game.

Also on Friday night, the jayvees from Prospect managed to edge out Magnolia jayvees 37-34 which enabled them to play in the final against Pembroke, which defeated Fairgrove Thursday night.

Purcell Locklear collected 13 points for Prospect and Dexter Brewington of Magnolia collected 9 to lead their teams in scoring.

Pembroke jayvees held on to their championship by defeating Prospect Jayvees 38-27 in a thrilling final game.

Ray Brayboy who was high scorer Thursday night against Fairgrove, captured the scoring honor again by scoring 13 points for Pembroke. He was followed by George Oxendine who collected 11. Oxendine scored three baskets early in the third quarter which enabled Pembroke to establish a small lead which they held until the game ended.

Carl Chavis and Burlie Locklear collected 8 points each to lead Prospect's scoring.

During the first half, both teams played a tight game and the score was tied four times, but Prospect controlled most of the rebounds and managed to post a 17-15 lead at intermission. The first half ended after Johnny Oxendine of Pembroke missed a shot on a fast break play.

In the second half Pembroke began to control the boards, and they scored 23 points while holding Prospect to 10. Prospect committed some costly fouls in the second half when they started a pressing defense and also on rebounds, and before the game ended, three of their starters had fouled out.

VARSITY GAME

Pembroke	13	15	12	16	52
Prospect	9	10	10	14	43

Pembroke		**Prospect**	
Johnny Sampson	10	Freddie Oxendine	12
James Smith	12	Mitchell Brewer	15
Jerry Deese	15	Harleywell Oxendine	6
Jerry Lowry	4	Claude Moore	5
Bruce Swett	10	P. R. Bullard	3

Pembroke subs: Mike Clark 5, Jimmy Sampson, J. Locklear, Tony Brewington, D. Webster, and Robbie Lowry.

Prospect subs: Truman Oxendine 1, Truman Lowry.

VARSITY GAME

Fairgrove	11	14	8	12	45
Pembroke	10	13	11	5	39

Fairgrove		**Pembroke**	
Ardeen Hunt	9	Johnny Sampson	13
James E. Hunt	12	Jms. "Rooster" Smith	12
Wilbert Strong	7	Jerry Deese	4
Jm H. Oxendine	9	Jerry Lowry	
Charlie Sanderson		Bruce Swett	12

Fairgrove subs: Levon Sealey 3
Pembroke Subs: Clark 8.

JAYVEE GAME

Pembroke	7	8	17	6	38
Prospect	7	10	4	6	27

Pembroke		**Prospect**	
Ray Brayboy	13	Wyvis Oxendine	
George Oxendine	11	Mitchell Brewer	2
Van Lowry	2	Purcell Locklear	5
Johnny Oxendine		Burlie Locklear	5
Robert Earl Deese	5	Talford Dial	4

Pembroke subs: Robert Deese 7, E. B. Smith.
Prospect subs: Carl Chavis 8, Charles Locklear, W. Lowry, Harold Chavis.

JAYVEE GAME

Prospect	12	7	8	10	37
Magnolia	11	7	6	9	33

Prospect		**Magnolia**	
Wyvis Oxendine		Leon Jones	2
Mitchell Brewer		Willie Revels	
Purcell Locklear	13	Jr. Rogers	6
Burlie Locklear	10	Dexter Brewington	11
Talford Dial	3	B. Oxendine	10

Prospect subs: Dell Harris, Carl Chavis 9, W. Lowry
Magnolia subs: Ertle Hunt 4, Stanley Morrison.

The Robesonian, Lumberton, NC
Monday, March 19, 1962, Page 9

Freddie Oxendine
Prospect High School

Photo: 1964 Pembroke State College Yearbook, *The Indianhead*

Robeson Indian Tournament Begins Abbreviated Play

Semifinal action in the Robeson County Indian Basketball Tournament begins here at the Lumberton Recreation Center tonight with junior varsity games scheduled.

The Pembroke jayvees, defending champions in that circle, meet Fairgrove at 7 p.m., and Magnolia's varsity takes on defending champion Fairgrove at 8:30 p.m.

Magnolia's jayvees and Pembroke's varsity, which do not play until Wednesday night, got a bye in the first round on the basis of the best won-loss records of terms in the tournament.

This year's tournament was cut from four to three teams in each division when Prospect elected to withdraw from the playoff. Prospect staged its own invitational meet last week with teams from Hawkeye, Les Maxwell and Sampson High Schools.

Wednesday night will see the champions of the abbreviated Robeson tournament crowned. Tonight's jayvee winner plays Magnolia Wednesday at 7 p.m. and tonight's varsity victor plays Pembroke at 8:30 p.m.

Pembroke's varsity and Magnolia's junior varsity lost only one game each during the season.

Trophies will be presented to each of the winning teams.

The Robesonian, Lumberton, NC
Tuesday, March 19, 1963, Page 7

Pembroke, Fairgrove Teams Win First Tournament Tilts

By Walter Oxendine, Special Correspondent

The 1962-63 Robeson County Indian Basketball Tournament got under way Tuesday night here in the Lumberton Recreation Center with the Fairgrove varsity and Pembroke jayvees taking victories in the first night of action.

In the preliminary game the jayvees of Pembroke high school, coached by Jydor Locklear, defeated Fairgrove 31-14. Fairgrove is coached by Ralph Hunt.

A small crowd of about 300 fans watched the second contest of the evening as Fairgrove's varsity, defending champions, defeated Magnolia 46-26.

Fairgrove had a height advantage which proved efficient as they controlled both boards throughout the game.

Levon Sealey of Fairgrove led both teams in scoring with 15 points, while Leon Jones was high for Magnolia with 10.

At the beginning of the game Magnolia took the lead on a layup by Dexter Brewington. Levon Sealey scored on a free throw, and Leon Jones of Magnolia collected one and the score was 3-1 in favor of Magnolia. A long jump shot from outside by Sealey tied the score at 3-3 with five minutes 37 seconds left in the quarter, and after the tie was broken Fairgrove held the upper hand throughout the remainder of the game and increased its margin steadily.

A zone defense was used by Fairgrove to cut Magnolia's scoring, and fast breaks and screen plays helped build the lead.

Fairgrove led 23-12 at halftime as the half ended with both teams scraping for a loose ball.

The defending champions kept up their scoring pace in the second half, and Magnolia was unable to come from behind.

Ralph Hunt also coached the Fairgrove varsity, while Magnolia is coached by Ned Sampson.

In the first game of the evening the Pembroke junior varsity showed strong determination to capture the opening jayvee portion of the tournament. Jimmy Oxendine of Pembroke got scoring honors for both teams with 10 points, and Earl Deese was high man for Fairgrove with five.

Tonight's final championship action brings together Pembroke's jayvees and Magnolia at 7:15, and the Pembroke varsity and Fairgrove in the second game at approximately 8:45.

JAYVEE GAME

Pembroke	5	6	10	10	31
Fairgrove	8	4	0	2	14

Pembroke		**Fairgrove**	
Larry Sampson	6	B. Hunt	
Johnny Oxendine		Earl Deese	5
Robert Deese	6	R. Hunt	
Harvey Lowry	1	J. Oxendine	4
Jimmy Oxendine	10	J. Hunt	

Pembroke subs: J. Dial, B. Locklear 2, Kent Sampson 6.
Fairgrove subs: Jim Hunt 5, C. Hunt 2, K. Hunt.

VARSITY GAME

Fairgrove	11	12	10	13	46
Magnolia	5	7	8	6	26

Fairgrove		**Magnolia**	
Ardeen Hunt	1	Grady Harris	6
Jesse Freeman	10	J. Hunt	6
Levon Sealey	15	Dexter Brewington	6
Bobby Mitchell	8	Leon Jones	10
Bobby Lewis	9	Junior Rogers	

Fairgrove subs: Larece Hunt, J. Carter, Alford Hunt 1, Montford Sanderson, Jimmy R. Hunt, Jesse A. Oxendine 2.

Magnolia subs: G. Hunt, W. Carter, Ronnie Baker.

The Robesonian, Lumberton, NC
Wednesday, March 20, 1963, Page 8

Ardeen Hunt
Fairgrove High School

Photo: 1964 Pembroke State College
Yearbook, *The Indianhead*

Fairgrove Retains Varsity Crown; Pembroke JV's Win Fourth Straight Title

By Walter Oxendine, Special Correspondent

Fairgrove remained as champion of Robeson County Indian High Schools Wednesday night as they defeated Pembroke 44-40 in double overtime in the championship game of the Robeson Indian tournament played at the Lumberton Recreation Center.

In the first game of the evening the Pembroke Jayvees maintained championship honors by downing Magnolia 26-15.

A capacity crowd witnessed one of the best games in the history of the tournament. Fairgrove, backed by the sharp shooting of Levon Sealey, considered as the tournament's most valuable player, defeated Pembroke for their second straight championship.

Sealey led the way in scoring with 14 points, but he was followed closely by teammate Bobby Lewis with 13. Jerry Deese and Bruce Swett shared scoring honors for Pembroke with 12 each.

The lead changed many times during the back-and-forth game. Fairgrove obtained the first lead on a jump shot by Bobby Lewis and Swett tied it up with a jumper. After this, the lead changed 20 more times before the final count. Highest margin earned by either team was six points which Pembroke racked up in the third quarter.

Tension mounted as the game progressed, and the hustling and sharp shooting by both teams led to the double overtime climax. Each team used a man-to-man defense which accounted for numerous fouls.

Pembroke led by three points, 21-18, at intermission, but Fairgrove came back strong during the third quarter and took the lead with approximately 2:39 minutes left in the period.

During the fourth quarter both teams played equal ball, and with 12 seconds left to play in the regulation game, Fairgrove had possession and set up a play for one shot. Their attempt failed and the regulation game ended in a 38-38 deadlock.

In the first overtime only two field goals were scored, one by Levon Sealey of Fairgrove and one by Johnny Sampson of Pembroke. The second overtime began with the teams tied 40-40, and Ardeen Hunt scored on a layup for Fairgrove. Fairgrove regained possession and froze the ball for a minute and a half. Later during another freeze a Pembroke player fouled Fairgrove's Bobby Mitchell with 12 seconds left to play, and he sank both shots from the foul line to assure the victory.

During regular season play Pembroke defeated Fairgrove three times out of four times.

In the opening preliminary game Pembroke's jayvees romped to their fourth straight tournament championship. Johnny Oxendine of Pembroke led both teams in scoring with 11 points, and Willie Revels was high for Magnolia with five.

The score was close all the way, but Pembroke held Magnolia scoreless from the floor in the final quarter while scoring four field goals themselves for the extra margin.

Championship trophies were presented to the winners and runnerup of each game.

JAYVEE GAME

Pembroke..........6	6	6	8		26
Magnolia 5	5	4	1		15

Pembroke		**Magnolia**	
Larry Sampson	4	Stanley Morrison	
Johnny Oxendine	11	Willie Revels	5
Robert Deese	7	Ertle Hunt	4
Harvey Lowry	2	Glenn Maynor	4
Jimmy Oxendine		S. Locklear	

Pembroke subs: Kent Sampson 2

Magnolia subs: D. Locklear 2, Harold Bell, Jack Morgan.

VARSITY GAME

Pembroke	11	10	10	7	2	0	40
Fairgrove	12	6	13	9	2	4	44

Pembroke		**Fairgrove**	
Johnny Sampson	9	Ardeen Hunt	6
Jerry Deese	12	Jesse Freeman	2
Bruce Sweet	12	Levon Sealey	14
Ray Brayboy		Bobby Mitchell	6
George Oxendine	7	Bobby Lewis	13

Pembroke subs: Robbie Lowry.

Fairgrove subs: Larece Hunt 3.

Fairgrove High School Boys 1963 Robeson County Indian Tournament Champions	**Pembroke High School 1963 Robeson County Boys Indian Tournament Runner Up**
Ralph Hunt, Coach	Jydor Locklear, Coach
Ardeen Hunt	Johnny Sampson
Larece Hunt	Jerry Deese
Jesse Freeman	Bruce Swett
Levon Sealey	Ray Brayboy
Bobby Mitchell	George Oxendine
Bobby Lewis	Robbie Lowry
Montford Sanderson	
Jimmy R. Hunt	
Jesse A. Oxendine	
Jimmy Cummings	

**The Robesonian, Lumberton, NC
Thursday, March 21, 1963, Page 11**

INDIAN TOURNAMENT COMMENCES
Fairgrove, Magnolia Win
By Walter Oxendine, Special Correspondent

The 1964 Robeson County Indian Tournament, with one team participating from Hoke County, got under way Friday night with Magnolia girls defeating Prospect girls in a consolation game and Fairgrove High defeating Hawkeye High from Hoke County in the second game of the evening played at Pembroke State College gymnasium.

In the second round Saturday night, Pembroke Jayvees downed Prospect, and in the second game, Magnolia High upset Prospect High 50-46.

In Friday night action, Letha Brewer led Magnolia girls in a consolation game in defeating Prospect girls 38-26 in triple overtime. Letha also scored the winning two points in the final overtime with 52 seconds left to play. Prospect was unable to tie the score before time ran out.

Magnolia led at half time 11-8, but Prospect came back strong in the second half behind the sharp shooting of Evelyn Bryant who scored 14 points, and the lead changed back and forth and the game was tied five times. Both teams had chances to go ahead in the game, but failed to do so, and this resulted in a thrilling game which ended in sudden death with Magnolia coming out on top.

Fairgrove, in the second game of the evening, made their chances good for retaining their title as "Champs" of the Robeson County Indian High Schools, by downing Hawkeye High from Hoke County, 72-36. This win for Fairgrove gave them the right to play in the finals against the winner of the Pembroke - Magnolia game to be played this Friday night.

A height advantage and sharp shooting started Fairgrove on their way soon as the game began, and behind the scoring of Jesse Freeman with 13 points and Levon Sealey with 9 points, Fairgrove built up a lead which they held until the game ended. Fairgrove's starting five only played one quarter or more, and substitutes were used the remaining part of the game.

Hawkeye entered the Robeson County Tournament after they won the Hoke County Indian Tournament last weekend, but Fairgrove used their size and experience to down the young hard playing team from Hawkeye.

Albert Carter who played the post for Hawkeye was high scorer for his team with 11 points, and team mate Charles R. Locklear contributed 8 points.

All of Fairgrove's players scored except one, with Jesse Freeman leading them with 13 points, followed by substitute Carl Deese with 10 points.

At half time, Fairgrove had compiled a 39-15 lead, which Hawkeye was unable to overcome. When the third quarter started, Fairgrove started hitting from out front and from the side, and Hawkeye missed scoring opportunities by bad passes, when they were breaking for the basket. Fast breaks also accounted for points by both teams, and the final horn sounded when Charles Hunt was fouled as he was bringing the ball down court. He ended the game with a one and one situation by making his first shot and missing his second.

Fairgrove, coached by Ralph Hunt, will meet the winners of the Pembroke - Magnolia game, which be played Friday night, Saturday night for the championship.

Saturday night's action saw Pembroke J.V.'s in the first game of the evening winning the right to participate in the Jayvee's finals by defeating Prospect Jayvee's in a hard fought game 82-57.

During the first half, both teams looked like a couple of small colleges playing by the way they were consistently scoring and hitting on a good percentage of their shots. When the half ended, Pembroke was out front 34-28.

Kent Sampson captured the scoring honors both teams with 35 points, and team mate Roger Lowry added 21 points for the winners.

Danny Dial was high man for Prospect with 17 points. Pembroke Jayvee's will play the winner of the Fairgrove - Magnolia Jayvee game, which will be played this Friday night, Saturday night for the championship.

In the second game of the evening Magnolia, coached by Ned Sampson, defeated favored Prospect 50-46, in a thrill packed game.

Magnolia was small in size compared to Prospect, but used give and go plays for easy baskets. A tight zone by Magnolia forced Prospect to take some bad shots which hurt them, and Magnolia made the difference in the final score by easy baskets and from the free throw line.

Both teams played hard, and at half time Prospect held the lead 22-21 on a free throw by Talford Dial. The half ended when Purcell Locklear of Prospect lost the ball out of bounds under his own goal.

When the second half began, Prospect got the tip, but the ball was stolen by Leon Jones of Magnolia. Joseph Oxendine of Magnolia tied the score at 22 all with 6:30 left in the third quarter. This was just of the many times that the score was tied, and the lead changed several times.

Magnolia kept the ball out front, to run give and go plays, which caused Prospect to make costly fouls, and Magnolia took advantage by making the free throws especially in one and one situations.

Mike Flannagan started a drive for Prospect in the final quarter by hitting three straight field goals, but Magnolia managed to keep calm during this situation, as well as when Prospect used a full court press against them.

Talford Dial had 14 points for Prospect, and Tim Locklear was high for Magnolia with 13 points.

Magnolia will meet Pembroke this Friday night in the Semi-finals to determine who will play Fairgrove Saturday night for the Championship.

FRIDAY NIGHT

Magnolia — Prospect Girls

Magnolia	9	2	9	8	28
Prospect	4	4	8	10	26

Magnolia		Prospect	
Letha Brewer	20	Evelyn Bryant	16
Carter	2	A. Chavis	
Chavis	6	Judy Bullard	
B. Locklear		Hunt	2
L. Locklear		Carolyn Chavis	
Smith		Barbara Bullard	4

Magnolia subs: R. Locklear; & Oxendine
Prospect subs: L. Bryant 2; Judy Chavis 2

Fairgrove — Hawkeye Boys

Fairgrove	22	17	17	16	72
Hawkeye	6	9	13	8	36

Fairgrove		Hawkeye	
Larece Hunt	2	Bobby Cooper	6
Jesse Freeman	13	Luther Locklear	7
Bobby Mitchell	7	Albert Carter	11
Levon Sealey	9	Charles R. Locklear	8
Jimmy R. Hunt	3	Dial	4

Fairgrove subs: J.O. Oxendine 3; D. Oxendine 2;
C. Hunt 1; R. Hunt 4; J. Oxendine 5; B. Hunt; Brooks 5;
J. Hunt; & Deese 10.
Hawkeye subs: Jimmy Locklear; Ozell Jacobs; Charles
Locklear.

SATURDAY NIGHT

Pembroke — Prospect JV's

Pembroke	14	20	26	22	82
Prospect	10	18	17	19	57

VARSITY

Magnolia		Prospect	
Dexter Brewington	6	Burlie Locklear	1
Tim Locklear		Mike Flanagan	6
Hunt	10	Gary Woods	
Stanley Morrison	5	Talford Dial	14
Jones	7	Wyvis Oxendine	3

Magnolia subs: Chavis 1, Joseph Oxendine 7
Prospect subs: Dell Harris 3, Johnnie Jacobs 9,
Arlie Jacobs, Virgil Dial

__The Robesonian__, Lumberton, NC
__Monday, March 2, 1964, Page 8__

Larece Hunt
Fairgrove High School

Photo courtesy of Larece Hunt

Fairgrove Wins Third Time

PEMBROKE - A capacity crowd at Pembroke State College gymnasium watched as Fairgrove High School retained their title as "Champs" of the Robeson County Indian High Schools for the third year in a row by defeating Pembroke High School 35-33 in the most thrill-packed game in the history of Indian High School Tournaments, in the final round of tournament action Saturday night.

In the preliminary game of the finals Pembroke Jayvees scored their sixth championship in six attempt by downing Magnolia Jayvees 25-20.

In the third round of tournament action Friday night, Magnolia Jayvees earned a right to play in the finals by defeating Fairgrove in overtime 40-38.

John Bass of Magnolia captured scoring honors for both teams with 20 points. Bass was the team play maker for Magnolia, but scored on out side shots frequently, and on drive in layups. He also scored the winning two points in the overtime with 5 seconds remaining to be played.

Kenny Hunt was high man for Fairgrove with 12 points.

Friday's night second game of the evening, Jimmy Oxendine, who was playing in his first tournament game, scored 16 points to lead Pembroke High to a 37-19 victory over Magnolia High.

A tight zone defense by both teams kept the scoring down in the first half, but Pembroke came back in the second half with a man for man defense and managed to get possession of the ball more often than they did in the first half, which enabled them to pull away from Magnolia in scoring.

Magnolia used a Shuffle offense, and worked for the good shot, but Pembroke's height advantage kept them from scoring frequently, and Pembroke controlled most of the rebounds.

The half ended in favor of Pembroke 16-9 after Leon Jones of Magnolia was called for traveling. Magnolia was working the ball for one shot, but Pembroke got possession of the ball with 10 seconds remaining, and Robert Lowry took a shot with 4 seconds left to play and missed. The ball was going out of bounds, but Jerry Deese threw it back, and Larry Sampson took a shot after the horn sounded which was good, but did not count.

In the final half, Pembroke used screen plays for easy points, and Magnolia was unable to catch up in scoring.

Stanley Morrison scored 7 points for Magnolia in a good effort for his team, but Pembroke's size made the difference, and the game ended by Jimmy Oxendine of Pembroke scoring 2 points, and making the score 37-19 in favor of Pembroke.

Saturday night action in the final championship games proved to be two of the best games ever played by two Jayvee and Varsity teams.

In the opening game of the finals, Pembroke Jayvees managed to defeat Magnolia Jayvees 25-20 without the help of Kent Sampson, who scored 35 points for Pembroke against Prospect in the opening round of the tournament last week-end.

Sampson was out because of illness, but Pembroke worked together and scored the win which gave them their sixth championship in six years of tournament play.

Michael Clark, who was the smallest player on both teams, proved to be as big as anyone by scoring valuable points in the first half which enabled Pembroke to lead 14-8 at half time. Although Clark had 9 points for Pembroke, Gary W. Locklear was high man with 10 points, and John Bass was high man for Magnolia with 10 points also.

Both teams played good defensive ball, but on offense, Pembroke used their tall center Gary W. Locklear to score needed points. Locklear also scored the final two points in the game, and the horn sounded as Magnolia was bringing the ball down court.

The Championship game Saturday night between Fairgrove High and Pembroke High provided much excitement and action until the final horn had sounded, Fairgrove came out on top 35-33 for their third championship in a row.

It was Fairgrove all the way in the first half, and early in the game they started running up the score behind the sharp jump shooting of Bobby Mitchell.

Jimmy Oxendine scored the first two points for Pembroke at 5:57 in the first quarter, and contributed a free throw afterwards, but Fairgrove had a 7-3 lead, and stayed out front. They led 23-15 at the half.

Fairgrove played a tight zone against Pembroke, and forced them to make bad passes and they lost the ball quite a few times. Pembroke also used a zone defense, but Fairgrove connected on shots from out front, which helped them to obtain their lead which they had at half time.

The second half proved to be a different game. Pembroke came back strong, and started connecting on easy shots which they had been missing during the first half, and also started getting a few of the rebounds which Fairgrove had been controlling the majority of the first half. Jerry Deese started the drive for Pembroke by tipping in two points at 7:28 in the third quarter, and added other valuable points in the same quarter to cut Fairgrove's lead to 30-27 when the quarter ended.

The Robesonian, Lumberton, NC
Monday, March 9, 1964, Page 6

INDIAN TOURNAMENT
Prospect, Magnolia Makes The Finals

PEMBROKE - Prospect's varsity and Magnolia's jayvees won games here Thursday night to advance to the finals of the Robeson County Indian Basketball Tournament.

Prospect will play tonight's Pembroke Hawkeye winner in the varsity championship game Saturday night, and Magnolia will play tonight's Pembroke-Hawkeye jayvees in the Saturday preliminary.

Prospect edged Fairgrove 44-43 in last's night varsity battle as Mike Flannagan of Prospect and Jimmy Hunt of Fairgrove led their respective teams. Flannagan, the big horse this year for Prospect, and Hunt staged a two-man battle under the boards in addition to topping their teams in scoring.

Flannagan proved to be the turning point in the game for Prospect with three minutes to go. As Fairgrove led, Flannagan made the shot to tie the score and then put Prospect in the lead. Fairgrove came back to tie the score 40-40 with a minute to play, and Flannagan broke the tie for the final lead.

Larece Hunt combined with Jimmy Hunt to pace the floor play for Fairgrove.

VARSITY GAME

Prospect	10	8	14	12	44
Fairgrove	15	6	13	10	43

JAYVEE GAME

Magnolia	12	8	8	15	43
Fairgrove	1	6	7	8	22

Prospect		Fairgrove	
Mike Flannagan	18	Larece Hunt	9
Burlie Locklear	8	Bobby Hunt	5
Wyvis Oxendine	8	Robert Lewis	4
Purcell Locklear	8	Jimmy Hunt	21
Talford Dial	7	Jerry Hunt	4

Prospect subs: Jimmy Jones, Jimmy Goins, Danford Dial, Virgil Dial, Harold Chavis.

Fairgrove subs: Alford Hunt, K. Hunt, Chavis, J. Locklear.

Magnolia		Fairgrove	
Jimmy Hammond	10	Freeman	1
Billy Blanks	7	Brooks	2
Harry Canady	7	W. Oxendine	8
Tonto Locklear	10	K. Hunt	
Maynor	7	B. Hunt	5

Magnolia subs: James McGirt 2, Jimmy Maynor, and Bill Blanks.

Fairgrove subs: Larry Freeman, Jacobs 6, McNeill, Cummings, Lewis, and Deese.

**The Robesonian, Lumberton, NC
Friday, February 26, 1965**

Joe Swinson
coached Prospect High School upset win over Pembroke

Photo: 1961 Pembroke State College Yearbook, *The Indianhead*

Prospect Upsets Pembroke 53-50 in Indian Final

CHAMPS PLACE THREE BOYS ON ALL-TOURNAMENT OUTFIT

By Bill Norment, *Robesonian* Sports Editor

PEMBROKE - Prospect High School, which finished the regular season in a second place with Fairgrove, upset Pembroke's defending champions 53-50 in the championship game of the Robeson County Indian Basketball Tournament here Saturday night.

All games were played here in the gym of Pembroke State College before standing room only crowds.

Pembroke beaten only by Rockingham's 3-A team among high schools this season, had a 20-4 record prior to meeting Prospect. Three of their losses were to military schools, and PSC was seeded first in the Robeson tournament. Pembroke had beaten Prospect twice during the regular season.

Big Mike Flannagan, who paced Prospect in scoring most of the year and in the first tournament game, yielded the floor to teammate Burlie Locklear who collected 17 points, but Flannagan retained his mastery of the backboards for Prospect.

Both Flannagan and Locklear, along with Talford Dial of Prospect, were placed on the all tournament team along with Kent Sampson of Pembroke and Larece Hunt of Fairgrove.

Prospect maintained a sizable 17-7 lead after the first quarter, but led by only two points at the half and by one after the third period.

Coach Jydor Locklear's Pembroke boys yielded five more points to Prospect at the start of the final quarter, but zipped back quickly to gain nine points and a 44-41 lead with 4:24 minutes to play.

Prospect tied the score 44-44 with 3:27 to go on Burlie Locklear's in and out layup, and the score was tied twice more before the victory. Pembroke knotted the count 50-50 on Jimmy Oxendine's jumper with 45 seconds to play for the final deadlock.

Talford Dial collected one of two free throws to snap the tie, and Dial added another foul toss when a technical was laid against the Pembroke bench. Wyvis Oxendine completed the scoring for Coach Joe Swinson's Prospect club with another free throw with nine seconds remaining.

Prospect had three players in double figures - Burlie Locklear with 17, Flannagan with 11, Wyvis Oxendine with 10. Kent Sampson led Pembroke with 17 points.

During awards presentations the championship game ball was presented to Mrs. Forace Oxendine in honor of her late husband and coach at Hawkeye High School for many years. Oxendine was also a star pitcher for the Pembroke Braves' semi-pro baseball teams.

The Pembroke junior varsity defeated Magnolia in the preliminary half of the championship doubleheader for the jayvee tournament title. Gary Locklear led Pembroke with 11 points, and Richard Oxendine had 10. Tonto Locklear was high for Magnolia with nine points.

VARSITY GAME

Prospect	17	5	14	17	53
Pembroke	7	13	15	15	50

PROSPECT		**PEMBROKE**	
Burlie Locklear	17	Kent Sampson	17
Mike Flannagan	11	Jimmy Oxendine	9
Purcell Locklear	7	Larry Sampson	7
Wyvis Oxendine	10	Geo. Oxendine	4
Talford Dial	8	Ray Brayboy	8

Prospect subs: None

Pembroke subs: Robert Deese 2, Gary Locklear 3

Prospect High School 1965 Robeson County Indian High School Tournament Champions

Joe Swinson, Coach
Cancel Chavis, Assistant Coach
Burlie Locklear
Purcell Locklear
Wyvis Oxendine
Talford Dial
Jimmy Jones
Danford Dial, Jr.
Jimmy Goins
Virgil Dial
Arlie Jacobs
Harold Chavis
Vincent Locklear
Guy Chavis
Mike Flanagan

Pembroke High School 1965 Robeson County Indian High School Tournament Runner-Up

Jydor Locklear, Coach
Kent Sampson
Jimmy Oxendine
Larry Sampson
George Oxendine
Ray Brayboy
Gary W. Locklear
Mike Clark
Robert Deese
Harvey Lowry, Jr.

The Robesonian, Lumberton, NC, Monday, March 1, 1965, Page 7

Photo courtesy of Joy Brayboy Locklear

Jydor Locklear
Coach, Pembroke High School

Indian Cage Tourney to Open Tonight

PEMBROKE - The Robeson County Indian basketball tournament begins here tonight with both junior varsity and varsity teams participating. There will be no girls games.

The opening round tonight will pair Fairgrove and Les Maxwell at 7 p.m., and Prospect and Hawkeye play at 8:30. Prospect is defending champion of the tournament, but the 1965 champions finished last in the new 6-team conference's regular season race this year.

Thursday night Wednesday's first game winner will play Pembroke's Eagles at 8:30. That game will be preceded by a jayvee game at 7:00. Friday the Prospect and Hawkeye varsities play at 8:30, and a jayvee game will also be played at 7 o'clock.

The championship games, both jayvees and varsity, will be played Saturday. Jayvees will start at 7 p.m., and the main title clash will begin at 8:30.

The Robesonian, Lumberton, NC
Wednesday, February 23, 1966

Fairgrove, Hawkeye Take Opening Wins At Pembroke

PEMBROKE - The 1966 Robeson County Indian tournament began Wednesday night at Pembroke State College with four games. The scores of the games played indicate that this will be of the best tournament in recent years.

In varsity competition, Fairgrove downed Les Maxwell 58-54 in the first game, and in the second contest Hawkeye defeated Prospect 63-54. In Junior varsity action, Hawkeye topped Prospect 26-17, and in the second game, Les Maxwell defeated Magnolia 50-18.

Varsity games were packed with action throughout each game, in that the winning margin for both teams that won was only 13 points.

Fairgrove used accurate shooting from outside to break the zone attack of Les Maxwell in the first varsity game, and managed to stay in front throughout the game. Les Maxwell depended on the fast breaks and ball movement to account for their scoring.

Ted Jones of Les Maxwell clinched the scoring honors in the game with 20 points, while Billy Hunt led the way for Fairgrove with 16 points.

In the second varsity tilt, Hawkeye relied on rebounding and ball movement to defeat Prospect, the defending champions. Prospect began the game with a zone defense, but Hawkeye was able to work the ball in for the close shot, and at half time, Hawkeye held a 30-26 lead. In the second half, Hawkeye took advantage of fast breaks, and built a lead of 20 points at one time. Later Prospect went to a full court press, and managed to get within 6 points of Hawkeye, but when the final horn blew, Hawkeye came out on top 63-54.

Phil Pierce set the scoring pace for Hawkeye with 22 points, while Ronnie Chavis was top man for Prospect with 14.

Hawkeye JV's, with the scoring of Carlton Locklear, who had 12 points, defeated the J.V's from Prospect 26-17 in the first game. Tony Locklear led the way for Prospect in scoring with 6 points. At the start of the game, both teams got off to a bad start with the score 11-8 at intermission in favor of Hawkeye. Both teams settled down in the second half, and began scoring, and turned in a good game for the evening with Hawkeye coming out victorious.

In the second J.V. game, Les Maxwell displayed good ball movement in fast breaks, and posted a 50-18 victory over Magnolia. Both teams played hard, but Les Maxwell's easy baskets on lay-ups, which developed on fast breaks, proved to be the deciding factor in the game.

Mitchell Hunt was top scorer for Les Maxwell with 16 points, and Tony Hunt was top man for Magnolia with 5.

Tonight's action sends Pembroke's Junior varsity against the J.V.'s from Hawkeye at 7:00, and in varsity competition, Pembroke plays Fairgrove at 8:30.

Fairgrove	15	12	17	14	58
Les Maxwell	9	12	17	16	54

Fairgrove		**Les Maxwell**	
Lewis, R.	13	Hunt	19
Freeman	9	Locklear, B.	9
Hunt, B.		Evans, Andy	2
Jacobs		Jones	20
Oxendine, J.	14	Locklear, N.	2

Fairgrove subs: Hunt, K.
Les Maxwell subs: Whitehead 2.

Hawkeye	20	10	12	21	63
Prospect	19	7	7	21	54

Hawkeye		**Prospect**	
Jacobs, Muriel	14	Chavis, Ronnie	14
Jacobs, Ozell	10	Jacobs, Arvin	6
Pierce, Phil	22	Bryant, Ronald	6
Dial, Joel	5	Chavis, G.	
Barton, Ronald	10	Dial, Carlton	8

Hawkeye subs: Charles Dial, Walter Lowry, Harold Dean Brewer 2, and Don Woods.
Prospect subs: Oxendine 2, Locklear 4, Woods 6, Jones 6, and Goins 2.

JAYVEE GAME

Les Maxwell	9	13	12	16	50
Magnolia	4	7	0	7	18

JAYVEE GAME

Hawkeye	2	9	4	11	26
Prospect	0	8	2	7	17

The Robesonian, Lumberton, NC
Thursday, February 24, 1966, Page 7

Sampson Scores 51 Points As Eagles Defeat Fairgrove

PEMBROKE - Kent Sampson of Pembroke High School did just about everything possible for a high school basketball player last night in leading his team to a 93-58 victory over Fairgrove in the Robeson County Indian Tournament semi-finals.

Sampson set an all time high scoring record in the tournament with 51 points on 22 field goals and 7 free throws. Exceptional shooting and accuracy from the floor proved to be the main factor in Sampson's scoring - which enabled him to also break his previous single game of 46 points.

The victors only had one other player in double figures. This was 6'7" center Gary Wayne Locklear with 18 points. Locklear also proved to be outstanding with his rebounding and his ability to block shots.

Pembroke had their problems at times in trying to move the ball against Fairgrove, but with the use of screens and picks they were able to get in for the lay-up which enabled them to post a 46-31 lead at half time.

In the first half, Fairgrove stayed within range of Pembroke behind the scoring of Robert Lewis, who had 15 points in the game, and Billy Hunt, with 13 points of their final total.

In the second half, Pembroke guards Mike Clark and Richard Oxendine led the defense. Fairgrove played an outstanding game, but were unable to cope with the height advantage which Pembroke had with Sampson and Locklear.

Pembroke's J.V.'s earned the right to play in the championship game Saturday night with a 66-27 victory over Hawkeye in the opening game.

Pembroke relied on the fast breaks in many cases which accounted for most of their scoring, while Hawkeye worked the ball into their center, Jimmy

Locklear, who scored 9 points in leading the scoring pace for Hawkeye.

James "Bunk" Maynor, who has been leading Pembroke in most of their recent games in scoring, also led in the game with 26 points. Maynor was followed in the scoring column for Pembroke by Bobby Oxendine with 16, Charles Graham 14, Selwyn Sampson 6, David Graham 2, Gerald Hunt 1, and Robert Sampson 1.

The following players along with Jimmy Locklear's 9 points also contributed to Hawkeye scoring: Elisha Dial 1, Roger Dial 2, Oscar Jacobs 8, Carlton Locklear 3, Jensen Locklear 2, and Steve Dial 2.

In defeating Fairgrove, Pembroke's Varsity will advance thewinner of the Magnolia - Hawkeye game, to be played at 8:30 tonight, for the championship Saturday night at 8:30, and Pembroke J.V.'s will play the winner of the Fairgrove - Lee Maxwell game that begins at 7:00 this evening at 7:00 Saturday.

| Pembroke | 29 | 17 | 20 | 27 | 93 |
| Fairgrove | 18 | 13 | 8 | 19 | 58 |

Pembroke		Fairgrove	
Kent Sampson	51	R. Lewis	15
G. W. Locklear	18	Freeman	6
Gary Locklear	2	B. Hunt	13
Richard Oxendine	7	Jacobs	10
Hunt	3	J. Oxendine	12

Pembroke subs: Chester Chavis 4, Hammonds, Clark 6, H. B. Locklear, J. Chavis 2.
Fairgrove subs: W. Oxendine, K. Hunt, J. R. Lewis 2.

JAYVEE GAME

| Pembroke | 15 | 14 | 17 | 20 | 66 |
| Hawkeye | 6 | 4 | 10 | 7 | 27 |

The Robesonian, Lumberton, NC
Friday, February 25, 1966

Pembroke Eagles Gain Title 52-23 Over Hawkeye Hawks

PEMBROKE - The Eagles of Pembroke High School defeated the Hawks of Hawkeye 52-23 in the finals of the Robeson County Indian Tournament Saturday night at Pembroke State College.

The Junior Varsity of Pembroke won the championship in the first game of the evening by defeating Fairgrove 44-37.

A capacity crowd watched as Pembroke was able to break the zone defense set up by Hawkeye in the first quarter, and post a 23-3 lead which was considered the determining factor in the game.

Gary W. Locklear led the way for Pembroke in the first quarter with his superior height by rolling away and shooting over his opponents' head. Locklear was also top scorer in the game with 22 points.

Pembroke used a 2-3 zone through out the game which limited Hawkeye to mostly outside shots, and this enabled Pembroke to post a 35-13 lead at intermission.

During the first half, Hawkeye had their problems in making field goals, and as a result, they connected on only 3 goals and 7 free throws. Pembroke was more settled, and managed to follow up most of the shots from outside on tippins by Locklear, and follow-up shots by Kent Sampson.

Hawkeye had plenty of scrap and hustle throughout the game, especially in two brothers, Ozell Jacobs and Muriel Jacobs. The Jacobs brothers accounted for most of the Hawkeye rebounds, and Muriel accounted for most of their points with 8 with the rebounding ability of Hawkeye, Pembroke was still able to control both boards in most situation with 6'7" center Gary W. Locklear, 6'5" forward Kent Sampson, and 6'1" forward Chester Chavis.

The second half began with Pembroke getting the tip-off, and Richard Oxendine lost the ball on a fast break. Hawkeye took possession and held it for 1 minute and 58 seconds before they attempted a shot which Ozell Jacobs made good.

During the remainder of the half, Hawkeye set up a man for man defense, and relied on ball control to hold Pembroke's scoring down, but they were unable to overcome the difference in scoring made by Pembroke in the first half.

Gary W. Locklear of Pembroke was followed in scoring by Kent Sampson with 18 points. Hawkeye did a good job in holding down Sampson's scoring, because in the semi-finals he netted 51 points, and finished with a tournament average of 34.5 points along with a season average of 32 points.

Muriel Jacobs of Hawkeye was followed in scoring by Ozell Jacobs and Joe Lowry with 4 points each.

J. V. CHAMPIONSHIP

In the first game of the evening, Pembroke's Junior varsity won the championship for the seventh time in as many starts in a thrill-packed game over Fairgrove Fairgrove stayed in the game all the way until the final seconds.

Charles Graham led the scoring for Pembroke with 13 points, and was followed by James Maynor and Bobby Oxendine with 12 points each and Selwyn Sampson with 7.

For Fairgrove's scoring, Robert Jacobs led the way for a game high of 14 points followed by Jimmy Cummings with 10, Jimmy Sealey 7, Bobby Blanks 4, and Willie Jacobs 2.

FRIDAY NIGHT GAME

Hawkeye earned the right to play Pembroke in the finals by defeating Magnolia 42-39 in one of the best games of the tournament.

Hawkeye used their rebounding advantage, and the scoring of Ozell Jacob with 10 points to win the game, after holding a 28-21 lead at half time.

Tim Locklear and Leon Maynor led the scoring for Magnolia with 12 points each in winning the consolation trophy.

In the first game Friday night Fairgrove J.V.'s defeated Les-Maxwell 47-40 to earn the right to play Pembroke for the J.V. championship.

Robert Jacobs of Fairgrove was high scorer in the game with 17 points and was followed in scoring by Jimmy Sealey with 9, Jimmy Cummings and Bobby Hunt with 6, Willie Jacobs with 5, and Bobby Blanks with 4.

Lennis Watts led the scoring for Les-Maxwell with 17 points and was followed by Lester Chavis with 12, Mitchell Hunt 6, R. Locklear 3, Ralph Slate 2, and B. Watts 1.

After the completion of the championship game Saturday night, the following were named to the All-Tournament Team: Kent Sampson and Gary W. Locklear of Pembroke, Phil Pierce of Hawkeye, Tim Locklear of Magnolia, Clyde Jacobs of Fairgrove, and Ronnie Chavis of Prospect.

SATURDAY NIGHT GAME

Pembroke	23	12	11	6	52
Hawkeye	3	10	4	6	23

Pembroke		Hawkeye	
Kent Sampson	18	Phil Pierce	3
Gary W. Locklear	22	Muriel Jacobs	8
Chester Chavis	2	Ozell Jacobs	4
Gary Locklear		Ronald Barton	2
Richard Oxendine	5	Joel Dial, Jr.	2

Pembroke subs: Gerald Hunt, Clark 5, H.B. Locklear, J. Chavis, Hammonds.

Hawkeye subs: Charles Dial, Harold Dean Brewer, Don Woods, Joe Walter Lowry 4.

JAYVEE GAME

Pembroke 9   11   12   12   44
Fairgrove..........7   10   14   6   37

FRIDAY NIGHT GAME

Hawkeye.........11   17   11   3   42
Magnolia 6   15   8   10   39

Hawkeye		Magnolia	
Muriel Jacobs	6	Tim Locklear	12
Ozell Jacobs	10		
Phil Pierce	8		

The Robesonian, Lumberton, NC
Monday, February 28, 1966

Prospect, Magnolia Win First Games

PEMBROKE - The Tri-County Indian Conference tournament passed the opening rounds here Friday and Saturday nights and semifinal action will come up this Thursday at the Pembroke High School gymnasium.

Varsity winners in the opening round were Magnolia and Prospect, and jayvee winners were Fairgrove and Prospect.

Coach Bill Stanton's Prospect team, which won the tournament in 1965, defeated Fairgrove 68-59 Saturday evening. Ronnie Chavis led the Prospect scoring with 23 points, and Hunt was high for Fairgrove with 16.

James Howard Locklear's 15 points was high for the Prospect jayvees, and D. Chavis led Magnolia with eight.

In the first night's games Friday Magnolia's varsity beat Hawkeye and Fairgrove's jayvees beat Les Maxwell.

Semifinal games Thursday will be Prospect varsity vs. Les Maxwell, and Prospect jayvees vs. Hawkeye. The jayvee game will open the doubleheader at 7 o'clock.

The winner of the tournament will go into the District Four Class. A tournament at Buies Creek in March.

Prospect: Ronnie Chavis 23, Dial 9, Brewer 16, Bryant 10, Locklear 8, A. Locklear 2.

Fairgrove: Larry Freeman 11, Jimmy Sealey 9, Jimmy Ray Cummings 9, Bobby Hunt 16, Robert Jacobs 15, Charles McNeill 4, Willie Jacobs 4.

The Robesonian, Lumberton, NC
Monday, February 20, 1967, Page 7

Tri County Action Gets Underway

PEMBROKE - Semifinal games are scheduled tonight as the Tri County Indians Basketball tournament begins again here at Pembroke High School.

Games tonight are Prospect varsity vs. Les Maxwell, and the Prospect jayvees vs. Hawkeye. The jayvee game will open the doubleheader at p.m.

In first round games last week Prospect defeated Fairgrove 68-59, Magnolia's varsity beat Hawkeye, and Fairgrove's jayvees defeated Les Maxwell. The tournament finals will be played Saturday night.

Pembroke High, which won the tournament last year, is not playing in the event this time, but Pembroke gets a crack at a playoff spot in the state 2-A district tournament this Friday night. The Tri-County winner goes to the state class A Tournament at Buies Creek.

The Eagles will meet Hope Mills of the Pioneer Conference in a preliminary playoff Friday at 7:30 p.m. at Hope Mills. The winner will receive a berth in the tournament proper which begins at Fayetteville Senior High next week. The Hope Mills-Pembroke winner will play in the district tournament next Wednesday against Tabor City of the Waccamaw conference.

The Robesonian, Lumberton, NC
Thursday, February 23, 1967, Page 8

Pembroke Wins Tourney Spot Over Hope Mills

HOPE MILLS - Pembroke High School, playing as an independent 2-A team, knocked Hope Mills out of a District Four tournament playoff spot 102-48 here Friday night. The game was played to determine the fourth team from the Pioneer Conference.

The top four teams of the Pioneer, including Pembroke, will play the top four teams of the Waccamaw Association in a tournament starting here at Fayetteville Senior High Wednesday night.

James "Bunk" Maynor led Pembroke past Hope Mills with a 25 point performance. Richard Oxendine chipped in with 17, and Bobby Oxendine had 16.

Pembroke jumped off to an 18-9 lead at the end of the first period, and they stretched the margin to 40-21 at half-time. At the end of three periods Pembroke owned a 75-33 lead. Pembroke outscored Hope Mills 27-15 in the fourth quarter.

Pembroke has a 21-2 record for the season. Their only losses were to 3-A Hamlet.

Pembroke: Richard Oxendine 17, James "Bunk" Maynor 25, Gary Locklear 3, Bobby Oxendine 16, Chester Chavis 12, Hank Smith 12, Gerald Hunt 4, Selwyn Sampson 4, Charles Graham, 4, Marvin Howington 2, Ed Chavis 2.

Hope Mills: Miles 6, Arrant 16, Ivey 12, Dalton 2, Woreen 3, Childers 2, Gautier 1, Sessoms 4, and Kinlaw 2.

The Robesonian, Lumberton, NC
Monday, February 27, 1967, Page 8 Extra

Magnolia Earns Tri-County Title Over Les Maxwell

PEMBROKE - Saturday night's championship game between Magnolia and Les Maxwell in the Tri County Indian Conference Tournament at Pembroke High School went into overtime, and Magnolia emerged after the three minute extra session with a 56-53 victory and the tourney title.

The winning margin was produced by Magnolia's all-conference player Harry Canady on a three point play. As Canady connected on a layup as the overtime period was about to end, he was fouled, and he turned his effort from the line into another point.

Les Maxwell tallied a basket to tie the regulation game 49-49 with four seconds left to play. Magnolia called time and received a technical because it had no time outs left. Les Maxwell missed the shot from the line, but they got the ball out of bounds also; however, they were not able to work the ball to the basket in the final four seconds.

Magnolia outscored Les Maxwell 7-4 in the overtime period. Les Maxwell took a 16-15 first quarter lead, and Magnolia led 28-25 at the half and 40-35 at the end of the third period.

Harry Canady led the Magnolia championship scoring with 21 points, and Sam Oxendine contributed 18 and Harry Maynor 12. Leading scorer for Les Maxwell was Ronny Locklear with 19 points, and Ellison Hunt had 11.

The league's all-conference team was announced following the tournament's championship game, and players selected were Harry Canady of Magnolia, Sam Oxendine of Magnolia, Ronnie Chavis of Prospect, Ellison Hunt of Les Maxwell, and Lester Chavis of Les Maxwell.

Magnolia succeeds Pembroke High as tournament champion. Pembroke did not compete this year, since they are playing in the district 2-A tournament at

Fayetteville Senior High this week. Magnolia will represent the Tri County Indian Conference in the Class A district tournament which will be held at Campbell College at Buies Creek next week.

Fairgrove's junior varsity won the jayvee championship in the preliminary round Saturday night. Fairgrove defeated Prospect for the title.

Magnolia: Sam Oxendine 18, Tonto Locklear 4, Bill Blanks, Harry Canady 21, Harry Maynor 12, Jimmy Hammonds 1.

Les Maxwell: Ellison Hunt 11, Norman Locklear 9, Ronny Locklear 19, Leonard Gibbs 6, Lester Chavis 6, William Oxendine 2, Howard Maynor.

Magnolia	15	13	12	9	7	56
Les Maxwell	16	9	10	14	4	53

The Robesonian, **Lumberton, NC**
Monday, February 27, 1967, Page 9

Photo courtesy of Barbara Braveboy-Locklear

Ned Sampson coached the Magnolia High School boys team to a tournament title in 1967. This was the final basketball game played in the Tri-County Indian High School Athletic Conference. The Indian High School basketball teams joined the NC High School Athletic Association the following season.

INDIAN HIGH SCHOOL TOURNAMENTS

The Robeson Indian High School Athletic Conference began interscholastic participation in the 1920's. Original members of the conference were Fairmont, Green Grove, Magnolia, Pembroke, Piney Grove, Prospect and Union Chapel. Teams competed in several sports, but the post-season basketball tournament at Pembroke State was always a highlight of the year. With consolidation reducing the number of schools to four, the league added Hawkeye (Hoke County) and Les Maxwell (Cumberland County) in 1966 to become the Tri-County Indian High School Athletic Conference. Then, in 1968, the schools joined the NCHSAA, just as the schools in the North Carolina High School Athletic Conference for black high schools did.

ROBESON COUNTY INDIAN HIGH SCHOOL CONFERENCE MENS BASKETBALL TOURNAMENT CHAMPIONS

YEAR	CHAMPION	SCORE	RUNNER-UP	SCORE	
1939–40	Pembroke		Prospect		
1940–41	Prospect	31	Pembroke	29	OT
1941–42	Pembroke	27	Green Grove	21	
1942–43		no tournament results			
1943–44	Pembroke		Prospect		
1944–45	Fairmont	22	Green Grove	16	
1945–46	Green Grove	33	Prospect	15	
1946–47	Pembroke	51	Green Grove	19	
1947–48	Prospect				
1948–49	Prospect	27	Pembroke	15	
1949–50	Prospect		Fairmont		
1950–51	Pembroke	38	Fairmont	19	
1951–52	Fairmont		Pembroke		
1952–53	Pembroke		Prospect		
1953–54	Pembroke	81	Magnolia	48	
1954–55	Fairgrove	44	Magnolia	43	
1955–56	Pembroke	45	Fairgrove	42	
1956–57	Fairgrove	50	Pembroke	39	
1957–58	Fairgrove	63	Pembroke	36	
1958–59	Fairgrove	52	Pembroke	32	
1959–60	Pembroke	52	Magnolia	41	
1960–61	Pembroke	49	Magnolia	43	

YEAR	CHAMPION	SCORE	RUNNER-UP	SCORE	
1961–62	Fairgrove	45	Pembroke	39	
1962–63	Fairgrove	44	Pembroke	40	
1963–64	Fairgrove	35	Pembroke	33	
1964–65	Prospect	53	Pembroke	50	

TRI-COUNTY INDIAN CONFERENCE

1965–66	Pembroke	52	Hawkeye	23	
1966–67	Magnolia	56	Les Maxwell	53	OT

ROBESON COUNTY INDIAN HIGH SCHOOL WOMENS BASKETBALL TOURNAMENT CHAMPIONS

1945–46	Magnolia	21	Pembroke	12	
1946-47	Magnolia	21	Pembroke	19	
1947–48	Union Chapel		Prospect		
1948–49	Prospect	19	Union Chapel	14	
1949–50	Union Chapel		Magnolia		
1950–51	Pembroke	60	Magnolia	50	
1951-52		no tournament results			
1952–53	Pembroke				
1953–54	Pembroke	64	Fairgrove	41	
1954–55	Pembroke				
1955–56	Pembroke	64	Fairgrove	62	OT
1956–57	Magnolia	57	Prospect	35	
1957–58	Pembroke	45	Fairgrove	39	
1958–59	Pembroke	59	Fairgrove	45	
1959–60	Fairgrove				
1960–61	Fairgrove	68	Magnolia	38	

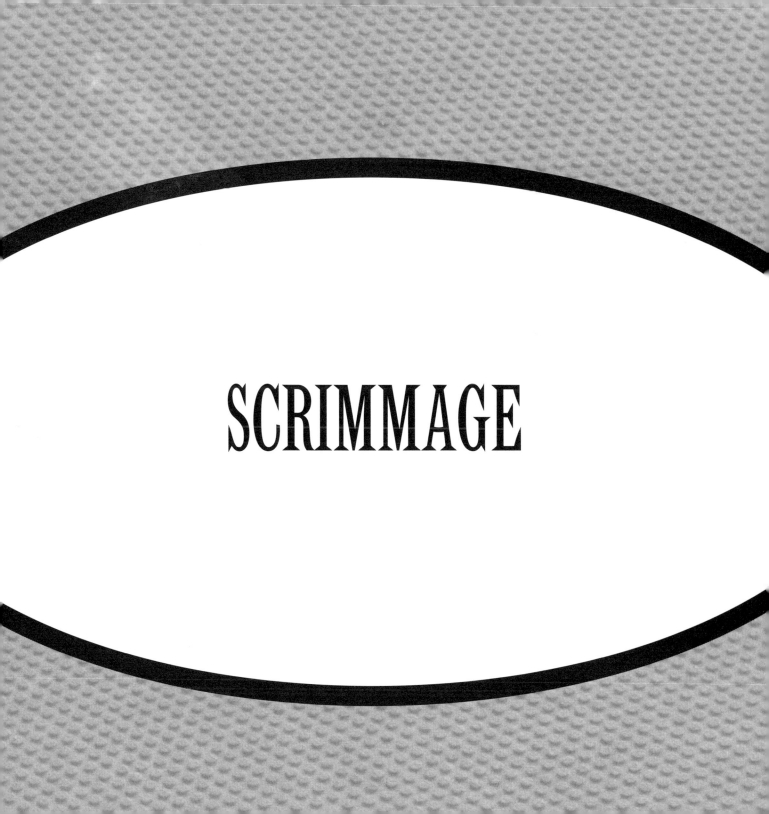

SCRIMMAGE

A Recognition Long Overdue

THE ROBESONIAN, OCTOBER 1999
by Glenn Swain, sports editor

Photo by Glenn Swain

From left, Charlie Adams, North Carolina High School Athletic Association Executive Director, Tim Brayboy, Ronnie Chavis, and Barry Harding unveil a plaque recognizing the Robeson County Indian Athletic Conference.

It was a journey for long-awaited recognition.

The two white Robeson County public school vans that traveled to Chapel Hill Thursday carried precious county sports history. Inside the vans were men – proud Indian men – who were finally going to be recognized.

The North Carolina High School Athletic Association was to unveil a plaque honoring the Robeson County Indian Athletic Conference.

The basketball conference began in 1920s and formally organized in 1939. It was disbanded after the 1967 season.

The conference consisted of seven charter Indian schools. The schools were not members of the NCHSAA and did, not have the opportunity to participate in the state playoffs.

In the beginning, playing conditions were horrible. Most games were played not in comfortable, dry gyms, but outside – on dirt. Instead of sneakers, many players wore their work shoes – brogans, they called them – or sometimes they played barefoot.

The highlight of the basketball season was the annual Indian tournament. Held on the campus of what was then Pembroke College, the event would draw 1,000 people to the old gym.

This Indian conference and its past may have been forgotten, if not for the efforts of a handful of Indians who refused to let it die. But in the process of bring this fertile basketball history to light, a darkness was exhumed. It was a discovery of ignorance, prejudice, and bigotry that has remained as hidden as the conference itself.

The dark

It was a conference born out of racism. During the time, schools were segregated. On and off the court, races usually stayed with their own.

Racism was accepted and prevalent. Views were cemented. Robeson County was no different than most of the county.

In 1954, the Brown vs. Board of Education ruling overturned the 1896 Plessy vs. Ferguson law, which spawned the oxymoronic "Separate but Equal" decree.

Racism was so entrenched in Robeson County that it took 13 years before segregation was attained and the conference disbanded, allowing county Indian schools to be accepted into regular high school athletics.

Since the Indian schools could not compete with the white and black schools, Fairmont High, Green Grove, Magnolia, Pembroke High, Piney Grove, Prospect and Union Chapel became the original members of the new Indian conference. Teams competed in several sports but basketball dominated.

"The only teams we could play were in our race," said Earl Scott, a 1950 graduate of Green Grove who played guard. "I was proud to be an Indian and that the schools got together to start their own conference. I was glad when the schools combined. That gave students the chance to play more sports.

"That's the way people lived back then. My mother and father told me that I was just as good as anybody else. We children never did talk about these people over there or those people over there. My parents wouldn't allow it. My mother would say, 'Earl, God loves you as much as that one over there and over there.' That has not left me."

"It was just a given," said 1959 Magnolia High School graduate Kermit Chavis. "We came from a very religious setting. We were taught to accept what you have and make the best of it. It just wasn't something we were going to make static about. I guess we were just proud of the fact that we had an opportunity to play."

Racism permeated every facet of life. At the Carolina Theater in Lumberton, the races were separated; whites sat downstairs on the cushioned seats, while blacks and Indians were directed to the uncomfortable balcony, where, even there, the two races were separated by a chicken-wire partition.

"Some people didn't want to integrate," Barton said. "It wasn't just whites and blacks. Some Indians didn't want to, either. Everybody wanted to stay unto themselves. People were comfortable with segregation."

"We didn't get the kind of coverage by the media as did Lumberton High, Red Springs or St. Pauls," Chavis said. "I can still remember some of the players I read about in The Robesonian that was playing the same game I was playing, but they got the newspaper coverage. It boiled down to that we were Indian and not part of the state athletic organization."

But through the turmoil, a bond was formed.

"The lower end of each race would buddy up together," said Fairgrove graduate Larece Hunt. "It's not like it has been a total isolation. We've always been friends.

There was resentment when you would be working in the cotton fields and the land owner's son would drive by drinking a Coca-Cola. To this day, I still don't like Coke because of that."

"I actually thought all white people were smarter than I was until I got into college because I had always been told that," said Larece's brother, Ardeen, another Fairgrove graduate. "Then I saw some test scores and I said, 'Wait a minute... my scores are better than these others.' I began to feel I was just as good."

"I went through high school with the three different school systems; the whites, the Indians and the blacks," Larece said. "Any new text books that came in, white schools had first access to the new books. The old books they had would be passed down to the Indians and the books we had would get passed down to the blacks. During that time, decisions made at the central office were made by whites because that's who worked there."

Times have changed for the better, but more work needs to be done.

"Ironically, now racism operates within the race itself," Larece Hunt said. "I may find more racism in the Indian population than I would find coming from the other two non-Indian races. That exists more now than Indians not liking blacks or whites."

"I was proud to be an Indian and that the schools got together to start their own conference."

Earl Scott, Green Grove High School
Class of 1950

The light

Pembroke High graduates Tim Brayboy and Bruce Barton refuse to let the conference, and the proud Indians who were part of it, be forgotten. Barton, who founded the Carolina Indian Voice newspaper, convened a meeting a year ago and, along with Brayboy and NCHSAA Executive Director Charlie Adams, set in motion a collection of basketball history that resulted in the NCHSAA officially recognizing the Indian Conference on Thursday.

"This has been long overdue," Adams said. "It should have never taken this long. We're really pleased that we can do this today. It etches that history."

"I'm concerned that sometimes our memories are short and we forget the people who's shoulders we stood on," said NCHSAA Associate Executive Director, Rick Strunk. "This will be a written and permanent record of the contributions of these Robeson County schools."

"Charlie (Adams) mentioned to me that this was an oversight," Brayboy said. "That this should have been done a long time ago. He apologized for it, and we started the ball rolling.

"The Indian population of Robeson County are a proud people," Brayboy added. "This makes the contributions and deeds in athletics by the Indian people more visible."

"Today is one of our proudest days in the history of the High School Athletic Association," Adams said. "This gives a chance for any Native American to come to see a plaque that recognizes their accomplishments, history and their place in North Carolina athletics."

"It's a long time coming," Earl Scott said after the ceremony. "When they asked me to go to Chapel Hill for this, I said, 'Let's go.' This is something we can leave to our grandchildren. They'll know that we played the game back then."

Photo courtesy of North Carolina High School Athletic Association

Charlie Adams, working with school administrators, arranged for Indian high schools to join the NCHSAA in 1968. Adams made the decision for a plaque to be displayed in the NCHSAA headquarters recognizing the Robeson County Indian High School Athletic Conference.

"Today is one of our proudest days in the history of the High School Athletic Association. This gives a chance for any Native American to come to see a plaque that recognizes their accomplishments, history and their place in North Carolina athletics."

Charlie Adams

Robeson County Indian Conference Is Recognized by NCHSAA

NCHSAA Bulletin, winter 2000

CHAPEL HILL – The North Carolina High School Athletic Association has honored an organization which made outstanding contributions to the history of high school sports in our state.

Many people are aware that at one point there were three statewide organizations that were governing high school athletics in North Carolina, including the NCHSAA, the old Western North Carolina High School Activities Association and the North Carolina High School Athletic Conference. The WNCHSAA included approximately 40 schools in the western Piedmont portion of the state and the NCHSAC was the organization for historically black high schools.

There was another group that competed in high school athletics, but its schools could not compete in the NCHSAA for many years, and that was the Robeson County Indian Athletic Conference.

NCHSAA game programs and records, after some extensive research, reflect some information and championships from the WNCHSAA and the NCHSAC. Even though the Robeson County organization was not a statewide group, it conducted its own competitions in several sports.

Tim Brayboy, former state Department of Public Instruction employee who worked for many years in athletics, and others began to do some research on the history of Robeson County league, with the idea of someday producing a written history. Some of the information about the organization's basketball tournament was published in the 1999 edition of the NCHSAA basketball program.

Earl Scott, 70, photographs the plaque at the North Carolina High School Athletic Association in Chapel Hill. Scott played basketball in the conference, "sometimes with barefeet" at Green Grove High School. "We had about the best basketball court around," he said, "because our dirt was the hardest."

Then the idea surfaced to recognize the accomplishments of these schools on a plaque for permanent display in the Simon F. Terrell Building. A group of individuals from Robeson County came to Chapel Hill for the official unveiling of the plaque in October. The ceremony had been delayed because of Hurricane Floyd.

The plaque reads:

"Robeson County Indian Athletic Conference

"This organization began interscholastic competition in the 1920's, under the auspices of the Robeson County Board of Education. Original members were Fairmont, Green Grove, Magnolia, Pembroke, Piney Grove, Prospect and Union Chapel.

"Championships were held in several sports, organized and administered by the school principals. The popular post-season basketball tournament was held at Pembroke State College. Consolidation reduced the membership to four, and then in 1966 Hawkeye (Hoke County) and Les Maxwell (Cumberland) joined the Robeson County schools to form the Tri-County Indian High School Athletic Conference.

"In 1968, the schools joined the North Carolina High School Athletic Association. But many athletes and coaches first got the opportunity to participate in this conference, another important part of the tradition that is now the NCHSAA."

Many of those in attendance for the ceremony either were involved with the old organization or assisted with the research about these schools.

Among the attendees Dr. Barry Harding, superintendent of the Public Schools of Robeson County; Ronnie Chavis, athletic director of the Public Schools of Robeson County; former Robeson superintendent Purnell Swett; and current Purnell Swett High School athletic director James Locklear, Jr.

Others included Bruce Barton, James Bell, Hartman Brewington, Wilson Chavis, Kermit Chavis, Robert Deese, Ardeen Hunt, and Larece Hunt.

Photo: 1956 Pembroke High School Yearbook, The Challenger

1956 PEMBROKE HIGH SCHOOL GIRLS REGULAR SEASON AND TOURNAMENT CHAMPIONS

Pembroke defeated Fairgrove 64 to 62 in overtime in the tournament championship game. Frances Locklear 33; Shelby Jane Sampson 25; and Rose Oxendine 6 led the Pembroke offense.

KNEELING: Janice Lowry, Jennie Ree Baker, Shelby Jane Sampson, Frances Locklear, Ellen Jane Deese, Ruth Brewington.

STANDING: Coach Delton Ray Locklear, Nancy Louise Locklear, Eudora Sampson, Rose Oxendine, Kathryn Brewington, Della Rae Oxendine.

We are grateful to the North Carolina High School Athletic Association for the recognition given the citizens of Cumberland, Hoke, and Robeson Counties by placing this plaque in its headquarters. This plaque recognizes the deeds and contributions the citizens made in providing and supporting interscholastic athletic opportunities for the young people who attended the public schools in their respective communities.

Realizing education and school activities were limited to a certain degree during this period in history, the school administrators saw the educational experiences that contributed to having interschool athletic programs for the students and patrons.

Although some bitter feelings still exist regarding race separation practices in the schools and society during this period in time, the Tri-County communities were not isolated. Prejudice and race separation were prevalent throughout the country and the world. However, as citizens of this great nation – where the Constitution for the people governs – let the past experiences and memories make us all stand strong with pride at the accomplishments in race relations and character, knowing that we have made much progress in recent decades.

Let all of us here today dedicate ourselves to improving human relations and educational opportunities for our brothers and sisters. Let us reflect on this moment and the purpose athletics have made in our lives.

Photo: 1957 Pembroke High School Yearbook, *The Challenger*

Tim Brayboy

Being here today for this historic event brings back fond memories of a simple time and place – a time when ordinary people had the pleasure to show their skills in sports activities before a cheering crowd. We were ordinary people doing extra ordinary things.

The North Carolina High School Athletic Association played a large role in the desegregation of the public schools in North Carolina. Through the efforts of Mr. Simon Terrell, Executive Director and Mr. Charlie Adams, Assistant Executive Director of the North Carolina High School Athletic Association, the Indian high schools in the Tri-counties were admitted to the North Carolina High School Athletic Association in 1967.

During a conversation with Mr. Adams, I mentioned a desire for the North Carolina High School Athletic Association to arrange a plaque to be displayed in the Association building honoring the Tri-County High School Athletic Conference. Mr. Adams agreed that this honor was long over due, and that he had been thinking as I had. Visitors to the Association building who read the words on the plaque can learn the legacy of the Tri-County Indian High School Athletic Conference. Thank You.

Response given by Tim Brayboy at the ceremony recognizing the Tri-County Indian High School Athletic Conference, Chapel Hill, N.C., October 12, 1999.

Indian Basketball Facts

- Prior to 1939, Pembroke High School was part of the Pembroke State Normal School. Pembroke High School was the last of the seven original high schools to open on an individual campus.

- Fairmont Indian, Prospect, Piney Grove, Green Grove, Union Chapel, and Magnolia High Schools were established on their individual campuses.

- The gymnasium at Pembroke State College opened the 1939-40 school year. Before the gym opened, the high school teams held their post season basketball tournament rotating at different schools. The games were played on a dirt court. Teams continued to play most of their regular season games on dirt courts after the college gym opened.

- The school principals organized and administered the post season basketball tournament.

- Les Maxwell High School did not have a gymnasium. The teams practiced on an asphalt court located on the school campus. During inclement weather the teams would practice walk through drills in a classroom. They would do conditioning by running in the school hallways.

- School principals were allowed to coach.

- It was a big adjustment for players when they played in the college gym. Most were accustomed to playing outdoors. Oft times, they had to borrow gym shoes when they played in the gym, because some did not, and could not, afford gym shoes.

- In the 1940s, teams were allowed to use regular school buses for transportation. They also traveled by cars and trucks. By the 1950s, the mode of travel was cars. The school principal designated the driver, usually a school teacher. Players were not allowed to drive personal vehicles to away games.

- In 1967, Pembroke High School was the first Indian high school to join the North Carolina High School Athletic Association. The following year, the other Indian high schools in the Tri-County area joined the Association.

- For many years, the athletic teams at Pembroke State College were former players from the Robeson County Indian high schools. Some Indian athletes played at other colleges in North Carolina and other states.

- Joe Williams, of Laurel Hill, North Carolina, was a member of the 1954-55 Pembroke State College mens basketball team. He is reported to be the first non-American Indian to play basketball at PSC.

Whaʼs In A Name?

Despite the size of their community, the Lumbee are held together by the same mechanisms and values that have kept them together for the past one hundred years and more. First and foremost is the sense of kinship. An Indian family (sometimes referred to as clan) is closely related to a handful of other families, adding yet another degree of association. For instance, when a Lumbee meets another he doesn't know, his first inquiry is, "Who's your people?" Once the clan membership is determined, each places the other and conversation can proceed.

Individual Lumbees maintain that they can tell the place of residence of an individual by his or her accent; that people from a particular settlement have distinctive speech patterns. Certain families are able to maintain a concentration of property and kin in given areas. Some examples are the Lowrys in the Hopewell area, Hunts in Fairmont, Oxendines in New Hope, Bells and Emanuels in Saddletree, Brookses in the Red Bank area, and the Locklears, Dials, and Bullards in Prospect. Harris is also a prominent surname in the Prospect area. Marriages within the settlements are common. There are, of course, many who marry out-side settlements. In the cases where family-owned land is available, the husband commonly takes his wife to his community. To be near ones' family is of paramount concern and contributes to intra-community marriages. The extended family is by far the most important factor in the maintenance and expression of community values, information, and opinion. It is the nexus of community interaction. Most individuals can trace lines back to at least one of a half-dozen core families. From an anthropological perspective, these are examples of "kindreds," a type of kin organization commonly found among tribes who trace descent bilaterally. Not only can most Lumbee describe in detail their kindreds, they can describe how present-day members are related to them and to each other.

But where did the Lumbee people get their surnames? European immigrants flooded North Carolina during the 1700s. Among them were people from all of Great Britain, including England, Scotland, Ireland, and Wales. Smaller numbers came from Germany and France. However, it is believed that many well-known family names like Lowrie (later spelled Lowery and Lowry), Berry (Berrie), Cummings, McNeill, McMillan, McGirt, Burnett, Collins, Cooper, Blue, Bell, Clark, Graham, Carter, Sanderson, Moore, Brook (Brooks), Thomas, Smith, Brewer, Porter, Johnson, Sampson, Rogers, Taylor, Scott, and Wood come from Scotland because about half of all the Europeans who immigrated to North Carolina in the early 1730s were Scots. The Scots were surprised to discover English-speaking people already living in simple houses near the Lumbee River. Many of the Scottish immigrants were the so-called Buckskin Scots (the poor) and most likely had closer contact with Indians rather than the English-speaking wealthy landowners.

It did not take long after the Scottish immigrants began settling the upper regions of the Cape Fear Valley of North Carolina for these names to begin appearing in the census and tax records for Indian families in eastern North Carolina. Most land grants made to Scotsmen in what is now Robeson County were made between 1755 and 1775. There is documentation showing Major and John Locklear, patriarchs of the present-day Locklears, living in the Robeson County settlement of Prospect in January of 1754. Deed records show that in 1749, in Edgecombe County, North Carolina, Robert Locklear (spelled Locklere) granted a "deed of gift" to his children, who included

John and Major before mentioned. Further records show that in 1694, Robert Lowry was granted 260 acres of land on Little River in Pasquotank County, North Carolina. James Lowrie and Henry Berry received land grants directly from King George II of England in 1732, the former receiving a second grant in 1738. Charles Oxendine, in 1768, was issued 150 acres northeast of Drowning Creek in Bladen County, and John Brooks was granted land in Edgecombe County, North Carolina in 1725. William Chavers (Chavis), in 1743, was granted 540 acres of land on the north side of Tar River in Edgecombe County, North Carolina. Numerous Chavis family names appeared prominently among tax lists and land records in Granville County, North Carolina, from 1748-1789. John Braveboy (Braboy and Brayboy) purchased 50 acres of land in Chowan County, North Carolina in 1725.

It is very common for Lumbee individuals to be able to trace their parents' genealogies back five or more generations. Not only are individuals able to name grandparents, great-grandparents, great-great grand-parents, etc., but very often they can name siblings of their ancestors, the spouses of their ancestors' siblings, relate where they live in Robeson County, the church they attended, and the names of their offspring. As mentioned earlier, most individuals can trace their lines back to a least one of a half-dozen core families. Such is the case with the name Locklear, the most-widely recognized surname of the Lumbee tribe. The Locklears of Robeson County descend from six-to-seven core families who are not related by blood. In this case, an individual by the name of Locklear may marry a Locklear from a different core family and neither be related by blood.

Indians of Robeson and adjoining counties are made up of a little bit of each ancestor, and a grandmother and grandfather who lived ten generations ago gave them part of their spirit, hair and eyes; but the European immigrants most-likely gave them their names.

Some Indian Surnames

Baker	Freeman
Barnes	Gibbs
Bell	Godwin
Berry	Goins
Blanks	Graham
Blue	Groves
Brayboy	Hammonds
Brewer	Hardin
Brewington	Harris
Brooks	Holmes
Bryant	Hunt
Bullard	Jacobs
Burns	Locklear
Canady	Lowery
Carter	Lowry
Chavis	Maynor
Clark	McGirt
Collins	Moore
Cooper	Oxendine
Cummings	Ransom
Deese	Revels
Demery	Sampson
Dial	Sanderson
Emanuel	Smith
Epps	Strickland
Fields	Thomas
Flanagan	Thompson

Multi-Families Participants

Multiple family members played basketball for their respective schools. The following is a partial listing of noble contributors to the Indian high schools basketball program.

*Parent appears in bold print

FAIRGROVE HIGH SCHOOL BASKETBALL PLAYER(S)

Quinnie Hunt:
Geraldine, Clementine, Dorothy, Lillian Ruth, Horace

Clarence Locklear:
Clara Bell, Javie, Bonson, Rosa, Datry

Thomas Oxendine:
Thomas Jr., Bruce, Virginia

Sam Sanderson:
Edward, Lankford, Arbidella, James, Gary, Monford

MAGNOLIA HIGH SCHOOL BASKETBALL PLAYER(S)

Frank Bell:
Hardy "Red", Harold, Shirley

Furman Bell:
James F. "Buddy", Gladys, Katherine, Glennis

Wash Bell:
Henry, Hosey, Bertie

Isaac Brewer:
Ray, Ennis, Homer, Mattie Fay, Letha, Annie Sue

Pet Butler:
Gerald, Pet Jr., Leroy

Steve Hammonds:
Lloyd Ander, Frank, Ronald

Howard Locklear:
Howard Lee, Gerald

PEMBROKE HIGH SCHOOL BASKETBALL PLAYER(S)

Tecumseh Bryan Brayboy, Jr.:
Bobby, Tim, Tecumseh Bryan III, Ray

Clyde Brewington:
Jeannie, Myrtle, Ruth

Peter Brooks:
Bernice, Paul, Howard

Rev. Venus Brooks, Sr.:
Venus, Jr., Sam, Bellene

Rev. Clarence Locklear:
Ted, Bundy Ross, Rod

Dewery Locklear:
Willard, Clyde, Van Benson

Gus Locklear:
Bertha, Eddie Mack, Frances, Patsy, Gary Wayne

Hardywell Locklear, Sr.:
Hardywell, Jr., Lynwood, Katrina

Willard Lee Locklear:
Jydor, Lummie Jane, Barbara Ann

Winnie Catherine Locklear:
Carrie Mae, Delton Ray, Dorothy, Maxine

Benford Lowry, Sr.:
Narva, Janice, Sylvia, Benford, Jr.

Bernard Lowry:
Bob, Joan

Rev. Harvey Lowry:
Jimmy, Robbie, Harvey Jr., Jerry

Wayne Maynor:
Waltz, Faye, Ann, Jeff

J.C. "Sonny" Oxendine:
Sim, Jesse, William Earl

Lonnie Oxendine:
Denford, Geneauga, Carol Jane, Deola, George

Tom Oxendine, Sr.:
Tom Jr., Louise, Joe, Ray

Clifton Sampson, Sr.:
John "Ned", Clifton Jr., Shelby, Norma, Kent

Kenneth Strickland:
Nathan, Moland, Kenny Ray, Reginald

Rev. Tommy Swett:
Vardell, Purnell, Dorothy, Tommy D., Bruce

PROSPECT HIGH SCHOOL BASKETBALL PLAYER(S)

Tommy Brewer:
Evelyn, Margaret, Carl

Noland Bryant:
Myrna, Evelyn, David Earl

Lester Bullard:
Sara Neal, Nancy Lou, Paul Reese, Barbara, Judy

Godwin Chavis:
Ruth, Mary Frances, Oneal, Godwin, Jr.

Walter Chavis:
Wilson, William Cancel, Dosey, Grady

Emma Collins:
Alice Ruth, Ledford, James

Newton Cummings, Sr.:
Wilton, Newton, Jr., Carlton

Daniel Tucker Dial, Sr.:
Daniel Tucker, Jr., Alice Dale, Sally

Onnie Dial:
Danford, Jim, Leslie, Naomi, Ruth

Simmie Dial:
Byrtis, Talford

Will Goins, Sr:
Annie, Bertha, Will, Jr.

Asa Locklear:
James Howard, Joe, Thelma

David Locklear, Sr.:
Douglas, Edward Hayes, Paul, David Ray

James "Pike" Locklear:
Walter, Dallas, Reese, Priscilla, Bessie

John Winston Locklear:
Samuel, Herman, Marie

Mack Locklear:
Nash, Sadie Mae, Maurice

Magnolia Locklear:
Jeannie Dale, James, Mike

Paul Locklear:
James, Brantley, Agnes, Myrtle

Caplor Lowry:
Lola Mearl, Truman, Praford

Neal Lowry, Sr.:
Marvin, Neal, Jr., Annie Jarvie, Walter

Luther Moore:
Bill, Mabel, Cleo, Richard, Claude

Harleywell Oxendine, Sr.:
Harleywell, Jr., Freddie, Bobby, Ronald

Luther Channel Oxendine, Sr.:
Luther, Jr., Wyvis, Truman

UNION CHAPEL HIGH SCHOOL BASKETBALL PLAYER(S)

Chesley Oxendine, Sr.:
Iona, Lucy, Forace, Della Rae

John W. Oxendine:
John Ander, Vashti, Nora, Shirley, Rose

* One parent identified as representing their children

Ako, Margaret, Green Grove High School 1949.
Coach: Joseph Sampson. Teammates: Sarah
Locklear, Louise Chavis.

Amos, Maxine Locklear, Pembroke High School
1948-52. Coach: Fred Lowry.

Bell, James F., Magnolia High School 1950-54.
Coach: Eugene Chavis and Robert McGirt.

Bonos, Barbara, Fairgrove 1956-57. Coach: Ralph
Hunt. Teammates: Euretta Hammonds, Amy Hunt.

Brewington, Hartman, Pembroke High School
1956-59. Coach: Delton Ray Locklear. Teammates:
Howard Brooks, Lynwood Sampson, Bobby Eugene
Jacobs, Jerry Revels.

Brooks, Paul, Pembroke High School 1953-57.
Coach: Danford Dial. Teammates: Reginald
Strickland, Howard Sampson, Jr., Adna Lowry, Jr.,
Jerry Revels.

Bullard, Sally Ann, Fairgrove High School 1955-
59. Coach: Ralph Hunt. Teammates: Doris Locklear,
Clara Locklear, Lena Hunt, Dorothy Hunt, Laura Lee,
Vernie Lee Hunt, Janice Hunt, Martha Sealey.

Caulder, Clementine Hunt, Fairgrove High School
1952-56. Coach: Albert C. Hunt. Teammates:
Marie Jacobs, Geraldine Hunt, Mary Ellen Hunt,
Dorothy Hunt, Martha Rae Hunt.

Chavis, Chester, Pembroke High School 1965-69.
Coach: Ned Sampson. Teammates: Kent Sampson,
Ed Chavis, Titus Locklear, Gary Locklear, Herman
Hammonds.

Chavis, Crafton, Fairgrove High School 1955-59.
Coach: Ralph Hunt.

Chavis, Doris Locklear, Fairgrove High School
1955-58. Coach: Reese Locklear. Teammates:
Clara Locklear, Lena Hunt, Janice Sealey, Vashtie
Jacobs, Lee Hunt, Treva Hunt, Dorothy Hunt.

Chavis, Jerry, Pembroke High School 1963-67.
Coach: Jydor Locklear. Teammates: Lee Sampson,
Kent Sampson, Mike Clark, Richard Oxendine,
Gary Locklear, Gary Wayne Locklear.

Chavis, Mary Sue, Union Chapel High School
1947-50, Pembroke High School 1950-51.
Coach: Theodore Maynor. Union Chapel High
School, Tom Oxendine, Pembroke High School.

Chavis, Naomi Dial, Prospect High School
1949-52. Coach: Mary Sanderson. Teammates:
Pauline Bullard, Sara N. Bullard, Verdie Locklear,
Arminda Locklear.

Chavis, Randall, Pembroke High School 1953-56,
Prospect High School 1956-57. Coach: Danford
Dial at Pembroke High School, Marvin Lowry at
Prospect High School. Teammates: Prospect High
School: Bill James Locklear, James Alton Revels,
Grady Chavis, Carlton Cummings, Carl Maynor.

Chavis, Ronnie, Prospect High School 1964-68.
Coach: William Cancel Chavis and William Stanton.

Clark, Dennis, Pembroke High School 1959-63.
Coach: Jydor Locklear. Teammates: Curley Locklear,
Walter Oxendine, Jimmy Lowry, Johnny Sampson,
William Lowry.

Clark, Michael, Pembroke High School 1963-66.
Coach: Jydor Locklear. Teammates: Richard
Oxendine, Gary Locklear, Kent Sampson,
Chester Chavis.

Cummings, Annie Pearl, Prospect High School
1951-55. Coach: Lucy Oxendine Thomas.

Dial, Danford, Jr., Prospect High School 1962-66.
Coach: Hilbert "Joe" Swinson.

Dial, Dorothy Locklear, Prospect High School
1960-64. Cheerleader.

Flanagan, Michael, Prospect High School 1961-65. Coach: William Cancel Chavis and Joe Swinson. Teammates: Talford Dial, Burlie Locklear, Percell Locklear, Wyvis Oxendine, Gary Strickland, Danford Dial, Jr.

Flowe, Dorothy Hunt, Fairgrove High School 1957-59. Coach: Ralph Hunt. Teammates: Lena Hunt, Linda Hammonds, Doris Locklear, Clara Locklear, Lee Hunt.

Hammonds, Cecil, Green Grove High School 1944-48. Coach: Joseph Sampson and Herbert G. Oxendine. Teammates: Earl Scott, Rodney Locklear.

Hammonds, Earl E., Fairmont Indian High School, 1946-52, Coach: Sanford Hunt.

Hammonds, Elsie, Fairmont Indian High School. Coach: Albert Hunt. Teammates: Virgie Oxendine, Katrina Locklear.

Hardin, Benford, Pembroke High School 1959-61. Coach: Jydor Locklear. Teammates: Jimmy Ray Locklear, Steve Jones, Bemus Blue, Curley Locklear, Walter Oxendine, William Lowery.

Hardin, Lillian Hunt, Fairgrove High School 1957-60. Coach: Ralph Hunt. Teammates: Dorothy Hunt, Doris Locklear, Clara Locklear, Lena Gray, Lee Hunt, Linda Hammonds.

Harvey, Myrtle, Pembroke High School 1951-54. Coach: Tom Oxendine Jr. Teammates: Ann McGirt, Geneauga Oxendine, Jeanie Brewington.

Hill, Rose Oxendine, Pembroke High School 1953-57. Coach: Fred Lowry and Delton Ray Locklear. Teammates: Shelvie Locklear, Vashti Locklear, Kathryn Brewington, Frances Locklear, Shelby Sampson, Edna Berry, Della Rae Oxendine, Sylvia Lowry, Janice Lowry.

Hunt, Ardeen, Fairgrove High School 1959-63. Coach: Ralph Hunt. Teammates: Bobby Lewis, Levon Sealey, Larece Hunt.

Hunt, Chad, Fairgrove High School 1955-59. Coach: Ralph Hunt. Teammates: Charles Hunt, Earl Sealey, Pernell Locklear, Crafton Chavis, Gerald Ransom.

Hunt, Clara, Green Grove High School 1949-50 and Fairgrove High School 1950-53. Teammates: Nelva Barnes, Libbie Locklear, Clara Hammonds.

Hunt, Clois, Fairgrove High School 1950-53. Teammates: Nelva Barnes, Libbie Locklear, Virgie Jones, Essie Carter.

Hunt, Gerald, Pembroke High School 1963-67. Teammates: Jerry Chavis, Chester Chavis, Gary Locklear, Richard Oxendine.

Hunt, Welbert, Green Grove High School. Teammates: L.F. Swett, Buddy Swett, Delton Jacobs, Welton Jacobs, Delton Huggins.

Jones, Carrie Mabel, Prospect High School. Cheerleader.

Jacobs, Artie Mae Jones, Prospect High School 1959-62. Cheerleader.

Jacobs, Bobby Eugene, Pembroke High School 1956-60. Coach: Delton Ray Locklear and Jim Cook. Teammates: Walter Oxendine, William Lowery, Jerry Revels, Billy Ray Locklear.

Jacobs, Fannie, Prospect High School 1951-55. Teammates: Betty Locklear, Betty Jacobs, Joyce Chavis.

Largent, Mary, Prospect High School 1952-55. Coach: Mary Sanderson. Teammates: Fannie Jacobs, Ruth Dial, Annie Sanderson, Jarvie Lowry.

Locklear, Bundy Ross, Pembroke High School 1951-54. Coach: Danford Dial. Teammates: John H. Hunt, Kenneth Maynor, Harold Cummings, Jydor Locklear, Bob Jacobs, Adna Lowry Jr., Rod Locklear, Ray Oxendine, Joe Morgan, Tim Brayboy, Bob Lowry, Randall Chavis.

Locklear, Burlie, Prospect High School 1961-65. Coach: William Cancel Chavis and Joe Swinson. Teammates: Wyvis Oxendine, Purcell Locklear, Talford Dial, Mike Flanagan, Dell Harris, Johnny Locklear, Virgil Dial, Gary Strickland, Mitchell Brewer, Harold Dean Chavis, Guy Chavis, Jimmy Goins, Jimmy Jones, Danford Dial, Jr.

Locklear, Della Oxendine, Pembroke High School 1953-57. Coach: Fred Lowry. Teammates: Rose Oxendine, Kathryn Brewington, Vashti Locklear, Shelby Sampson.

Locklear, Delton Ray, Pembroke High School 1942-47. Coach: Joseph Sampson and James Thomas Sampson. Teammates: Ned Sampson, Joseph Oxendine, Hoover Lloyd, Zeb Lowry, Jr.

Locklear, Elvera S., Magnolia High School 1963-67. Coach: Ned Sampson.

Locklear, Gary Wayne, Pembroke High School 1962-66. Coach: Jydor Locklear. Teammates: Kent Sampson, Mike Clark, Gary Locklear, Jerry Chavis, Lee Sampson, Ray Brayboy, George Oxendine, Jimmy Oxendine.

Locklear, Grace Dial, Prospect High School 1947-50. Coach: Mary Sanderson. Teammates Rose Dial, Arminda Locklear, Pauline Bullard, Frances Locklear.

Locklear, Henry T., Prospect High School 1959-61, Hawkeye High School 1962-63. Coach: Forace Oxendine. Teammates: David Bullard, Bobby Cooper, Durant Cooper.

Locklear, Pauline Bullard, Prospect High School. Coach: Mary Sanderson.

Locklear, Ruth D., Prospect High School 1951-55. Coach: Mary Sanderson and Lucy Thomas. Teammates: Jarvie Lowry, Shirley Locklear.

Locklear, Verdia, Prospect High School 1947-50. Coach: Mary Sanderson. Teammates: Pauline Bullard, Rose Dial, Dora Lee.

Locklear, William, Magnolia High School 1958-62. Coach: Ned Sampson. Teammates: Wendell Lowery, Kermit Chavis, Jerry Baker, Carnell Oxendine, James Swett.

Lowry, Bernice Brooks, Pembroke High School. Coach: Joseph Sampson and James Thomas Sampson. Teammates: Katie Jones, Janice Lowry.

Lowry, Joan, Pembroke High School 1954-58. Coach: Fred Lowry and Delton Ray Locklear. Teammates: Frances Locklear, Pat Locklear, Janice Lowry, Sylvia Lowry, Ruth Scott, Edna Berry, Rose Oxendine, Della Rae Oxendine, Shelvie Locklear. Cheerleader.

Lowry, Marvin, Piney Grove High School 1940-41, Prospect High School 1941-44. Coach: Curtis Moore. Teammates: Lonnie Maynor, Walter Locklear, Dook Locklear, Talmage Locklear.

Lowry, Monroe, Pembroke High School 1939-43. Coach: Margolis Sanderson. Teammates: Garnett Lowry, Molan Strickland, English Jones, Jesse Oxendine, Curt Locklear.

Lowery, Sarah L., Green Grove High School 1948. Coach: Joseph Sampson. Teammates: Margaret Chavis, Louise Chavis.

Lowry, Truman, Prospect High School 1963-67. Coach: William Cancel Chavis. Teammates: Freddie Oxendine, Claude Moore, James Flanagan, Truman Oxendine.

Lowry, Walter, Prospect High School 1949-53. Coach: Conrad Oxendine. Teammates: Clarence Woods, Brantley Locklear, James Collins, Daniel Tucker Dial, Jr.

McGirt, Annie, Prospect High School 1951-55. Coach: Mary Sanderson and Lucy Thomas. Teammates: Ruth Dial, Annie Cummings, Sherrill Locklear, Lilly Bullard, Lucille Locklear.

Moore, Christine Hammonds, Prospect High School 1956-1960. Coach: Marvin Lowry. Teammates: Byrtis Dial, Ceola Locklear, Dorothy Scott, Odessa Chavis, Edna Scott.

Oxendine, Bobby D., Prospect High School 1964-68. Coach: William Cancel Chavis. Teammates: Ronnie Chavis, Floyd Locklear, Kirk Bullard, Arvin Locklear.

Oxendine, Delton, Fairmont High School 1951-52, Fairgrove High School 1952-53. Coach: Sanford Hunt and Leon Hunt.

Oxendine, Doris Hunt, Pembroke High School 1951-54. Coach Ned Sampson.

Oxendine, Lena Gray, Fairgrove High School 1956-59. Teammates: Sally Ann Bullard, Clara Locklear, Doris Locklear, Dorothy Hunt, Martha Sealey, Laura Lee Hunt, Virginia Hunt.

Oxendine, Louis, Pembroke High School 1944-45. Coach: Joseph Sampson. Teammates: William Price Locklear, Curliss Lowry, Dawry Lowry.

Oxendine, Oscar, Green Grove High School 1947-51. Coach: Joseph Sampson and Herbert G. Oxendine. Teammates: Cecil Hammonds, Aubrey Graham, Earl Scott, Willie Scott, Kelvin Hammonds.

Oxendine, Ray, Pembroke High School 1951-54. Coach: Danford Dial. Teammates: Bundy Ross Locklear, Jydor Locklear, Bobby Jacobs, John H. Hunt, Ken Maynor.

Oxendine, Riley, Pembroke High School 1952-53. Coach: N/A. Teammates: James Hardy Oxendine, Cliff Sampson Jr., Bundy Ross Locklear.

Oxendine, Samuel, Magnolia High School 1963-67. Coach: Ned Sampson. Teammates: Jimmy Hammonds, Harry Maynor, Harry Canady, Tonto Locklear, Jr.

Sampson, John Ned, Pembroke High School 1943-47. Coach: Joseph Sampson and Dorsey Van Lowry. Teammates: Hoover Lloyd, Zeb Lowry, Jr., Joseph Oxendine, Delton Ray Locklear.

Sampson, Lee Edward, Pembroke High School 1963-67. Coach Jydor Locklear. Teammates: Jerry Chavis, Gary Locklear, Kent Sampson, Mike Clark, Richard Oxendine, Gary Wayne Locklear.

Sanderson, Mary, Prospect High School 1947-52. Coach: Conrad Oxendine.

Scott, Earl, Green Grove High School 1946-50. Coach: Joseph Sampson and Herbert G. Oxendine. Teammates: Aubrey Graham, Calvin Hammonds, Willie Swett.

Sheppard, Earl, Pembroke High School 1939-40. Coach: Paul Sampson. Teammates: John Lowry, James Sanderson, Earl Cummings, Oscar Jacobs.

Stankiewicz, Ruth, Pembroke High School 1952-56. Coach: Joseph Sampson. Teammates: Ellen Deese, Annie Chavis, Frances Locklear, Shelby Sampson.

Strickland, Reginald, Pembroke High School 1953-57. Coach: Danford Dial. Teammates: Paul Brooks, Jerry Revels, Randall Chavis, Howard Sampson Jr., Tommy Swett, Oceanus Lowry, Jeff Maynor, Hartman Brewington, Lynwood Sampson, Tim Brayboy, Howard Brooks, Stacy Brayboy, Sam Brooks.

Strickland, Tommy, Fairgrove High School. Coach: Ralph Hunt. Teammates: Earl Sealey, Bonson Locklear, Thomas Oxendine, Calvin Hammonds, James Horace Hunt, Charles Hunt.

Thomas, Lucy Oxendine, Union Chapel High School 1946-47. Coach: Theodore Maynor. Teammates: Fannie Lou Oxendine.

Woods, Clarence, Prospect High School 1950-53. Coach: Conrad Oxendine. Teammates: Walter Lowry, James Collins, James Earl Locklear, Brantley Locklear, Daniel Tucker Dial, Jr.

Woods, Rosa B., Prospect High School 1945-49. Coach: Mary Sanderson. Teammates: Pauline Bullard, Rose Dial.

Note: Information taken from a questionnaire completed by Indian basketball participants.

HALL OF FAME

Robeson County Indian High School Athletic Conference Athletes
Selected to the University of North Carolina-Pembroke Athletic Hall of Fame

NAME	SCHOOL	INDUCTED
Theodore Maynor	Pembroke	1980
James Thomas Oxendine	Pembroke	1980
John "Ned" Sampson	Pembroke	1980
Victor Elk	Pembroke	1981
Forace Oxendine, Sr.	Union Chapel	1981
Leslie "Les" Locklear	Magnolia	1982
Marvin Lowry	Piney Grove and Prospect	1983
Ray Brayboy	Pembroke	1984
Tim Brayboy	Pembroke	1985
James Howard Locklear, Sr.	Prospect	1986
William Molan Strickland	Pembroke	1986
Robert Lee McGirt	Magnolia	1988
Joseph Sampson	Pembroke	1990
James Thomas Sampson	Pembroke	1992
Ronnie Chavis	Prospect	1996
Kelvin Sampson	Pembroke	1998
Delton Ray Locklear	Pembroke	2000

Selected to the Catawba College Athletic Hall of Fame

Joseph Oxendine	Pembroke	1978
Ray Oxendine	Pembroke	1984

Selected to the Elon University Athletic Hall of Fame

Ricky Locklear	Fairmont	1988

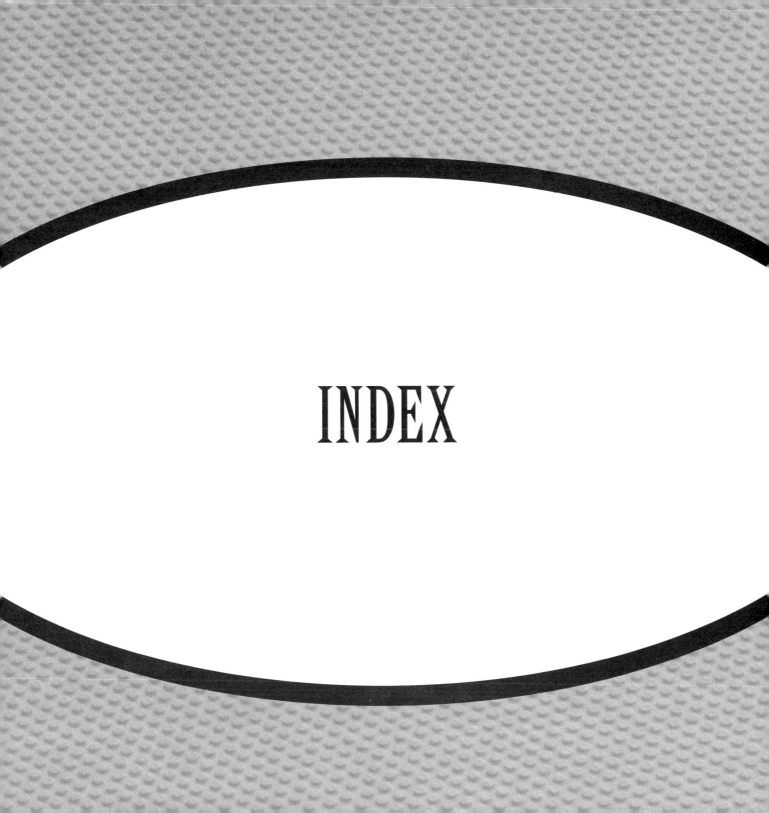

INDEX

The authors have made every attempt to list all the people in the index. However, some names may not be included because of being overlooked. Also, as so many given names are the same or similar, it is possible that a page number may not correspond to the right person. We offer our apologies and beg forgiveness.

MEET THE AUTHORS

Bruce Barton lives in the Deep Branch Community near Pembroke, N.C. with wife Barbara and daughter, Brandi. A man of varied interests, he is the founder and first editor of The Carolina Indian Voice Newspaper, a former social studies teacher, and now employed as Coordinator of Cultural Activities with the Indian Education Program in the Public Schools of Robeson County (N.C.). Barton, a Lumbee, claims his greatest accomplishment is as a grandfather. His son, Pete, and wife, Lori, are the proud parents of a son and daughter, John Edwin Marshall and Mallorie; daughter Sissy, and Roger, her husband, do the bidding of son, Seattle Grayeyes, and daughter, Jodie Whitehorse. Barton does the bidding of all of the above.

Tim Brayboy lives in Cary, N.C. with his wife, Byrtis ("Byrt"). They have one daughter, Mia. Retired as an educator with the N.C. Department of Public Instruction, Tim stays busy on special projects and officiates football games in the North Carolina Athletic Officials Association. A former basketball player, he was a tenacious point guard on the Pembroke High School Eagles teams in the late 1950s. Brayboy, a Pembroke native, also enjoys returning home to Robeson County (N.C.) as often as possible, especially on the weekends, to practice his wares as a gentleman farmer on the homeplace where his wife grew up in the Prospect community.